W9-ABF-702

WITHDRAWN

Gramley Library
Salem College
Winston-Salem, NC 27108

Literary Criticism in Perspective:
Critical Approaches to Goethe's Classical Dramas

Editorial Board

Literary Criticism in Perspective

James Hardin (*South Carolina*), General Editor

Stephen D. Dowden (*Brandeis University*), German Literature

Benjamin Franklin V (*South Carolina*), American and
English Literature

Reingard M. Nischik (*Konstanz*), Comparative Literature

* * *

About *Literary Criticism in Perspective*

Books in the series *Literary Criticism in Perspective*, a subseries of the
series *Studies in German Literature, Linguistics, and Culture*, and *Studies
in English and American Literature, Linguistics, and Culture*, trace literary
scholarship and criticism on major and neglected writers alike, or on a
single major work, a group of writers, a literary school or movement. In so
doing the authors — authorities on the topic in question who are also
well-versed in the principles and history of literary criticism — address a
readership consisting of scholars, students of literature at the graduate and
undergraduate level, and the general reader. One of the primary purposes
of the series is to illuminate the nature of literary criticism itself, and to
gauge the influence of social and historic currents on aesthetic judgments
once thought objective and normative.

IRMGARD WAGNER

CRITICAL APPROACHES TO GOETHE'S CLASSICAL DRAMAS

Iphigenie, Torquato Tasso,
AND *Die natürliche Tochter*

CAMDEN HOUSE

Gramley Library
Salem College
Winston-Salem, NC 27108

Copyright © 1995 by
CAMDEN HOUSE, INC.

Published by Camden House, Inc.
Drawer 2025
Columbia, SC 29202 USA

Printed on acid-free paper.
Binding materials are chosen for strength and
durability.

All Rights Reserved
Printed in the United States of America
First Edition

ISBN:1–57113–003–9

Library of Congress Cataloging-in-Publication Data

Wagner, Irmgard.
    Critical approaches to Goethe's classical dramas : Iphigenie,
Torquato Tasso, and Die naturliche Tochter / Irmgard Wagner. -- 1st
ed.
        p.   cm. -- (Studies in German literature, linguistics, and
culture. Literary criticism in perspective)
    Includes bibliographical references and index.
    ISBN 1–57113–003–9 (alk. paper)
    1. Goethe, Johann Wolfgang von, 1749-1832. Iphigenie auf Tauris.
2. Goethe, Johann Wolfgang von, 1749-1832. Torquato Tasso.
3. Goethe, Johann Wolfgang von, 1749-1832. Natürliche Tochter.
I. Title.   II. Series: Studies in German literature, linguistics,
and culture (Unnumbered).   Literary criticism in perspective.
PT1955. W34   1995
832'.6--dc20   95-32703
                                                                CIP

Contents

Introduction

A study that presents the critical history of Goethe's classical dramas needs to explain its selection: why those three? The reasons are frankly pragmatic. There is, first, the matter of sheer bulk. A century and a half of Goethe criticism has produced such masses of writing that to deal with even only the seven dramas traditionally considered major — *Götz, Clavigo, Stella, Egmont, Iphigenie, Tasso, Natürliche Tochter* — would have exploded the format of this series. The omission of *Faust* here is deliberate. Goethe criticism has placed this work in a category by itself, made it a text sui generis, whose critical history would have to be dealt with in a special study. Concerning the present study, it was likewise impossible to slim down the material by selecting only the major critics. Over the last century and a half under investigation here, it was precisely the major scholars who wrote about Goethe, the towering figure in German literature. In fact it was on Goethe's coattails that German literary studies rode into Fortress University. Under the leadership of Goethe scholar Wilhelm Scherer, the school of Goethe Philology became the first branch of German literary studies to achieve the rank of academic professionalism. Another reason for grouping together *Iphigenie, Tasso*, and *Die natürliche Tochter* has to do with disciplinary conventions. Scholarly tradition in literary histories, bibliographies, and Goethe monographs has established a particular category for Goethe's three classical dramas. To follow this tradition is especially indicated for a project such as this that aims to be a useable tool for workers in the vineyard of academe.

The central role of Goethe in German cultural and intellectual history, during his lifetime and later, is well known and richly documented. Karl Robert Mandelkow's four-volume work *Goethe im Urteil seiner Kritiker* (1975–79), is invaluable and indispensable in establishing the documentary background for any exploration of Goethe reception history, including this study. Wolfgang Leppmann's *The German Image of Goethe* (1961) is useful in addressing the problematical aspects of the German Goethe cult. Collections of criticism during Goethe's lifetime are presented in Julius W. Braun (1883–85, reprinted 1969) and Oscar Fambach (1953). More recently, the essays collected in *Goethes Dramen. Neue Interpretationen*, edited by Walter Hinderer (1980), make a special effort to inform on the state of criticism. The volume also contains a well-organized and user-friendly bibliography on Goethe in general, with particular emphasis on reception history, and on each of the dramas in particular.

In view of the massive history of Goethe reception, another selection had to be made among the multiplicity of reactions to the dramas, from performance reviews to articles in popular periodicals and guides to secondary school instruction. This situation was of particular concern to *Iphigenie*. Vying with *Faust* in this respect, the drama and the figure had developed into a cultural icon of mythic stature and, in consequence, had generated a body of secondary texts spanning the entire horizon of what goes by the name of cultural studies today. Keeping the focus on academic criticism was one way of dealing with the problem, a way consistent with the main purpose of this study. Academic criticism may properly be said to begin after Goethe's death. The type of questions asked during an author's lifetime, from a contemporary perspective, is fundamentally different from the kind of issues addressed in retrospect, from the historical perspective. It took precisely a decade for Goethe to become historical. The first German literary history, *Geschichte der deutschen Dichtung*, was the landmark achievement of Georg Gottfried Gervinus; its last volume, published in 1842, includes Goethe. Five years later the academic writer considered the first major Goethe critic, Karl Rosencranz, professor of philosophy occupying Kant's place at Königsberg, published (from memory!) his lecture notes in the influential book *Göthe und seine Werke*. Fifteen years after his death Goethe could be approached from a properly Hegelian, historicist distance.

Goethe's outstanding place in German culture entailed another consequence for this study. As Mandelkow has demonstrated conclusively, Goethe criticism did not remain academic. On the contrary, it became increasingly part and parcel of the historical context: demonstrably shaped by events in the turbulent German history of the last one hundred and fifty years, and to an as yet undetermined degree in turn exerting influence on that history. Or how else would we account for the role of Spengler's Western man shaped in the image of Faust, or for the ideological vicissitudes of the idea of *Humanität* formed in the image of Iphigenie? It is important to remember that Goethe's dramas occupied a different place in German life and thought than the novels or poems. The dramas were standard fare in school curricula and pièces de résistance on theater programs. Keeping in mind the significant function of theater in both middle and working class life until the very recent past, we can see that from about the mid-nineteenth century the Germans were learning their Goethe from *Faust*, *Götz*, *Egmont*, *Iphigenie*, and *Tasso*. Teachers and theater professionals in turn had learned their Goethe from precisely the critics whose work is our object of inquiry. The plaint of the Stuttgart ensemble as they were preparing a new production of *Iphigenie* in the troubled year 1977 that "die Literatur- und Theaterwissenschaft läßt einen ganz schön im Stich [literary and theater scholarship really lets you down here]" (Hobson 1980, 446), merely makes the point: that this was where they expected to find help — and they eventually did find it in Theodor Adorno's text.

Writing the story of criticism of Goethe's dramas thus became, to a rather disturbing degree, writing a history — intellectual, ideological, psychological — of Germany. Disturbing because over and over again the critical texts revealed in painful clarity how our own revered teachers had been part of and participants in that history. And because, of course, this recognition brought home the troubling knowledge that we, too, with our writing and teaching today, are implicit in whatever history is taking shape around, within, and through us. From the mid-nineteenth to the mid-twentieth century, it fell to *Iphigenie* and *Tasso* to help articulate a discourse of German self-understanding and identity, as the *Volk der Dichter und Denker* [nation of poets and thinkers] remade itself into a *Volk der Bürger, (Geschäfts-) Gründer und (Weltmacht-) Kämpfer* [nation of bourgeois, (business)founders, and (world power) warriors]. Fundamental issues such as the role of art in society; power, war, and peace; guilt, responsibility, and redemption; and most prominently *Humanität* as a problematical result of the history of secularization, all came before the forum of literary criticism. Discussion of *Die natürliche Tochter* remained safely and sparsely academic during most of this time. But to everyone's considerable astonishment, this previously ignored drama surged forward to a position of prominence in the period following the Second World War, proving a subtle linkage with *Iphigenie*. At a moment when Iphigenian ideals had become cause for general embarrassment, the sister drama could serve as substitute with the effect that critical discourse shifted its focus away from the ethical into the political field.

Given the close interweave between critical texts and historical contexts, the stop and flow of historical development itself seemed the most appropriate framework for organizing the material under examination here. The situation we observe in drama criticism confirms Mandelkow's findings that Goethe criticism generally reflects the major points of discontinuity in German history. As our study will illustrate in detail, the years 1918 and 1945 mark decisive ruptures. These signpost dates, each accompanied by a significant hiatus in the writing of critical texts, signal a turning point in the course of history: the end of an era and the beginning of a new period. The two world wars brought, first, years of silence for the duration of war action, and then, for Germany, the trauma of defeat. Both postwar periods revealed radical reversals of fortunes and values. Our texts are deeply marked by these upheavals. Indeed the writings on Goethe's dramas during those turbulent years open new avenues of insight into precisely these values and some of the reasons for their change.

Criticism of each drama will be presented in three segments. The first will encompass the period before 1918, when Goethe scholarship slowly emerged and then burst into its first bloom in the atmosphere of Bismarckian and Wilhelminian nationalist ambitions, while struggling at the same time to find and defend its place against the competition from scientific enthusiasm. The second segment covers the years between 1918 and 1945. We have become accustomed to seeing the culture of the Weimar Republic and the Third Reich in stark contrast to one another, separated by the historic rupture of 1933. Contrary to our expectations, German Goethe criticism shows an amazing degree of continuity over those years, while on the other hand English criticism takes decisive steps to counterpoint German developments. The third period, since 1945, brings us up to the present. Here more attention is paid to the more distant texts which have now, too, become historical, informing about postwar reactions to the most difficult experiences in modern German history.

Obviously, every scholar writing now will have to examine on her or his own those texts that the discipline considers part of recent criticism. A rather summary presentation, therefore, deals with criticism of about the last decade, showing major trends and approaches in the hope of offering at least some clues leading through the maze of contemporary criticism. Orientation is the purpose, too, of the brief introductory narratives that open each of the period segments. They aim to sketch in the historical background and to give an overview of the main roads taken by criticism in each period. Finally, the bibliography lists in chronological sequence the authors and texts discussed here, with major editions of Goethe's works presented separately. In the history of Goethe criticism, introductions to the major editions constitute a crucial category of critical texts. Themselves scholars of superior reputation, the editorial commentators have consistently set standards of interpretation for their colleagues. Their impact on successive generations of scholars has been immense. The neophyte in the profession reads introductory comments to the works together with, and therefore practically inseparable from, Goethe's own texts. These comments thus acquire an extraordinary status of normative power that is difficult to overestimate. This study makes a special effort to take the importance of editorial comments into account.

1: *Iphigenie auf Tauris*

UNTIL 1918

IT WAS A favorite tack of critics engaged in the war over the classics during the 1970s to accuse the nineteenth century of *Iphigenie* abuse. It was then, we read, as the bourgeoisie strove toward social status through education and created for themselves the new identity of *Bildungsbürgertum* [educated bourgeoisie] that this Goethean drama acquired the patina of classicity. The critics of the seventies defined classicity in negative terms; to them it meant the universal validity, timeless rigidity, and unchallengeable perfection that is the quality of myth (see Jauß 1973, Hobson 1984b). There is much truth to this view of early *Iphigenie* criticism. The whole story, however, is far more complicated than the highly ideologized version propagated in the seventies. A somewhat more complete version would point out three crucial aspects of the nineteenth century background that framed *Iphigenie* criticism: developments in (1) theology and philosophy, (2) education and national identity, and (3) science.

Given the close proximity between the disciplines of theology, philosophy, and nascent German literary studies, the first of these three aspects presents the most obvious context for approaches to Goethe's drama. As philosophy — many of whose practitioners were trained theologians — turned away from Hegelian spirituality and Christian orthodoxy toward historical criticism, materialism, atheism, or some sort of pantheism, the central theme of *Iphigenie* was perceived to be the relation between God and man. More precisely at issue was the definition of both humanity (*Menschlichkeit*) and the divine. The nineteenth century was more concerned by far with the side of the divine, while the other side of the issue, the definition of humanity, would dominate in the twentieth. The process of secularization that characterized German thought in the nineteenth century, spearheaded by such figures as David Friedrich Strauß (*Das Leben Jesu* 1836), Ludwig Feuerbach (*Das Wesen des Christentums* 1841), and Karl Marx, was a wrenching experience for a fundamentally conservative and Christian culture.

As critics debated the respective powers of human versus divine agency in *Iphigenie*, there was a gradual shift of emphasis from human empowerment to an increasing takeover of the human by divine power, to the point where Goethe's heroine finally became an incarnation of the divine. The nineteenth century's Iphigenian myth of the Christ substitute, *Christuser-satz*, was born. With this claim in a speech before the Goethe Society published in the *Jahrbuch* of 1888, professional philosopher Kuno Fischer transferred Goethe's fiction from the domain of literature into the kingdom of philosophy, which had itself already annexed the realm of religion.

The second aspect, questions of education and national identity, functioned more as a hidden subtext than as evident context for *Iphigenie* criticism. In the second half of the century, however, these questions loomed large in the public debate; historians have labeled them with the code words *Realismusstreit* and *Griechengermanentum*. The first designates the controversy over secondary school reform, more particularly over the role of the traditional Humboldtian Gymnasium with its emphasis on Latin and Greek language and literature on the one hand, versus the modernizers' claims for the *Realgymnasium*, which would emphasize science, modern languages, and German literature. The second term, *Griechen-germanentum*, refers to a brand of conservative ideology in the quest for national identity that assumed particular urgency with the establishment of the Wilhelminian Empire in 1871. This view asserted a special relationship, historically and culturally, between the ancient Greek and the German peoples, for the purpose of wholesale adoption of the admired Greek image for the new German nation.

To put it somewhat crudely: the *Volk der Dichter und Denker* was declared the natural heir of Greek high culture in contrast with the rest of the West — France and Britain particularly — which had sold out to crass commerce and industry. The issue was of more than academic interest. The kaiser, Wilhelm II, with his ambition to compete precisely with the commercial powers on the world stage, inserted himself in the debate on the side of the modernists when, at an important convention on education in 1890, he demanded "eine wehrhafte deutsche Jugend, nicht junge Griechen und Römer [German youth prepared to fight, not young Greeks and Romans]" as end products of secondary schooling (see Ameri 1991). In this contest *Iphigenie* served both camps. Neohumanists could offer a bridge and compromise: here was the Greek spirit Germanized through the work of the greatest German poet. Modernists could wield a battering ram: here German literature had proved itself congenial to the Greek model, had made the study of the Greek language superfluous.

Finally, the explosion of scientific knowledge and of public interest in the sciences during the later part of the century had a direct impact on *Iphigenie* criticism. Advances in the biological and psychological sciences in particular had wrought upheaval in the public mind to a degree that is hard to imagine today. Darwinism, the laws of heredity, and studies in psychophysiology linking mental phenomena to physical and environmental conditions, amounted to a metaphysical revolution on a Copernican scale. It was determinism threatening to displace ethics, philosophy, and, above all, theology.

These transformations affected *Iphigenie* criticism in two ways. One approach, on the metaphysical plane, contests the divinely empowered human, autonomous and in control of destiny, which Goethe's heroine had come to embody; and thus, from the 1890s the figure of Iphigenie recedes into the background. The second effect derives more immediately from scientific innovation with the consequence of making Orestes the center of interest. Focusing on him as the bearer of a family curse — code for hereditary disease in the public discourse of the time — suffering from mental illness, the challenge now was to explain his cure.

In the overall scheme of fundamental transformations leading up to the dawn of a new era in 1918, *Iphigenie* criticism accompanied the path of German thought from Enlightenment optimism to the skepticism and irony associated with modernism. Just as Hegelian faith in the emancipatory power of truth shines forth from the first major interpretation (Rosencranz 1847), so does Kierkegaardian pessimism pervade the strongest reading toward the close of the period (Schrempf 1907). In the narrower frame of literary criticism itself we can trace other lines that have to do with the development of the new discipline. The origin of academic German studies in classical philology is perhaps nowhere more evident than in the scholarship on Goethe's Greek drama. Indeed it was by means of this work that the first generation of Goethe scholars aimed to establish the category of classicism in German literary history, a trend deplored as early as 1855 by the (English) outsider George Henry Lewes, author of the first Goethe biography.

Moreover *Iphigenie* proved a godsend for the positivist orientation of the period. The pursuit of source relations found ample play in comparing Goethe with Euripides, in locating bits of Greek culture in the German drama, and in tracing Goethe's development toward a German renaissance of classicism (Hettner 1870: "beste italienische Renaissance") through the four extant versions of the work. Closer study of the critics reveals, however, the defeat of the positivist claim to scientific objectivity, as the new discipline found itself caught in the dilemmas emanating from the classicist-modernist education controversy and from the ideology of *Griechengermanentum*.

Thus we find a strange competition between the merits of the different versions, posed in nationalistic terms as the German (prose version) versus the Roman (verse version) *Iphigenie*. Similarly the central question about precisely how Goethe differed from Euripides is skewed by the subliminal battle of modernity versus traditionalism. The drama's installation as a classic may be seen as compromise solution of this dilemma. In contrast with all earlier Goethe dramas, *Iphigenie* was declared to be not of the eighteenth century, not of its own time, but of all time and of all mankind: the poem of "reine Menschlichkeit [pure humanity]."

Biographism, the other main line of literary scholarship, found itself rather at a loss, having to admit that of all Goethe's dramas *Iphigenie* was farthest from confession literature. Goethe's self-identification as Orest in his Sturm und Drang period had to be considered an exaggeration: guilt over the abandoned beloved, Friederike, could not, it was argued, compare with matricide. And for the exalted image of Iphigenie that the nineteenth century developed, Charlotte von Stein seemed an inadequate model. Charlotte's role in the genesis was duly acknowledged or decried, but it is interesting to see that as early as Herman Grimm (1877) other avenues to the birth of *Iphigenie* were suggested, for instance Gluck's French opera as transmitted by Wieland. There was, however, general agreement concerning the drama's role in Goethe's development: *Iphigenie* marked the overcoming of Promethean Titanism in the decisive step from Sturm und Drang toward classicism.

Concerning aspects of form, the installation of *Iphigenie* as the model work of German classicism made the question of genre paramount. In the context of and in contest with model classics of other national literatures — Greek and Shakespearean tragedy, French *tragédie classique* — what sort of drama was this rather late and obviously unconventional piece? Lewes (1855) took German scholarship to task for assimilating *Iphigenie* to classical Greek tragedy. By way of explicit contrast, he set the British course of approaching the work from the background of (English) Romanticism, specifically from the Byronic and Shelleyan genre of dramatic poetry, with emphasis on poetic qualities.

By coining the term *Seelendrama* [soul drama], Wilhelm Scherer (1883) reasserted *Iphigenie*'s place in the German tradition at the same time as he reoriented that tradition in a decisive new direction. Scherer's new genre made *Innerlichkeit* the focus of German classicism and criticism: inner events (*der innere Vorgang*) not outer happenings (*Handlung*) are supposed to constitute the ideal drama. Scherer's innovation was a success story. The new category of *Seelendrama* continued to be enriched with definitions and variations all the way to Friedrich Gundolf's radical concept of "Verseelung" (1916).

Some of the variations were intended to explain *Iphigenie*'s lack of success on stage, such as "Lesedrama" [drama for reading] or, following the triumph of Wagnerian opera, "Weihespiel" [sacral play]. A late variation on the soul theme, the term "Erbauungsliteratur" [spiritual literature] (Schrempf 1907), connotes the beginning of critical distancing in the early twentieth century. Aside from genre questions there was hardly any attention to formal and aesthetic aspects, notwithstanding the general interest in aesthetic topics around the turn of the century. By that time *Iphigenie*'s model status precluded genuine debate; criticism had cast this drama's form in marble as simply perfect.

First among the critics who set the frame, Georg Gottfried Gervinus in his *Geschichte der deutschen Dichtung* (1842) presents *Iphigenie* as a synthesis of classical and modern features. The classical form guarantees aesthetic quality, while the modern substance conveys relevance to current interests. Already central to the drama's modernity is *Innerlichkeit*: "Gesinnung" [mentality] rather than action is its motivating force. Current interests are well represented in the themes highlighted by Gervinus: family reconciliation as metaphor for the elusive goal of German unity, patriotism, and, with particular emphasis, feminine consciousness bordering on feminism.

Five years later Karl Rosencranz in his seminal work *Göthe und seine Werke* (1847) welcomes *Iphigenie* enthusiastically into the camp of progressive modernism. He cares nothing for the drama's praised classical perfection ("there is a difference between praising the drama and understanding it" 247); instead his focus is precisely the difference between classical, mythic consciousness and the modern consciousness of freedom in history. His intellectual analysis in the Hegelian method presents *Iphigenie* as a parable of humankind's progress from object to subject of history. He explores the drama's wide range of human relations — gender, generational, familial, national, power, moral, and spiritual — to show how they pass from necessity to freedom by means of truth. Truth as an absolute value is available to humans and holds the solution to all conflicts of the drama and, by implication, of human life. Rosencranz's principle of interpretation, his belief in the emancipatory power of cognition, shines forth in Orest's hermeneutic skill as he discovers truth in the cryptic divine text: "Er erkennt mit zweifelloser Klarheit den wahren Sinn des zweideutigen Götterausspruchs [He recognizes with doubtless clarity the true meaning of the ambiguous divine word]."

Salvation lies within human, not divine power, a point that Rosencranz stresses with a bit of ironically flavored philosophical terminology: Goethe's solution is "immanent anthropologisch" while Euripides' ending with Athena as dea ex machina was "transzendent theologisch" (254). The point of Goethe's drama understood as hermeneutic exercise is to conquer history, to realize human freedom not from but in history. According to Rosencranz, *Iphigenie* reinterprets (Greek) fate as history. This changes the meaning of human destiny from the mythic concept of a fight to the death against fate ("Vernichtung des Schicksals") to rising above past events ("Erhebung über das Geschehene") by means of modern historical consciousness, which in turn implies the possibility of new beginnings and thus asserts a belief in progress (258). In his reading of *Iphigenie*, Rosencranz performs a transactional demonstration of the birth of historical consciousness; he has left us an exciting document of a fundamental step in the evolution of modern mentality.

The modern approach taken by the philosopher from Königsberg (Rosencranz) had few followers. One exception was another voice from the margins of the German not-yet-Empire, which unfortunately did not enter mainstream criticism: Franz Bratranek's study published in Vienna in 1853. The reasons may be that his intended audience were the pedagogues of the Hapsburg Empire rather than his scholarly colleagues, and that his essay on *Iphigenie* was hidden in a volume with the uninformative title *Ästhetische Studien*. Quite possibly, too, his reading of the heroine, on the one hand, as well as his views of authority, on the other, were felt to be too critical.

Bratranek reads the drama in the frame of genre theory, anticipating the explorations of inner form a half century later. His focus is on the theme of individual autonomy shaped and emerging through conflict with the suprapersonal authorities of family, state, law, culture, and religion. Iphigenie herself is much in need of learning before her autonomy can emerge: she first has to overcome her own curse of misunderstood autonomy. Only a few years after the traumatic events of 1848, such views must have appeared positively subversive in the strict authoritarian school system of the Hapsburg Empire.

The dominant voice, however, came from the side of the classicists. It was Heinrich Düntzer in his book of so-called *Erläuterungen* [Explanations], a voice that still today gives the classicist effort a bad name. Düntzer virtually cornered the market on *Iphigenie* until philosopher Kuno Fischer's best-seller appeared in 1888. First published in 1859, Düntzer's book achieved its fifth edition in 1894. Notwithstanding its commercial success, its quality is well below that of the other volumes in Düntzer's series *Erläuterungen* of Goethe's dramas; it was so bad that even the positivists of the later nineteenth century denounced it as "Düntzerian uncriticism." It is precisely Düntzer's attempt to assert *Iphigenie*'s citizenship in the classical kingdom that vitiates his commentary. He altogether ignores the ideas, issues, and problems addressed by his predecessors. Instead he offers pedestrian paraphrases of Goethe's poetic text and spreads etymological, philological, and mythological trivia throughout his voluminous notes, in order to prove the drama's classical Greek essence.

In later editions, when Düntzer does take account of contemporary criticism, he lashes out at scholars of the modernist persuasion. His favorite target in the fifth edition (1894) is Kuno Fischer's reading of Iphigenie as a Christ figure. For Düntzer, Iphigenie is thoroughly human. She is not, however, the learning subject of emancipation as in Rosencranz and Bratranek, but woman in submission to divine will. She embodies "das Ewig-Weibliche" (42), ideal femininity characterized by "Gottvertrauen" [trust in God], which Düntzer sees rooted in Goethe's worshipful relation with Charlotte von Stein and the Duchess Luise. In Düntzer's reading it is not human but divine agency, activated by Iphigenie's "Gottvertrauen," which solves and saves: Orest from the furies, Iphigenie from her truth crisis, the Greeks from Thoas's revenge (128, 158, 164f.).

The attempt of German philologists to appropriate *Iphigenie* for the classical Greek tradition provoked the irate opposition of Goethe's first biographer, George Henry Lewes (1855). While Lewes gives full rein to his admittedly hyperbolic admiration of Goethe's poetry, he yet casts a critical look on the drama's form and substance. His emphasis on Goethe's difference from Euripides rests on formal grounds, and Goethe comes off worse in the comparison. But in substance, too, the drama is declared decidedly modern, a product of late eighteenth-century morality and sensibility. Its characters are kinder, gentler, and weaker, because they are separated by Christian centuries from their pagan Greek models. The heroine is a "Christian maiden [whose] Christianized conscience" shudders at deceit. Goethe's Thoas, "a moral figure," looks benignly boring, and Iphigenie's dilemma appears positively harmless compared to her situation in Euripides, where "the fierce Scythian looms from the dark background, terrible as fate" (270). Lewes's judgment on Goethe's protagonists would haunt German critics for decades to come, as they repeatedly tried to prove him wrong. The view of Thoas survived subliminally, one might say, until its resuscitation a century later in Martin Walser's incendiary attack of 1965: "Aber Thoas ist Weimaraner [But Thoas is a Weimar citizen]."

A more immediate effect of Lewes's critical stance can be seen in Karl Goedeke's introduction to *Iphigenie* in the 1866 Cotta edition of Goethe's collected works, the last before Cotta's exclusive copyright ran out and the first to offer introductions. Goedeke practices precisely what Rosencranz had tried to preach against: untrammeled panegyrics. His encomium installs the work as a cut-in-marble classic: "perfect" it forbids analysis, the critic's words serve only to praise. And so Goedeke initiates the vocabulary that would become typical of *Iphigenie* criticism for the rest of the century: "tragisch, sittlich, edelst, (er)heben, Menschlichkeit, Läuterung, unendliche Seelen(fülle), Vollendung, harmonisch, rein, Schönheit [tragic, ethical, noblest, uplift, humanity, purification, infinite (plenitude of) soul, perfection, harmonic, pure, beauty]."

In more measured terms, *Studiendirektor* [highest rank of Gymnasium teacher] Friedrich Strehlke in his introduction to the Hempel edition (1868–79, Vol. 7) sets a precedent for German educators' position over the next century by suggesting the category of modern classic. According to this definition *Iphigenie*, like other masterworks of the Goethe-Schiller production in classicism, is neither classical nor purely modern but universal, of timeless human relevance. The heroine in particular is a paradigmatic figure, since she exhibits human nature's original purity of mind

Gramley Library
Salem College
Winston-Salem, NC 27108

("die in ihr ursprünglich liegende Reinheit der Gesinnung"). Strehlke's characterization of the drama's form: "plastische Schönheit . . . lichtvolle Klarheit . . . unter dem heitern Himmel Italiens gelungen [plastic beauty . . . light-filled clarity . . . achieved under the serene Italian sky]" (107–9), heralds a new field of discourse.

The sensational success of Jacob Burckhardt's *Die Kultur der Renaissance in Italien* (1860) had brought the cult and culture of the Renaissance home to the educated classes, with an explosion of interest in art, art history, and Italian journeys. The Italian Renaissance vogue left clear marks in the criticism of *Iphigenie* and more particularly *Tasso*, the Goethean works with a substantial Italian genesis. (The spirit of the age was distinctly hostile to the most Italian of Goethe's works: his *Römische Elegien. Iphigenie* and *Tasso* promotion thus also served the purpose of hiding the embarrassing erotic poetry of the *Roman Elegies*.) In addition, the ideology of *Griechengermanentum* found welcome support in emphasizing the significance of Italy for Goethe, who could now be claimed as mediator between German and Renaissance culture. For the *Griechengermanen* his works had generated a second rebirth or Renaissance of Greek culture, had demonstrated Germany to be the true heir of classical Greece.

Thus Hermann Hettner in his highly respected and influential *Geschichte der deutschen Literatur im achtzehnten Jahrhundert* (1870) summarily declares the drama in its formal aspects "beste italienische Renaissance." But the form interests him far less than the figure of Iphigenie. She is the focus of his account and he completes what Goedeke had begun: he extends the aura of apotheosis from the work to the heroine. Much as he strives for unadulterated praise, his characterization of Iphigenie is yet fraught with contradictions. She emerges as a Christ-like figure, suprahuman and yet ("und doch") fully human. Her superhuman features prevail by far and mark Iphigenie as saint, indeed goddess. At the same time as she personifies Fate, however, she also embodies humankind's highest moral ideals: "the idea of humanity, moral justice."

Just as influential as Hettner's divinization of Goethe's heroine was his procedure of what is currently known as *othering*. Identifying with Goethe (most obviously 344), Hettner constructs Woman, that is Iphigenie, as Other. He makes her the ideal that Man must strive to reach in a life of struggle against reality and through "hard efforts of *Bildung*," while She is by nature ("Natur" "angeboren") pure, whole, good, secure, harmonious, etc. (A skeptical feminist historian might suspect an attempt to legitimate the nineteenth century's exclusion of women from higher education.)

In Hettner's fascinating account, Goethean "reine Menschlichkeit" is defined and thereby limited as unattainable other, "reine Weiblichkeit": "das unmittelbare Naturdasein der höchsten sittlichen Harmonie [ist] die unbefangene Sicherheit reiner und hoher Weiblichkeit [the immediate natural existence of highest moral harmony is the unselfconscious security

vatanley Library
Salem College
Winston-Salem, NC 27108

of pure and high femininity]" (349). The issue of gender introduced into *Iphigenie* criticism as early as Gervinus and Rosencranz now is radicalized and at the same time withdrawn from critical examination into the realm of nature-ordained absolutes. Where Rosencranz presented gender division as a historical dialectic working toward progress in human relations, Hettner institutes an essential and therefore unalterable difference between female and male.

Introductions to the Goethe editions of the eighties proceeded apace on the road to Saint Iphigenie. With equal enthusiasm they played on the theme of the German Renaissance in Goethe's masterwork. Masterwork status now was undisputed; even among Goethe's other dramas *Iphigenie* had become the compass point, the norm by which other works were measured. Ludwig Geiger in the Grote edition (1883) sings the German Renaissance tune as he praises this "Nachbildung" [re-creation of a shape] of a Greek original. By using the neologism *Nachbildung* instead of the common term *Nachahmung* [imitation] Geiger insists on the originality of the modern text, which succeeded in "bringing Euripides closer to modern views." Geiger reminds us of a similar feat of *Nachbildung* when Goethe's precursor Wieland modernized Alceste. Young Goethe's fierce satire of that modernization in his *Götter, Helden und Wieland* is passed over in silence.

The mid-nineteenth century had done its best to promote the classical Goethe over the Sturm und Drang model, a trend that had already begun to shift with the advent of the Wilhelminian Empire. In contrast to Geiger's rearguard emphasis on classicism, his turn to Wieland had a promising future. With the Wieland-Goethe line, a history of the German Renaissance began to be shaped, a history that the next century saw develop into *Deutsche Geistesgeschichte* [history of the German spirit].

Karl J. Schröer in the *Nationallitteratur* edition (1886) keeps his focus firmly on Goethe's biography, but he, too, pays at least lip service to the German Renaissance creed: Goethe's love for antiquity made him a second Winckelmann, who re-created German culture as a reign of art and humanity. In the context of Greece reborn, it is only natural that new myths should emerge, and indeed we see both editors busily fashioning the myth of Saint Iphigenie. Geiger refines Iphigenian *Weiblichkeit* [femininity], adding virginity as an essential ingredient, with a slant towards masculinity: "nicht weichlich und weibisch, sondern stark und besonnen [not softish and effeminate but strong and deliberate]." His holy virgin is a missionary who spreads blessing, who learns and teaches, and who can change and sanctify mankind through faith.

It should be noted that Geiger's religious vocabulary is limited to the figure of Iphigenie: "bekehrend; Glauben nach langen, bangen Zweifeln; heiligend und weihend [converting others; faith after long, anxious doubts; sanctifying and consecrating]." Schröer's saint is of the charismatic kind who works sheer, but definitely feminine, magic: "heilwirkende Kraft weiblichen Zaubers." The medium of this magic is female love, infinite and creative yet non-sensual ("ewige schöpferische Liebe . . . des Weibes"), its purity safeguarded by a childlike component of heightened inwardness ("kindliche Seeleninnigkeit"). The effect of this magic in Schröer's narration brings Goethe's drama perilously close to the despised French boulevard comedies of the time: "[Orest] wird besänftigt und Thoas wird besänftigt und alle Irrungen lösen sich in Harmonieen auf, ganz allein durch . . . ihr liebevolles, lauteres Wesen [Orest is calmed and Thoas is calmed and all errors dissolve in harmonies, solely through her loving, pure nature]" (lx–lxi).

Dissenting views are rare; with the exception of Herman Grimm's evasive account in his *Goethe* lectures (1877), they come from outside the mainstream. Heinrich Bulthaupt, a man of the theater, and Alexander Baumgartner, Jesuit priest and the first German Goethe biographer, both reject the new classic for obviously different reasons. For Bulthaupt in his *Dramaturgie der Classiker* (1882), it is precisely because academic critics created the myth of the perfect work of art, of the marble-cold classic, that *Iphigenie* has problems on stage. There are, he finds, no actresses in real life who can do justice to the rarefied, idealized image of the heroine that the audience of "Gebildeten" [educated persons] carry in their heads.

His focus therefore shifts to Orest, the "youthful Greek hero" in the "proud, masculine" Achillean mould, and more enthusiastically still to Pylades. In the context of seemingly unanimous idolization of Iphigenian sublimity it comes as a shock to read that the pragmatic antagonist of the saintly heroine is in fact the favorite of contemporary audiences. They see in him the hero of empirical reason, who is not above using ruse and trickery if it avails: "das herzgewinnendste Ideal . . . der sicher und listig arbeitende und rettende Verstand [the ideal that most surely conquers all hearts . . . reason working and rescuing with certainty and ruse]" (119).

In his massive biography of the same year, *Göthe: Sein Leben und seine Werke*, Alexander Baumgartner openly campaigns against Iphigenie's canonization. Coming on the heals of a papal encyclical (1879) issued to counteract the spread of religious liberalization and secular humanism, Baumgartner's stance is evidently motivated by catholic orthodoxy, and less evidently by clerical machismo. He has to reject salvation through human power, but beyond that, Baumgartner finds the idea of an *ErlöserIn*, a female Christ substitute, unacceptable. Equally intriguing is his love-hate ambivalence toward the drama as a whole.

In an astounding rhetoric of rage he fulminates against Goethe scholars for having ruined any possibility for enjoying the work's "religious dignity and majesty." He credits the Greek original, however, with this exalted quality without explaining how in that case sublimity might still be found and enjoyed in Goethe's text. To discredit the modern author's creation, he makes paradoxical use of the selfsame Goethe scholarship he so heartily despises, linking the drama to Goethe's much-discussed relations to women. While a female redeemer is unthinkable to the orthodox Jesuit, he relishes projecting Iphigenie as an erotic object of male fantasy. This drama, he declares, stands somewhere between a romantic-sentimentalist fantasy of the (in)famous lover Goethe and contemporary French — meaning frothy and frivolous — opera, imagining a heroine "far more beautiful than all *Frankfurterinnen, Leipzigerinnen* . . ." whom Goethe-Giovanni might have encountered in real life (413).

Mainstream criticism, however, held fast to Iphigenie's symbolic function within the spirit of secular humanism. The choice of Kuno Fischer as main speaker before the third convention of the Goethe Society in 1888 was significant in this respect. The famous professor and historian of philosophy represented the conservative mainstream of German thought at the time. His *Festvortrag*, published in the *Goethe Jahrbuch* and again, in book form, in 1900, would become the focus of *Iphigenie* criticism far into the next century. Fischer casts the quasi-religious perambulations of earlier critics into Christian concepts. Goethe meant to write an allegory of Christ's "stellvertretende Leiden [representative suffering]" to redeem mankind from its "Erbsünde [original sin]." Like Christ untainted by the sin of mankind, Iphigenie is free from the "Erbsünde" of her family's curse.

Goethe's drama thus proves human power superior to the seemingly all-powerful law of heredity, which in the popularized science of the period functioned as a veritable bogey. Not miracles, but Iphigenie's character ruled by composure and becalmed desire ("Gelassenheit, Windstille der Begierden") renders invalid the law of heredity. To prove his point with an example from real history, Fischer calls on the mystic Meister Eckehart, whom historicist cultivation of the German past had made familiar to Fischer's audience of the educated elite. Iphigenie is still a "Seelsorgerin [minister; literally: caring for souls]," who fulfills a religious mission in redeeming her brother.

Fischer nevertheless insists that Iphigenian religiosity rests not on orthodox Christianity but on ethical deism as expressed in two Goethe poems of the *Iphigenie* period: "Grenzen der Menschheit" and "Das Göttliche." Fischer quotes the latter in its entirety to conclude: "Von diesem Glauben war der Charakter unserer Iphigenie erfüllt, in diesem Glauben war er gedichtet [it was this faith that filled the character of our Iphigenie; this faith created her character]."

If we find Fischer's closing lines a mite too assertive, there is good reason for that. Criticism, incited by developments in theories of heredity and environment, of psychology and mental illness, had begun to zero in on the issue of Orest's cure. In the scientific spirit of the time, Fischer's religious solution came immediately under attack. In a related development, the focus of interest was shifting away from Iphigenie's calm spirituality to the figure of Orest for reasons that had much to do with the assertive posture emphasized in the cultural politics of the Wilhelminian Empire. Wilhelm II, we have seen, wanted "eine wehrhafte deutsche Jugend [a combat-ready German youth]" to come out of his schools. The figure and fate of Orest became a metaphor for the revival of the German spirit from quietism, passivity, and the infection of decadence and the entrance of a new age of youthful activism and energetic enterprise.

The two big Goethe biographies of 1895 exemplify in stark contrast the emergence of a split in the attitude toward *Iphigenie*. Albert Bielschowsky, whose *Göthe: Sein Leben und seine Werke* would become the most widely-read Goethe biography of the period, embraces and embroiders mainstream canonization of heroine and drama. Richard Meyer, in his three-volume work simply called *Goethe*, demotes Iphigenie from her exalted status and is highly critical of the work to a degree that in the discourse of the period appears nothing short of iconoclasm. Where Bielschowsky admits that the drama is difficult to understand, he faults the recipients — "anhaltende Versenkung [long and deep immersion in meditation]" is required for proper appreciation — or he situates large domains of the text beyond human understanding altogether. Iphigenie, "Heilige, Göttergleiche [Saint, Godlike]," is far above us humans. She feels and thinks differently, for instance in her much-discussed reaction when Orest reveals his identity. Average humans would express their emotions in a display of joy; godlike saints pray.

The postulated difference between Iphigenie and mere mortals serves to explain other puzzles, too. Her enigmatic communication with her brother is based in mystic communion, an immediate sort of cognition which in lower souls might be called hypnotism. On the issue of secular humanism versus Christianity, Bielschowsky stoutly maintains the reign of "reine Menschlichkeit," drawing support from the contemporaneity of Lessing's *Nathan*, that other acknowledged paean of humanist faith.

His paradoxical stance on this point, however, shows that criticism by now has created problems of its own. Not being a philosopher skilled in negotiating the subtleties of human versus divine essences, Bielschowsky falls into the trap that Kuno Fischer's straddling of extremes had prepared. At the same time as he asserts the supremacy of human over divine agency he yet imagines Iphigenie's role in a clearly Christian frame of reference and vocabulary. She is a Christ figure who redeems fallen mankind through giving her life for theirs. She saves individuals through mediating divine grace: Orest for instance, "der sich zum Glauben an die göttliche Gnade bekehrt [who converts to faith in divine grace]" (Vol. 1, 432f., 442f.). On the issue of Orest's salvation, then, Bielschowsky has no truck with modern views of psychological cure; he is squarely back with Christian tradition requiring faith, conversion, and divine grace.

Viewed against this background, Richard Meyer's reading of the same year is truly sensational. Meyer attacks the Iphigenie myth from all sides. "No more-than-lifesize heroine," Iphigenie is just your average woman — average in terms of the era's views of femininity, of course: "a pure and noble woman," who is nevertheless acutely conscious of her female weakness and who moreover talks far too much about female oppression, "Frauenschicksal." Having been thus downsized, Iphigenie is ready for marginalization, as Meyer displaces her from the center of the drama. Orest is the true protagonist, and the drama's main theme is his rebirth from suicidal melancholy and apathy to a new life of youthful vigor, emblematic of "aus Wertherscher Tatenlosigkeit wieder auftauchende Jugend [youth re-emerging from Wertherian inactivity]." *Iphigenie* has become a rallying call to German youth in the era of decadence.

Meyer tends to actualize in other, less obvious, ways, too. The family curse represents the law of heredity, and Meyer finds the root of the curse in what Wilhelminian culture considered cardinal vices: insubordination and lack of self-discipline. Iphigenie's major function is to conquer this curse by attacking its roots, a role for which woman is supremely well suited: she has to rehearse and model submission. Meyer expresses his approval in a nice paradox defining (female) strength as weakness: "Iphigenie hat die Kraft sich unterzuordnen [Iphigenie has the strength of submission]."

Finally, it turns out that Meyer's own hero is not Orest, weaker brother of Hamlet and seeker of the absolute, but the representative of empirical reason, Pylades, whom he sketches with empathetic admiration: "unschätzbar, fromm, umsichtig, tapfer, heiter, liebevoll [inestimable, God-fearing, circumspect, brave, cheerful, loving]." Meyer then uses his reading of Pylades as evidence for his thesis that truth in this drama is not an absolute value, not "Fichte's apodictic truth postulate." Pylades' pragmatism ("Lehre von der Welt") is right. Orest's reading of the oracle, praised by Rosencranz and followers as the crowning discovery of truth, is a mere pun. Meyer's judgment on the drama's aesthetic value is no less severe, most particularly on the language, whose universally praised beauties he faults as sententious, monotonous, too figurative, and altogether "ungoethisch," a problem he attributes — in line with current Francophobia — to the dangerous foreign model of French classicism that Goethe had adopted for his *Iphigenie* (201–5).

From the late eighties until the turn of the century, the forum for *Iphigenie* discussion widened from works editions and Goethe monographs to include a number of journals. It is somewhat surprising to see that the *Goethe Jahrbuch* contains very few articles on *Iphigenie* (three in the two decades since its beginning in 1880). The shift of interest from the classicist to the young and post-classicist Goethe and, above all, the tidal surge of a *Faust* cult among the Goethe establishment may help explain the fact. Other journals were more welcoming, particularly *Neue Jahrbücher für Philologie und Pädagogik*, the organ of classical philology (*Altphilologie*), where *Iphigenie* may be said to have found an adoptive home (three articles 1889–99). Publications of more general interest, too, offered essays (*Deutsche Rundschau, Preußische Jahrbücher, Nord und Süd*): *Iphigenie* had become a common possession *(Bildungsgut)* among the German educated classes.

Of special note is an essay in the *Deutsche Rundschau* of 1897 by Herman Grimm, doyen of Goethe scholars or, in Mandelkow's term: "Goethes Reichsstatthalter" (1975–79, Vol. 3, xxxvi). In a remarkable reversal of the slighting treatment he had given the drama in his *Goethe* lectures (1877), Grimm now attempts to help *Iphigenie* compete against the overwhelming *Faust* force. To counteract the drama's lack of theatrical success, he stages an imaginary performance based on close readings of significant passages. The aesthetic orientation of art historian and Renaissance enthusiast Grimm yields aperçus unique for his time, as when he compares the enigmatic dialogue of Iphigenie and Orest in act 3 to Beethoven's late quartets, or the conclusion to a Beethovenian symphonic finale.

Yet these impressionistic flights of aesthetic imagination recede before Grimm's main concern, which is to demonstrate this drama's significance within contemporary German culture and ideology, in order to construct the figure of Iphigenie as a competing paradigm alongside the frontrunner Faust. Both of these Goethean characters, he declares, have become "Weltcharaktere [world characters]" (title of essay) through many translations and editions in other countries. In his project of actualization he propounds Iphigenie as a model for today's woman, who needs strength of character to meet the challenges of the historical moment. In her decision crisis of act 4 Iphigenie becomes "im Geiste des heutigen Tages ein Charakter [a character in the spirit of today]."

But this woman is a model for the German man, too, in the spirit of monarchic cultural imperialism. She represents superior humanity as only royals can: "Königstochter" with "Machtinstinkt und Souveränetät... 'Nur Agamemnons Tochter' ... gehört zu den erhabenen Stellen deutscher Dichtung. Dieses 'Nur' ist kolossal [power instinct and sovereignty... 'Only Agamemnon's daughter' ... is one of the sublime passages in German poetry. This 'Only' is colossal]." Together with her brother she guarantees the people a brighter future ("Repräsentant höherer königlicher Zukunft") than could be provided by "the savage Scythian Prince," who is also a coward ("verkriecht sich hinter den 'Dienst'") but can be saved since he desires "the blessings of supreme humanity." The German colonizing enterprise in the background of this reading becomes explicit when Grimm reflects on the Homeric tradition of Greek supremacy in the face of Barbarian warriors, as mirrored in Goethe's Orest: "Wir sehen ja auch heute geringe deutsche Mannschaft sich ganzer Heerhaufen afrikanischer Naturkämpfer und ihrer Fürsten erwehren [We see today as well small German contingents fight off entire hordes of African nature warriors and their princes]" (107–123).

For Grimm's agenda of German-Greek supremacy it made sense not to make an issue out of the issue that well-nigh monopolized journal discussion of the time: the cure of Orest. A guilt-ridden matricide driven to insanity would ill accord with Grimm's representative of royal superiority. The sequence of curse and cure itself, however, serves his optimistic ideology. In the mythic history of mankind, he points out, the "Fall into original guilt" has ever been the prerequisite of progress. Orest's "dream" shows that a bad past can be undone, that the new world order envisaged by Goethe is "paradise regained": "eine nach rückwärts ihre eigenen Taten wieder aufhebende Weltordnung . . . die kein Böses und keine Sünde kennt [a world order which retroactively annuls its own acts . . . which knows neither evil nor sin]" (111).

It was precisely the question of Orest's cure, variously called "Heilung" or "Entsühnung," that preoccupied *Iphigenie* critics from the late eighties through the first two decades of the next century. To a literary scholarship trying to emulate science it was unacceptable that Goethe should have made an inexplicable event the axis of his play (Heinemann 1899). The two designations under which the topic appears identify the two problems involved. "Entsühnung [absolution]" refers to the ethical problem of guilt deriving from the most heinous crime known to civilization, matricide; the problem: is (maximal) guilt forgivable? "Heilung" refers to the individual aspect of guilt feelings, here in a worst case scenario sharpened to the point of insanity; the problem: is insanity curable? As Adolf Metz phrased it in his signal essay of 1900, it is a question of the objective and the subjective aspects of guilt.

Broadly speaking, we can distinguish five types of approach to this question. Most obvious is the metaphysical explanation, with Kuno Fischer (1888) as the main exponent. Religious concepts and analogies of forgiveness of guilt, structured in a specific sequence of steps, were identified and explored in Orest's speeches: repentance, confession, penitence, absolution.

Next there was the imaginary solution proposed by Karl Heinemann in the *Goethe Jahrbuch* eleven years later. Here Orest is not really guilty since the law of *Blutrache* [vendetta] demanded his deed. The tormenting furies must be seen as a product of his overactive imagination, an interpretation that allowed for a biographical explanation and for support from a much-discussed tenet of current science: from his own experience Goethe knew about the closeness of genius to insanity (Heinemann 1899).

A third way was the humanistic solution embraced especially by pedagogues writing in the *Neue Jahrbücher*, who tended to approach the drama from the poetic autograph Goethe had written in 1825 for the actor playing Orest. Since the little poem was to become a basic text for *Iphigenie* criticism in the twentieth century, it might be well to quote it in its entirety here.

> Was der Dichter diesem Bande
> Glaubend, hoffend anvertraut,
> Werd' im Kreise deutscher Lande
> Durch des Künstlers Wirken laut.
> So im Handeln, so im Sprechen
> Liebevoll verkünd' es weit:
> Alle menschliche Gebrechen
> Sühnet reine Menschlichkeit.
>
> (*Goethes Werke*. 1952, Vol. 5, 406)

[What the poet has entrusted to this volume in faith and hope, may it become known in the German lands through the work of the artist. May its action and its words announce far and wide: pure humanity atones for all human failings.]

In the view of the humanist philologists, pure humanity, to be thought of as a sort of chemical purity, is sufficient to purge itself of any and all failings ("Gebrechen"). What happens to Orest is the self-regeneration of basic good human nature. This reading does away with Iphigenie's help, an important item in the humanist educational agenda of (male) self-sufficiency, which had to reject the substitute Christ figure as well as the redeeming woman. "Die Summe aller der guten Eigenschaften, auf denen des Menschen Gottähnlichkeit beruht [vermag] sich in ihrer Reinheit wieder herzustellen [The sum of all those good qualities which constitute man's likeness to God, is able to regenerate itself in its purity]" (Wohlrab 1899, 93).

A fourth approach was the scientific solution meticulously undertaken in Adolf Metz's essay in the *Preußische Jahrbücher* (1900). Using concepts of physiological psychopathology, Metz aims to explain every aspect of the quandary that has bedeviled *Iphigenie* criticism. The process of Orest's cure can be subsumed to "scientific laws of necessity" by means of two explanatory formulas, one subjective and one objective. Metz gives a fascinating and rich reading of the crucial scenes between Orest and Iphigenie, where he traces the decisive agency of the unconscious, buttressed by arguments from empirical psychology.

If Metz nevertheless in conclusion takes recourse to a religious analogy it is to respond to those critics who refuse to accept the possibility of Orest's "inner cure." Metz refers them to the biblical conversion narrative of persecutor Saulus into persecuted Paulus. The analogy consists in both Paulus's and Orest's experience of transference ("Übertragung"). They become what German psychologists after the Second World War described as authoritarian personalities, by making an "unconditional surrender" to an ideal or, if the ideal is personified, by a complete "Seelengemeinschaft [communion of souls]" with that person, in Orest's case with Iphigenie.

The fifth way, finally, was taken only in the more iconoclastic atmosphere of the early twentieth century. Both Eduard Engel (1909) and Georg Brandes (1915) in their Goethe biographies fault Goethe's art. Engel decides that Orest's crime is simply unforgivable, even through recourse to a miracle: "Goethe hat eine ungeheure dramatische Aufgabe ungelöst zurückgelassen [Goethe has left unsolved a tremendous problem for drama]" (291). Brandes, demanding psychological verisimilitude, rejects Goethe's text as cure by magic; he "owes us a more exact motivation" (385f.).

The first contribution from English criticism provided just that by applying principles of Freudian psychology. George M. Baker from the University of Chicago, writing in *Modern Philology* (1918), works out the "natural mental process by which this seeming miracle was performed" through the phases of catharsis, sleep-cure, and imaginary atonement. First to suggest the motif of *Heilschlaf* [sleeping cure], which would play a great role in criticism after the Second World War, Baker was also the first to point to a literary parallel of Orest's "restoration of personality" in Kleist's *Prinz von Homburg*.

The turn of the century brought a marked change in the status of *Iphigenie* and in approaches to the work. With the exception of an epigonic essay in a journal for the educated public (*Nord und Süd*) in 1905 and two articles in the *Goethe Jahrbuch*, both published in 1912, *Iphigenie* was absent from the German journals scene during the first two decades of the twentieth century. The focus on *Faust* and the grooming of Faustian Man as the new German ideal could account in part for the paucity of interest. But beyond that Iphigenie had become persona non grata for reasons of her own. Her central message rang a discord with the prevailing tune of the times. In the rise of strident nationalism the idea of brotherhood of mankind found itself denigrated in terms such as "vaterlandslose Gesellen [fellows without a fatherland]," a phrase commonly applied to socialist internationalism. The ideal of "reine Menschlichkeit" as it had been propounded by humanist pedagogues, fell into ambivalence before the demand for aggressive ambition in the pursuit of German world power.

Gustav von Loeper's address to the Goethe Society, "Berlin und Weimar" (1890), is symptomatic for the conflicted relationship of power (*Berlin*) and Goethean spirit (*Weimar*). Aiming to save Goethe into the new spirit of the empire under Wilhelm II, Loeper has a noticeable Iphigenian subtext concerning precisely the issues of patriotism versus cosmopolitanism, and of humanitarianism.

It is difficult to imagine the disrepute that befell the concept of "Menschlichkeit" at the time. There is perhaps no more revealing text on the disastrous career of the Iphigenian ideal par excellence than the chapter with the same title in Thomas Mann's *Betrachtungen eines Unpolitischen*, written during the First World War (1915–17). Taking up a much-discussed incident at the Belgian front, Mann has no qualms that a modern-day Iphigenie named "die Cavell" should have been put before the guns of a German execution commando, while by contrast he blasts the wimpish idea of "Menschlichkeit" held against German war policies by Germany's enemies.

Iphigenie criticism properly speaking, in editions of Goethe's works, biographies, and now also dissertation-type studies, had dealt with ideological problems by distancing. The most common way of distancing was by historicizing, a path that had been opened up by Goethe philology and positivism. In contrast with the continuing actualization of *Faust*, *Iphigenie* was assigned to the eighteenth century or to other literary traditions reflecting Enlightenment ideas, Greek models, and French classicist forms. These phenomena belonged to the past; they had no bearing on the very different historical moment of the present.

Another distancing strategy was gendering, but with a marked difference from the nineteenth century's treatment of the gender issue. No longer part of a dialectic towards human progress, as when we saw the female function evolve from Rosencranz's Hegelian logic to the idealism of suprahuman modeling in secular humanism, Iphigenie the woman is now that which man is not nor wants to become. She is the rejected other in opposition to which man defines himself.

Finally, the disappearance of *Iphigenie* from the forum of public discourse into the groves of academe has to be seen as a way of distancing, too. Subject of doctoral studies with ever more specialized, aesthetic, and formalist perspectives, *Iphigenie* becomes an academic question. It is symptomatic of the drama's diminished stature that the most innovative approaches to Goethe in the early twentieth century, those undertaken by Dilthey and Gundolf, should prove the least productive on this Goethean work.

Introductions to the three major editions of Goethe's collected works around 1900 betray a certain nervousness. Karl Heinemann, author of the above-mentioned essay on Orest's cure (1899) and of a Goethe biography, which stands out by not discussing the works at all, retreats to the safe position on biographical background in the edition published by the Bibliographisches Institut (1900). He accommodates the interests of the day by highlighting the extreme and precarious aspects of Goethe's own psyche: "the relatedness of genius to insanity."

Heinemann's comment on the present fall of the drama from its former august heights ("no longer enjoys that enthusiastic admiration") prepares us for the critical tone of Albert Köster's introduction in the *Jubiläums-Ausgabe* (1902), whereas Ludwig Geiger in the Hesse edition

(1901) still conforms to the decorum of the introductory genre, which demands informative appreciation. Geiger adheres to the worshipful view of Iphigenie as ideal-human approaching the divine ("göttergleich").

Köster, by contrast, emphasizes her thoroughly human, typically female weaknesses and crises. It is these "feminist" issues that Köster considers the central innovation of Goethe's drama, while the question of modern versus classical otherwise does not interest him. Precisely this is Geiger's main focus. His extensive comparison of Goethe and Euripides is haunted by the word *modern* but his effort to define the modernity of Goethe's drama consists essentially in declaring modern culture superior to "barbarische Roheit und Unsitte [barbaric crudeness and amorality]."

Both critics explain the drama's problems of reception in terms of form. In Köster's view, the many versions indicate a fundamental flaw of incompleteness. Even the vaunted last version, he contends, is "precisely speaking . . . merely a fragment," since Goethe at the time was thinking of writing a sequence, "Iphigenie in Delphi." For Geiger the root problem is lack of dramatic tension. He therefore recommends as locus of reception not the stage, but quiet reflection analogous to the Pietist form of worship (stille Andacht) for the enjoyment of this work: "[in] von den Mühen praktischer Tätigkeit und von der Dumpfheit hastenden Lebens abgewandter Stimmung zu genießen [to savor the drama in an atmosphere turned away from the stresses of practical activity and from the dullness of bustling everyday life]."

Thus from a "Lesedrama" (Geiger et al.) meant to be read in company or in school classes, *Iphigenie* has turned into *Erbauungsliteratur* [literature for spiritual regeneration], literature that is by definition irrelevant, even antagonistic to the realities of life. Understanding *Iphigenie* means to be "abgewandt [turned away]" from practical life, which Geiger moreover describes in wholly negative terms. As German academics constructed the ivory tower of apolitical *Innerlichkeit*, they recruited Goethe's noblest figure as one of its first inhabitants.

It is from this background that the theologian and Kierkegaard scholar Christoph Schrempf approaches the drama in the second volume of his *Goethes Lebensanschauung in ihrer geschichtlichen Entwicklung* (1907). The reader who takes up Schrempf after the preceding phalanx of eulogists and apologists is utterly amazed at his severe criticism. Schrempf does not share the official Goethe rejection espoused by the German Protestant Church (the *Evangelische Kirchenzeitung* had led a venomous anti-Goethe campaign on the subject of *Stella*). Neither is he motivated by orthodoxy's protest against the use of *Iphigenie* in the service of secular humanism.

His critical distance is rooted in an existentialist position inspired by Kierkegaard, a position Schrempf translates into historical pessimism. This attitude placed him way out of the dominant optimistic ideology and helps explain why, in contrast to the strong impact of his interpretation of

Clavigo, his *Iphigenie* reading was not received in mainstream German scholarship. When British critics entered the *Iphigenie* debate in the twenties and thirties, however, Schrempf was one of the few German scholars they consulted in their own work (see below on Robertson and Boyd).

Schrempf adopts a strategy of double reading in order to debunk the ersatz-religious function of the drama's central events: Iphigenie's truth action and Orest's cure. Without informing his readers of his project he first offers a naive reading in the traditional vein and finds that a number of lessons can be drawn from the text for the purpose of "spiritual regeneration [Erbauung]." But then he deconstructs this reading by presenting his own, "philosophical" analysis of the same text (233). Point by point he argues that the drama, instead of solving the conflicts it sets up, merely represses doubt which nevertheless persists.

In particular he demolishes the faith in "reine Menschlichkeit" as asserted in the by-now ubiquitous verse motto. Schrempf was the first to point out that these verses date from a much later time in Goethe's life and thought, and that it was inappropriate to use them as commentary on the earlier work. Yet Schrempf's objection to the dedicatory poem aims beyond philology to the very heart of the drama's message. "Reine Menschlichkeit," he asserts, does not work retroactively, cannot undo the damage of the past. It was this knowledge that Goethe embodied in his heroine, who is herself incapable of "fertigwerden mit [overcome]" her past experience.

The existentialist critic Schrempf claims Goethe as an ally in historical pessimism. The drama shows that "gegen die schwere Tragik des Menschenlebens . . . in der Geschichte . . . hilft weder Gottvertrauen noch Menschlichkeit [against the harsh tragedy of human life in history neither trust in God nor humanitarianism avails]." For Schrempf, Goethe has staged a conflict between the fatalism of ancient Greek myth and the eighteenth century's optimistic humanism, and Goethe, defying his own contemporaries as well as Schrempf's in the twentieth century, is on the pessimistic side of the Greeks.

With a final twist of his critical knife, Schrempf discredits "das Humane oder auch Christliche [the humane or also Christian features]" that had been the mainstay of critics seeking *Erbauung* through *Iphigenie* and of the tradition of adulation for Goethe's heroine. In these passages, he tells us, we do not hear Goethe speaking; we should read them as maudlin Charlottisms: "Aus Iphigenie, wo sie so gar fromm und gut redet, spricht Frau von Stein [through Iphigenie, where she talks so full of piety and goodness, speaks Frau von Stein]," the "Besänftigerin [pacifier]" who despite her best efforts could not quite domesticate ("zähmen") the stubborn Tantalid Goethe (239).

During the second decade of the twentieth century, *Iphigenie* criticism became more narrowly academic. Source relations, literary traditions, and questions of form dominate the approaches in two articles published in the *Goethe Jahrbuch* 1912 (Carl Fries and Camilla Lucerna) and in a dissertation on *Iphigenie* and *Tasso* (Carl A. Steinweg) of the same year. Another dissertation six years later (Otto Spieß) groups *Iphigenie* together with *Clavigo* and *Egmont*, devoting considerably less text to our drama than to either of the other two.*

Among the four authors, Lucerna stands outside mainstream German criticism; she hails from the margins of the Hapsburg Empire (Zagreb University) and she is a woman: the first in Goethe scholarship. The three insiders Fries, Steinweg, and Spieß all struggle to break out of the Greek classicist paradigm of *Iphigenie* interpretation. Fries discovers a Nordic tradition modeled by Wagnerian opera, the other two place the drama in the French classicist tradition of Corneille and Racine — with strikingly different results.

The book-length studies by Steinweg and Spieß are significant mainly for illustrating the deplorable state of affairs in *Iphigenie* criticism. The drama could be read, it seems, only in contrast with or propped up by other dramas: Goethe's, Corneille's, Racine's, Lessing's, even Wagner's. And the conclusions these comparatist critics drew from their groupings stand out by their confusion, contradiction, egregious wrongheadedness, and, one is tempted to say, perversity. No wonder British critics of the next two decades found German *Iphigenie* criticism useless, and said so.

The approach taken in the earlier of the two books (Steinweg 1912), is to elaborate on the hackneyed appellation of "Seelendrama." In Steinweg's redefinition *Iphigenie* is a "Qualdrama," a representation of divine pedagogy, where a soul's torment serves as a "pedagocical tool of the gods" (28) for the twofold purpose of "character formation [Bildung]" (142) and "to bring about the victory of truth" (54).

Gender plays a strange role in Steinweg's educational torture play. Reading against the grain of Goethe's text, he assigns the role of main sufferer to Iphigenie, not Orest, because "woman in the depth of her nature" has more soul and thus can suffer more (176). Goethe chose a woman to model the pedagocical process of character formation because his own nature, according to Steinweg, "war eben hervorragend weiblich betont [carried an outstanding feminine emphasis]" (185). Considerations of form, where dramatic categories are linked with other arts, including architecture, painting, and music, finally help Steinweg's subgenre of *Qualdrama* achieve the end of genre history. Goethe's intention in *Iphi-*

---

* While I have no absolute proof, all the publication data indicate that these were indeed dissertations.

genie has reached its perfection ("Vollendung") in Wagner's opera *Tristan* (vi).

The second of the book-length studies (Spieß 1918) groups *Iphigenie* with *Clavigo* and *Egmont* and, like Steinweg, calls on the Corneille-Racine tradition. But Spieß's purpose is to upend the established tradition of *Seelendrama*. In its place he proposes a new dramatic type: "Zieldrama [goal drama]," a genre for which Lessing would have served as the French-German mediator. In Spieß's definition, the *Zieldrama*'s goal-oriented dramaturgy prescribes a rationalistic plot structure, which in turn makes every action and every character completely explicable. There is no place in such a dynamic for religious or psychological mystery, magic or miracles. Foci of earlier criticism such as Iphigenie's crisis-driven monologues or Orest's recovery become "Beiwerk [accessories]" and "dichterisch nicht genug untergeordnete [poetically not sufficiently subordinated]" distractions (60, 66).

Spieß discovers a new focus in the "Pylades-drama," which in his view would ideally conform to the *Zieldrama* type but which Goethe unfortunately failed to assert against the interfering "Iphigenien-drama." For all its unconvincing, not to say perverse, argumentation, Spieß's text is a revealing document of his time. In the center of his reading we find the same rejection of Iphigenian humane ideals in favor of tough pragmatism as in Thomas Mann's *Betrachtungen*. The publication date of Spieß's study (1918) indicates that, like the reflections of the unpolitical Mann, it was written during the First World War and expressed the remarkable change in attitude brought about by that wrenching historical experience.

Of the two innovative articles that appeared in the *Goethe Jahrbuch* of 1912, Carl Fries's "Parzenlied und Völuspa" is decidedly the more strange. It would be easy to dismiss the piece as a product of anti-French, anti-Italian propaganda and Wagner-induced fantasizing. (Ten years later the Wagner cult would produce a Parsifalized Iphigenie in the same journal.) There is much that grates in Fries's vocabulary and the underlying ideology. Yet Fries's association of Goethe's early Weimar drama *Iphigenie* with "Nordic poetry" ("Nordlandsdichtung") mediated by Herder, particularly in the legend of the Parcae and in Orest's vision seen as a ritual of "Totenbeschwörung [invocation of the dead]," opens intriguing perspectives.

Most commendable for its novel approach and far too little known, however, is the article by Lucerna on concepts of morphology, religion, and development in *Iphigenie*. Using graphs and tables in her concise and decidedly inelegant analysis, Lucerna applies contemporary aesthetic theories, with special reference to Freytag and Nietzsche, in order to trace the "inner form" of Goethe's drama. As she correlates outer and inner action she finds a model for the particular way of representation of this drama in the tradition of German mysticism. Lucerna shows how the mystic writer makes outside phenomena stand for inner events as a method to describe the way of the soul to God. She sees the same technique at work in Goethe's and Enlightenment's secularized version of human progress, which is, according to Lucerna, "der Zug der Erdenkinder dem Lichte zu [the procession of Earth's children toward light]" by means of both inner effort and help from outside: "Streben und Heben [striving and uplifting]."

Ideas are paramount for Lucerna, too, and she crowds all the hot topics of *Iphigenie* interpretation into the brief space of her article. Her most ingenious suggestion is her reading of the permanent problem of Orest's recovery on the level of the signifier. Religion, she says, enters into the action only as a means of representation, not as an element of substance. The event of the cure itself is entirely psychological. Merely as imagery, in order to make visible the psychological process, as he would later in the ending of *Faust II*, Goethe here uses "Christian-religious elements of (imagination and) representation." Lucerna turns to the history of religion for evidence of this technique of representation through imagery. Besides recordings of mystical experience, she points to the narrative of Paulus's conversion as an account of visualizing truth through signs.

Finally, Lucerna anchors her interpretation in the context of Goethe's development as a writer. At the early point in his career when he wrote *Iphigenie*, she says, Goethe could represent a complex psychological transformation only by means of a silent event. It took the learning process of his entire life, until the ending of *Faust II*, for him to be able to emulate the mystic writers, to do it in words.

Four years later, in his epochal *Goethe* monograph (1916), Friedrich Gundolf placed *Iphigenie* in the service of Goethe's inner biography. Following on the chapter "Humanität," "Iphigenie" — the chapter and the drama — represents the decisive first step in Goethe's self-realization as artist-creator, which for Gundolf is tantamount to "Humanität" in Goethe's case. The author-centered perspective has significant consequences for Gundolf's reading of the drama. The first is radical subjectivization. All that matters is Goethe's subjectivity; characters, events, conflicts, themes are merely and explicitly symbols ("Symbol, Verkörperung, sprachliches Zeichen") of psychological processes in Goethe. It is this that Gundolf's neologism "Verseelung [soulification]" intends, which is his overall characterization of the *Iphigenie* text.

The exclusive focus on Goethe's inner self entails the withdrawal from the perspective of mankind, the traditional horizon of *Iphigenie* criticism, into the inner sphere of individual concerns: *Innerlichkeit*, that problematical facet of German cultural history. And indeed Gundolf is not interested in social or ethical themes. Linked to his focus on subjectivity is the second major aspect of Gundolf's reading: privatization. There is no Kantian ethic in this drama, no moral absolute. The motivating forces are entirely personal. The constellation of characters serves to install personal bonds — love, friendship, gratefulness — and it is these personal bonds that empower or impede every choice, decision, action.

The most telling instance is Gundolf's comment on Iphigenie's crucial truth decision. He sees it as an entirely private decision based on her personal feelings toward Thoas; any exemplary, let alone universal, value of truth and goodness is thereby erased. "Wenn Iphigenie des Fluchs ledig werden könnte durch Beraubung und Überlistung eines Mannes, der ihr gleichgültig ist, so wäre das Drama Goethes in seinem Keim vernichtet [If Iphigenie could get rid of the curse through robbing and tricking a man toward whom she feels indifferent, then Goethe's drama would be annihilated in its inner core]" (317). In this drama, then, it would be unobjectionable to rob and deceive anyone except your personal friends. Gundolf's Goethe revokes Kant's categorical imperative.

The reduction of *Iphigenie* to Goethean subjectivity further results in aesthetization. In Gundolf's view, Goethe worked his way out of psychological conflicts that threatened to destroy him — they are his reality referent of the drama's curse — through poetic creation. Goethe had to find a suitable "Stoffmasse [subject material]" and shape it ("umbilden, beseelen, gestalten") into an equivalent image of his own inner processes. Thus he created his *Iphigenie* from the Euripidean material (*Stoffmasse*), and he had Iphigenie do likewise in the "Parzenlied-monolog [song-of-the-Parcae monologue]," which Gundolf therefore considers the drama's center of gravity ("Schwerpunkt" 314).

The shift of focus from the work to the author yields its most egregious result in a final twist of the nineteenth century's *Iphigenie* apotheosis. Gundolf enacts the apotheosis of Goethe. With the proviso of a secularized frame, this is to be taken quite literally. How else are we to understand Gundolf's summarizing comment:

> die Iphigenie konzipieren zu können . . . diesen [Euripides] Stoff so lesen und deuten zu können, das setzt eine innere Hoheit und einen menschlichen Adel ohnegleichen voraus, und darum bleibt . . . die Iphigenie vor allem für Goethes Charakter das verherrlichende Denkmal, wie es denn das Evangelium der deutschen Humanität schlechthin ist [being able to conceive Iphigenie, being able to read and interpret the Euripidean material in this way, this presupposes a unique inner majesty and human nobility, and that is why Iphigenie above all remains the glorifying monument to Goethe's character, just as the drama is the gospel of German humanity par excellence] (318).

This *Könner ohnegleichen*, unique creator whom monuments glorify, has given to his German community a text to replace the Bible. Displacing the Bible is the subtext, too, in the Luther analogy Gundolf uses to explain Iphigenie's crisis leading up to her song of the Parcae. Both Luther and Iphigenie, in Gundolf's view, are prey to "Verzweiflungs-gefühl," a

state of mind that is "durchaus unantik, ja . . . protestantisch [funda-
mentally unclassical, even protestant]." But Gundolf states an essential
difference in the substance of the despair. In Iphigenie's case, despair is
"merely psychological, not metaphysical" as it had been for Luther. The
common quality of "protestantisch" then is what Gundolf, in his concluding passage quoted above, calls "deutsche Humanität." Given to the Germans by their new messiah, Goethe, this text is a protest in the name of
human autonomy, for "bei Goethe kann der Mensch von sich aus die Er-
lösung erringen, bei Luther nicht [in Goethe's view man can achieve redemption by himself, but not in Luther's view]" (313).

Gundolf's new German gospel, the text of *Iphigenie*, redefines
"Humanität" and "reine Menschlichkeit" (the latter term occurs only
once) in terms of an aesthetic of power. Central to Gundolf's argument is
Iphigenie's aesthetic creation, the song of the Parcae. By having his heroine create at the moment of peripeteia Goethe makes her a simile
(Gundolf's word "Gleichnis" is the common German word for the biblical
parable) of the powerful creative genius. Like Goethe, she needs to become a "Charakter" through self-control, that is, through harmonizing
and thus overcoming in the creative act a crisis of faith that originated in
fears and anxieties and has led to the extreme of "Welt-verzweiflung
[world despair]." Enhanced through creativity, the "character" becomes
the center of a force-field whose strength emanates, inspires, and motivates all others to the point of annexation. The strong personality constitutes others' destiny.

> Diese Kraft strahlt von ihr [Iphigenie] aus nach allen Seiten . . . Iphi-
> genie wirkt nicht nur auf alle andren Gestalten des Stücks, sondern
> auch in ihnen. Sie, d.h. ihr Charakter, ist das gemeinsame Schicksal
> aller [This power emanates from her to all sides . . . Iphigenie's effect
> does not only bear on all other figures of the play, but also in them.
> She, i.e. her character, is the common destiny of all] (318).

Personality cult, leader worship, glorification of submission, and endorsement of the authoritarian personality: Gundolf's view of Iphigenie
exhibits a significant spectrum of fascist ideology.

Gundolf's version of fascism hinges on an aesthetic moment, i.e. the
self-creation of the dominating personality through aesthetic production
rather than through ethical (heroic) action. The aesthetic displaces the
ethical, finally, in Gundolf's use of the concept of *kalokagathia*. In Platonism and in German neo-humanist pedagogy the term designated the path
to the Good through the Beautiful and eventually the synthesis of the two
ideas; this synthesis was the ideal that classicist education strove to approach. In Gundolf's "Iphigenie" chapter, *kalokagathia* has taken the
place of the motto of redemption through "reine Menschlichkeit." The
drama, Gundolf states at the outset, transacts the process of "Bildung" in

its most classical sense: as "Kalokagathon," the way to the Good through the Beautiful, to ethics through aesthetics.

In Gundolf's conclusion, however, the Good is absorbed by the Beautiful; the latter term is the true goal of the path through the text. Here *Iphigenie* represents a new kind of beauty which transforms the ethical into the aesthetic: "eine neue Schönheit" where "das Moralische tritt heraus in die Sinnlichkeit . . . als Schönheit [the moral is exteriorized into the sensual . . . as beauty]." For the author Goethe, *Iphigenie* may have been the overcoming of a moral problem. For Gundolf and his contemporary readers, the text is to be enjoyed as a pure performance of aesthetics:

> Das ganze Werk [ist] von Goethe aus gesehn, eine Bändigung und Läuterung quälender Überkräfte, von uns aus gesehn das sprachliche Zeichen der erreichten Kalokagathia [The work as a whole is from Goethe's perspective a taming and purification of tormenting passions, from our perspective it is the linguistic sign of kalokagathia achieved] (319).

FROM 1918 TO 1945

Compared to the sheer mass of writing on *Iphigenie* before the First and after the Second World War, the years of the Weimar Republic and the Third Reich present a very different picture. During the twenties and thirties there is a distinct paucity of German *Iphigenie* criticism: in the roughly two decades merely eight articles appeared in journals of the discipline, three of them in the *Goethe Jahrbuch*. And while the one hundredth anniversary of Goethe's death in 1932 was widely celebrated, it produced no texts on our drama. The anniversary year in fact, with articles on *Iphigenie* published in French and Austrian but not in German journals, brings into focus another eminent phenomenon: during the Weimar years and beyond, the mainstream of *Iphigenie* criticism passed outside of Germany. It is not too much to say that at this point English criticism took charge of the drama, which had apparently been abandoned by the Germans. This development culminated in the publication in 1942 of the first book on *Iphigenie* since Kuno Fischer's in 1900, *Goethe's "Iphigenie auf Tauris"* by Oxford Professor James Boyd.

Among the reasons for the drama's unpopularity, some have to do with German attitudes to Goethe in general at the time, others with specifically Iphigenian issues. As Mandelkow shows in the introduction to the fourth volume of his Goethe reception history (1979), the much-heralded "spirit of Weimar," invoked as patron saint for the new republic, was far from universally accepted. The Weimar appeal was attached to the conservative wing and the bourgeois establishment, with the Goethe Society and its *Jahrbuch* the very bastion of conservative reaction. The progressive groups, for political, ideological, or formal-aesthetic reasons, were in outspoken opposition to the Goethe tradition. To this first generation of modernists in Germany the spirit of Weimar was anathema; writers like Bertolt Brecht, Carl Sternheim, Karl Kraus, Egon Erwin Kisch, Kurt Tucholsky did their best to exorcise that spirit with satire, ridicule, and bitter criticism. The well-known example of Harry Haller's disgust with the Olympian Goethe on his former teacher's piano in Hesse's *Steppenwolf* (1927) is entirely representative. Moreover, the interest of Goethe scholarship itself had turned to the late Goethe, with *Faust II* and *Wanderjahre* commanding the most attention. There are, however, indications that it was more than Goethe rejection in general, or classicist Goethe rejection in particular that made *Iphigenie* a problematical text for German critics now.

The scholars and pedagogues of the preceding era had declared the drama the embodiment of all the ideals they wanted to believe in. School curricula had instituted *Iphigenie* as textbook for idealism, as guide for right behavior, as guarantee that whoever had learned this text would know, and practice of course, what "reine Menschlichkeit" meant. In the speeches and essays on Goethe of the period up to 1918 presented in Mandelkow's collection, references to *Iphigenie* intend exactly this: to invoke, by the code word "Iphigenie," the insurance policy that certifies right attitudes. Gundolf's book, for the most part a product of prewar times, was the apex of this development as he declared *Iphigenie* the German bible.

It is a historical commonplace that the generation who went to war full of enthusiasm and illusions carried *Faust* in their backpacks. But they also, a special publication of the Goethe Society in the war year 1915, *Weimar und Deutschland 1815–1915*, proudly informs us, carried *Iphigenie*. Indeed when the drama was staged on the conquered citadel of Namur with soldiers taking roles in the performance, "lauschten andächtig viele Reihen deutscher Offiziere und Mannschaften [many rows of German officers and men harkened reverently]" (Mandelkow Vol. 3, 431). This was in summer 1915, still at the height of war enthusiasm and in the certainty of victory. It could not be imagined after, say, 1917. It is well known how traumatic the war experience had become for the younger men; nervous breakdowns and suicides of artists and similar sensitive souls were legion. In the end, after 1918, the profound disillusionment of defeat trashed the erstwhile ideals like so many false idols, and *Iphigenie* was one of them.

Early salvage efforts in the Weimar years undertook to redefine "reine Menschlichkeit" in line with current concepts of New (Expressionist) Man, or they sought support from fashionable Wagnerian opera and the new religiosity of *Parsifal*, yielding up the Iphigenian message of autonomous humanity in favor of a return to the last century's focus on divine agency. Readings of the late twenties and thirties tended to evade issues and ideas, and instead embraced formalist discourses on the musical and atmospheric aspects of the drama's language, once more leading up to a Wagnerian aesthetic. These withdrawals into the inner exile of aesthetics bear witness to the changes in the ideological and political climate.

As the strife between radical right, radical left, nostalgic conservatives, and embattled liberals kept heating up, cultural life became more and more polarized: "politicized" in the terminology of the time. Toward the end of the interwar period, we see critics actualizing or even instrumentalizing *Iphigenie* in the ideological struggles (Sprengel 1932; Beck 1939). Over the entire period, however, a process of ideological contamination was taking place: a largely unconscious and often tormented adaptation of Iphigenian concepts to the perceived needs of the moment. It appears that *Iphigenie*, this most ideologically loaded of Goethe's dramas, would not allow abstinence from ideas, issues, and problems despite leading scholars' efforts to seek refuge in aesthetic formalism. In response to the changing historical situation the phenomenon of contamination resulted in some interesting auto-revisions, as major critics presented different readings at different points in time (Korff 1921 and 1930; Petsch in the *Festausgabe* 1926 and 1937).

A separate English line was launched in the *Publications of the English Goethe Society* in 1924 when John G. Robertson published an essay on *Iphigenie*, announcing modestly but significantly in his title " . . . Some New Points of View." It was the year that the journal, under Robertson's editorship, resumed publication after the hiatus of the war. Robertson's choice of *Iphigenie* in this context thus carries considerable weight, not the least of which is his intention to reset the course of *Iphigenie* criticism. Since that criticism thus far had been a near-exclusive German domain, Robertson's unannounced project was to correct the German course if possible, or to chart a new direction if the Germans persisted in their approach. Robertson's opposition to contemporary German criticism remained largely implicit in his critical reading of the drama and his focus on the French sources. The essay went essentially unchanged into his widely used Goethe monograph of 1927. Even a new version of the book, published in 1932 and known to Anglo-American Goethe scholars as the standard "Robertson," did not take account of the important readings by Petsch (*Festausgabe* 1926) and Korff (1930, Vol. 2 of *Goethezeit*).

More explicitly in its opposition to the German tradition, Barker Fairley's brief and eclectic, but enormously influential study, *Goethe as Revealed in His Poetry* (1932), dealt a severe blow to Iphigenie and Charlotte worshippers, while E. M. Butler's iconoclastic *The Tyranny of Greece Over Germany* (1935) hit the entire tradition of viewing German classicism. James Boyd's 1938 essay in the H. G. Fiedler *Festschrift* follows Robertson in taking account of German scholarship only up to 1924. In his 1942 book on *Iphigenie*, Boyd explicitly rejects twentieth century German Goethe criticism as useless. The British critics, however, widely disagreed among themselves. Fairley's study was inspired by opposition to Robertson, whose book he reviewed for a Canadian journal. Boyd conducts a running war with Robertson, but mentions Butler and Fairley only in rare instances: their stances proved, for the time being, incommensurably radical.

Opening the Weimar debate, Hermann August Korff published an essay, which has remained remarkably unnoticed, in the *Zeitschrift für Deutschkunde* of 1921.* Korff, who was a *Privatdozent* in Frankfurt at the time (i.e., waiting for an opening at the university), rehearses the revolution of *Iphigenie* criticism. "The entire literature on *Iphigenie*" has simply misunderstood the meaning of that "Universalschlüssel [universal key]" to the drama: "reine Menschlichkeit." What it really means, according to Korff, is the essence of New Man empowered with Nietzschean absolute will. Korff's hero is Orest, who achieves his own salvation without help from Iphigenie. In the figure of Orest, Goethe glorifies the decisive act by prescribing "Sühnetat [expiatory deed]" instead of "Sühnetod [expiatory death]." Playing on the phonic contrast of "Tat" and "Tod" Korff insists on the centrality of activism as against the Christian tradition of passivity and suffering symbolized in Christ's Passion ("Sühnetod"). Like Orest, Iphigenie too belongs to that higher species of humankind which according to Korff constitutes "reine Menschlichkeit." They qualify by dint of their idealist ideology ("Weltanschauung [des] absoluten Idealismus") and their willingness to stake their lives on it ("Blut der Märtyrer").

The Korffian ideology, for which his martyrs are willing to shed their blood in activist pursuit, stands out for its conceptual emptiness. His "absolute idealism" is not defined by any goals, such as the traditional Iphigenian ideals of humanity, truth, family, cosmopolitanism, civilization, and so forth. "Absolute idealism" means, then, zealous engagement for any and all values that might function as goals or ideals. It is almost too easy to see the connection between this stance and the historical context of extremist ideologies competing for the allegiance of the rising generation. Korff's summary view of *Iphigenie* holds out a similarly empty or all-encompassing promise. The Goethean work is a drama of willpower, a demonstration of the human will's "weltbewegende Kraft [world-moving power]," able to liberate from the past and to change the present and the future (311–14).

---

* Formerly named *Zeitschrift für den deutschen Unterricht*, the journal has been credited with initiating the ideologization of Germanistik.

There is little left of this triumph of the will in Korff's reading of *Geist der Goethezeit* nine years later (Vol. 2, 1930). Activism has been replaced by resignation ("Gottergebenheit" or "Entsagung"), autonomy of individual will has disappeared in favor of a new religion whose supreme good is beauty. Values are back; "reine Menschlichkeit" again means "Humanität" as defined in Lessing's *Nathan*, the work which in Korff's chapter on "Humanität" precedes *Iphigenie*. But the moving force behind the humane ideal is beauty, "ein neues Menschheitsideal, das uns nicht durch seine Zweckmäßigkeit, sondern durch seine Schönheit überzeugt [a new ideal of mankind which does not convince us by its serviceability but by its beauty]" (160). Beauty harmonizes and thus reconciles tragic conflicts that by definition ought to be irreconcilable: the ending achieves "the beautiful solution of a terrible tragedy" (156). The martyr of the new religion is Thoas. His resignation, through its beauty, validates Korff's aesthetic theodicy.

> Diese Entsagung . . . des Thoas ist so schön, sie überzeugt uns so von ihrem metaphysischen Eigenwerte, daß wir nicht mehr wie Iphigenie mit der Gottheit hadern, die es nicht vermochte, Sittlichkeit und Leben schlechtweg harmonisch zusammenzufügen [This resignation of Thoas is so beautiful, it convinces us of its metaphysical value in itself, so that unlike Iphigenie we no longer quarrel with the divinity, who was unable to conjoin harmoniously and immediately ethics and life] (168).

Korff's aesthetic metaphysic succeeds where the conventional gods as understood by Iphigenie failed: beauty with all-encompassing harmony makes the clash between ethical demands and reality ("Sittlichkeit und Leben") disappear.

The religious base of Korff's aestheticism shows up in his concepts and vocabulary. "Weihe [consecration]" is everywhere, in one paragraph three times. Iphigenie's "Sendung [mission]" is to be a "Heiland [savior]" for the Scythians and her brother; the text as a whole sings "das hohe Lied auf die Wundermacht des Gewissens [the Song of Songs on the miraculous power of conscience]" and on the "Göttlichkeit der Welt [divinity of the world]." But the new gospel of *Iphigenie* institutes a decidedly secular religiosity, a creed that actively refutes and then displaces established religion. Orest is Korff's strongest case for secular individualism, for, as he emphasizes in italics: "*sein Gewissen widerlegt seine Religion* [his conscience refutes his religion]" (158). Iphigenie, too, whose task and essence it is to realize the exalted humane ideal, achieves her goal on her own strength, without divine help. She is, in Korff's emphatic language, the creator of her own self and thus of a higher, more ideal human than the God of traditional religion managed to produce in the first creation. A Prometheus of the spirit, Iphigenie, the new creator of a better mankind, does away with old and outworn biblical myths. "Dieser Mensch ist ihre Schöpfung, die Schöpfung ihres Geistes, die Schöpfung ihres Gefühls für höhere Menschlichkeit [This human is her creation, the creation of her mind, the creation of her feeling for higher humanity]" (161).

The contradiction inherent in Korff's aesthetic theodicy, the tension between the aesthetic superstructure and its religious base, works itself out in a breakdown at the level of rational discourse. In marked contrast to the sober language of his 1921 essay, a rhetoric of hyperbole raises *Iphigenie* to the height of *opus absolutum*, the classic where superlatives silence all questions. Even though Thoas's final "Lebt wohl [fare well]" harbors "a world of the most conflicting feelings," Korff cuts off the "conflict" by moving it off limits into the unquestionable realm of absolutes: "In der gesamten deutschen Dichtung gibt es kaum zwei inhaltsschwerere Worte [in all of German poetry (read "literature") there are hardly two words more laden with content]" (168). Iphigenie's truth decision exhibits another feature of Korff's rhetoric, with Gundolf the unspoken godfather: the aim to appropriate the work and its idea(l)s for a specifically German *Humanität*. Iphigenie's deliberation on whether to opt for truth is "the classical passage in the history of German poetry . . . one of the most wonderful moments in the history of German poetry" (163, 166). Concerning the final act nothing less than the ultimate in rhetoric will do: "eine der höchsten Gipfelhöhen deutscher Dichtung und deutschen Geistes [one of the highest summit heights of German poetry and German mind]" (167).

More ominous than Korff's rhetoric is the breakdown of rational discourse at the level of signification, as central concepts defining his Iphigenian ideal become contradictory, tautological, or empty. Foremost here is "Humanität." From his preceding discussion of the first German "Humanitätsdrama," Lessing's *Nathan*, Korff takes over the defining categories "Gottergebenheit" and "Selbstlosigkeit [devotion to God, selflessness]." Both terms, however, contradict Iphigenie's central task of self-realization, her God-defying creation of a superior self. The "higher humanity" that Iphigenie is supposed to create is, in a circular argument, identified both with "ideal" and "truth," but is finally anchored in Iphigenie's self, which in turn is merely defined as "the moral genius." Given Korff's effort to bypass religion via aesthetics it is to be expected that concepts of divinity will be as problematical as his categories of humanity. The ubiquitous phrase "Göttlichkeit der Welt" means, tautologically, nothing more than *humanity*. The one place where Korff does offer a definition displays the emptiness of the concept. Iphigenie's creed, he tells us in a familiar but undocumented quotation, is: "Wie es auch sei, das Leben, es ist gut." Or: life is pro-life and therefore good (164).

In the interval between the two Korff readings, German criticism spins its wheels, reworking earlier patterns and showing a remarkable preference for the religious angle. Essays in the *Goethe Jahrbuch* of 1922 and 1924 (the yearbook skipped the inflation year 1923) compare Orest's healing to the "Easter miracle" of resurrection performed by the charismatic touch of "Heiland" Iphigenie (Pedro Warncke). Another author sees an analogy with the cure of Amfortas, whereby Iphigenie becomes a "weibliche Gegengestalt [female pendant] zu Wagners Parsifal" (Johannes Tiedge 1922). This author, drawing the logical consequence of his analogy, installs a new trinity of greatest German poets: Goethe, Schiller, and Wagner.

The author of the introduction to the Ullstein edition of Goethe's works (1923) is writer and critic Paul Ernst, whose own career is a vivid illustration of the ideological and aesthetic turbulence of the time, passing from social-democratic activism and naturalism to neoromanticism, neoclassicism, and finally national socialism, on the way producing works, mostly epigonic, in all the major genres except lyrical. Ernst's essay on *Iphigenie* likewise focuses on religion. In the context of religious history he first analyzes Euripides' play from the perspective of cultic imagery and myth, and then blasts Racine's courtly aberration of Christian "Seelentragödie [soul tragedy]" because his souls are "Hofschranzen [court lackeys]." Ernst credits Goethe with having rescued the soul drama from its French aberration in the spirit of German Protestantism and thereby marked a significant moment in literary history. But Goethe's solution no longer answers today's spiritual needs. The new religion and religiosity ("eine neue Religion und eine neue Art von Frömmigkeit") which Ernst sees developing "among the best of today," needs a new kind of dramatic correlate. Goethe's *Iphigenie* is too subjective, too internalized, too monologic. Drama now needs activism, antagonism, struggle: "Die moderne Seelentragödie braucht einen Gegenspieler, dessen andersgeartete Seele mit der Seele der Heldin kämpfen kann [The modern tragedy of the soul needs an antagonist with a soul that is different in kind and can struggle with the soul of the heroine]" (37).

Ernst's indictment of the formal aspects of the drama is detailed and devastating, considering the tradition of praise for its perfection. His chief objection is precisely to the lyrical beauties; they make the work undramatic and prevent its being an organic whole. The "Gesamtorganismus [total organism]" further suffers from too many epic passages, with the main offender Iphigenie's ancestor narrative. At this point in time, Ernst can feel confident that his critical view of *Iphigenie* is generally shared. Reflecting on the history of *Seelendrama* he declares that Goethe had been assigned the task of renewing the Euripides-Racine tradition; "everyone will certainly admit that this task has not been completely accomplished" (38). It is indicative of Ernst's judgment on Goethe's irrelevance to the present era that for his introduction of 1923 he should recycle an essay that was written ten years and a momentous era of historic cataclysms before. It is obvious that despite the attempts at Wagnerian refurbishment in the *Goethe Jahrbuch*, the moderns of the day consigned *Iphigenie* to the reference shelf of history.

With Robert Petsch's introduction to the *Festausgabe* (1926) academic criticism rose to the defense. Its seemingly objective style and methodical subdivision in historical, thematic, and formal perspectives model mainstream Goethe scholarship's service function for the enhancement of the pre-established classic. On the other hand, Petsch's text exhibits the pervasive, even though still subliminal ideologization of the discipline. Throughout the piece we hear echoes of that notorious saying: "Am deutschen Wesen wird die Welt genesen [German nature will cure the world]." The rhetoric of the concluding paragraph makes the tendency explicit, as Petsch appropriates *Iphigenie* for German ideology, for a specifically German spirituality ("weder griechisch noch französisch") that originated in Herder-Goethe's "German Idealism" and is still alive and struggling today ("des lebendigen, des noch ringenden und sich in sich selbst befestigenden 'Deutschen Idealismus'"). Goethe's drama has installed German humanity as paradigm for a militant human spirituality in general, which is what gives this classic its universal and eternal value:

> Kämpfe, die gerade der deutsche Mensch und weiterhin der innerliche Mensch überhaupt zu jeder Zeit aufs neue wird ausfechten müssen . . . . von hier aus gesehen hat [Goethes] Dichtung, so national und so zeitlich bedingt sie zunächst sein mochte, Ewigkeitswert erlangt [struggles which particularly German man and furthermore inner man generally at all time again and again will have to fight . . . . from this perspective Goethe's drama, as conditioned by nationality and time as it may have been initially, has achieved eternal validity] (30).

Petsch's most striking innovation is his new definition of the old motto concerning "reine Menschlichkeit." To the traditional components of *Humanität* derived from German Idealism he adds a new ingredient: communitarianism. The humane ideal, according to Petsch, is to be realized "in jeder menschlichen 'Gemeinschaft,' die in heftigen Auseinandersetzungen mit verwandten und entgegengesetzten Strömungen sich klären und in sich selbst vollenden will [in every human 'community' which, in vehement controversies with related and opposite tendencies, strives to define and complete itself in itself]" (16). Petsch's actualizing move, the attempt to make *Iphigenie* applicable to the German turbulence, is evident, as is his effort to accommodate the new, political emphasis on the collective as opposed to the individual ideal of tradition. His use of the term *"Gemeinschaft,"* emphasized by quotation marks, is a clear reference to the debate of the time concerning the competing ideologies of *Ge-*

sellschaft, Gemeinschaft, Volk, and *Kollektiv* [society, community, folk, collective].

Petsch promotes a new Iphigenian quasi-religion ("gleichsam eine neue Religion") which prescribes service to the community as precondition for individual achievement: "jede menschliche Gemeinschaft . . . [deren] Glieder einander vorwärtshelfen, um im Dienste an dem andern selbst zur Vollendung zu reifen [every human community . . . whose members help each other advance in order to reach maturity of self in service to the other]" (17). Thus Orest, preferred focus of Petsch's predecessors, "is only a member" in the generational tragedy of the Tantalids, his salvation merely part of Iphigenie's true goal, which is not primarily to save him but to achieve "expiation and consecration of the house."

It is only logical then for Iphigenie, agent of collective salvation, to displace once again Orest, mere passive sufferer, from the position of masculine hero. Endowed with "Mannesmut [man's courage]" she first has to perform her very special "new miracles" before Orest can decipher the oracle. Concerning the happy end of Goethe's tale, Petsch makes no secret of his objection to its optimism. Shakespearean endings seem more adequate to the truth of history and to Petsch's own time, where revolutions have to be paid for in gore and violence: in *Hamlet* and *King Lear* "muß Blut fließen [before] neues Leben sich kraftvoll zu regen beginnt. Goethe hat uns das Gewaltsame erspart — uns und sich [blood must flow before new life begins to stir vigorously. Goethe has spared us the violence — us and himself]" (23).

Concerning source relations, Petsch insists against recent critics Ernst (1923) and Robertson (1924) on Goethe's substantial difference from his Greek model. Indulging in some more German ideology, Petsch maintains that Goethe created a truly original work by transplanting the old "Tantalid fable . . . from foreign soil to home country [eignem Land]" and by transforming it in the spirit of a "new, German, his generation" (15). Taking a strong turn against Ernst's religious focus, Petsch declares *Iphigenie* an anti-Euripides drama where a new, secular spirituality replaces the old, myth-bound religion. The guiding principle of dramatic action for Petsch is a process of humanization, where human agency progressively displaces divine power.

In Petsch's new spirituality there is no place for Christian concepts of "'stellvertretendes Leiden' [vicarious suffering]" or superhuman "Heiland" figures, who in Wagnerized readings especially had agglomerated Nietzschean Superman qualities. Yet Petsch still needs to balance the individual and the social within his new German idealism. Thus he proposes that individually, the ideal is total renunciation ("Gesamtverzicht"); like Iphigenie, Orest, and finally Thoas, the individual can achieve freedom in victory over the passions ("Triebgebundenheit" 18). Surprisingly however, Petsch leaves the social ideal undefined. While he asserts its status as faith, its substance remains vague. The new humanism still contains a "Gottesidee [idea of God]" and is vaguely unworldly ("unirdisch") — Pylades' pragmatism is soundly rejected — but that's it. German idealism of the day was still, Petsch intimated earlier, struggling to find its bearings ("noch ringend und sich in sich selbst befestigend").

Beyond this conceptual indefinition in matters of ideology, we observe a slide into irrationalism particularly in the sections of Petsch's text that deal with the formal aspects of the drama. Petsch finds that the dramatic action is overwhelmingly internal and communicates itself through non-discursive aspects of language such as movement, rhythm, tone, tuning, or atmosphere ("stimmen" 28). The essential meaning of this drama, in fact, lies beyond words; understanding it likewise requires nonverbal communication, which Petsch describes in pseudoscientific terms as a sort of empathetic magnetism. "In our inner space [unserm Innern] a movement is incited between opposite poles, a movement which stands in close relation with the line of inner action and which teaches us to understand much that cannot be rendered in words" (27).

In a rhetoric of paradox which is typical for the mystifying tenor of much of Petsch's discussion of form, he asserts that language must intone the unspeakable contents of the soul, "in dieser Sprache die unaussprechlichen Strebungen und Wertungen der Seele . . . immer wieder anklingen zu lassen" (27). With the installation of a musical instead of a discursive semantic, Petsch detaches *Iphigenie* from the Enlightenment tradition that saw drama as verbal argument and transaction of moral issues within a shared rational discourse. He inserts the drama instead into the new genre of "Festspiel [festival play]" that had made Wagner's Bayreuth and Reinhardt's Salzburg places of ritual enactment of the German spirit, as he concludes: "the drama reaches far beyond all sensual and real possibilities of dramatic art. It is in the nature of this *Festspiel* that it . . . transcends into the infinite, into a dimension that only our intuition can grasp" (31).

During the Weimar years the new discipline of comparative literature established itself and under grand master Fernand Baldensperger became especially active in the Franco-German area. Two studies followed the tradition of relating *Iphigenie* to Racine. The uneven and pedestrian comparison with Racine's *Mithridate* by Ernst Lüdtke is of interest mainly as a symptom of *völkische* ideology and terminology penetrating Goethe studies. A belated contribution (1933) to the Goethe year, published with private sponsorship in the Eastern provinces where nationalism was particularly rabid, Lüdtke's study wants to be "Geburtshelfer [midwife]" in the "Wiedergeburt klassisch *deutscher* Geistgestalt [renaissance of the classical *German* form of spirit]" and show how the two dramas demonstrate "verschiedene volkheitliche Wesensart . . . aus verschiedenen Mutterböden [different folkish nature . . . from different maternal soils]" (6, 9).

By contrast, Fritz Ernst's elegant contribution to the Baldensperger *Festschrift* of 1930 represents an analytical counterweight to the aesthetic desubstantiation performed in Korff's *Geist der Goethezeit* of the same year. In a daring innovation, Ernst proposes another, self-critical Goethe word as motto instead of the overused "reine Menschlichkeit." It is the state-ment from an 1802 letter to Schiller signing over the "gräzisierende Schauspiel [Greekified drama]" to the theatrical expert for revision: "es ist ganz verteufelt human [it is quite devilishly humane]." When *Iphigenie* criticism resumed after the Second World War this phrase would take up center stage. Ernst reads it to indicate that Goethe had come to realize his drama's essentially utopian intent. Whereas Racine, in reworking the "myth critic" Euripides, adhered to a social and spiritual "Maß [measure, standard]," Goethe created a new mythology that was to herald "a higher man." For Ernst, *Iphigenie* is Goethe's once-only, deliberate transgression of human boundaries toward a "human theodicy," an attempt to realize the old "dream of mankind" of universal peace and brotherhood (139f.). It is surely a comment on the times when suddenly, under the impact of troubling historical events, the Iphigenian ideals that had seemed rea-sonably realizable since their first appearance in the Enlightenment, now appeared hybrid, transgressive, utopian.

The emergence of what would soon be called "the dialectic of Enlight-enment," the skeptical distancing from the defining experience of modern Europe, found confirmation in an essay by Alexandre Hérenger published in Baldensperger's journal, *Revue de Littérature Comparée*, in the anniver-sary year. (The issue was devoted entirely to Goethe.) In a bitter riposte to the nationalistic development of German Goethe scholarship, Hérenger ironizes *Iphigenie* criticism for claiming a monopoly on truth ("La Relig-ion de la Vérité" of his title) for Goethe's drama.

Now that *Iphigenie* had been metamorphosed from embodiment of truth to apple of discord, it should perhaps not surprise us that, with a single exception, the anniversary year produced nothing on this drama in mainstream German publications. The exception exemplifies Hérenger's criticism in preaching the religion of truth and trust by means of Iphige-nian transubstantiation. In a brief essay in the *Zeitschrift für deutsche Bildung*, Johann Georg Sprengel explicitly aims to mobilize *Iphigenie*'s "veritably topical significance" for ideological warfare. He wants to per-suade "our politicized youth of today," who are only interested in power, that truth is a superpower. His main concern is the rising tide of national-ism among the younger generation. Sprengel translates nationalism from the political discourse into Iphigenian terms of moral emotions and thereby reveals the dangers threatening from hostile nations under the curse of "hatred, distrust, and blind willfulness [Eigenwillen]" (127). There is still time, in his view, to overcome the nationalistic menace by following Iphigenie's example of creating trust among nations by relying on the power of truth instead of ideology.

The anniversary produced, however, an interesting outside perspective, remarkable, too, for its substantive and thematic approach in contrast with the increasingly formalist insider interpretations. It is the Goethe anniversary address given to the *Wiener Verein für Individualpsychologie* by psychoanalyst Carl Furtmüller, published in the *Internationale Zeitschrift für Individualpsychologie* (1932). This was the journal edited by Alfred Adler, founder and head of this non-Freudian branch of psychoanalysis. Furtmüller's is an outsider's view in several respects: a non-German's non-Freudian psychoanalytical reading presented to an Austrian audience of non-literary scholars. Furtmüller approaches Goethe's text from the main focus of Adlerian psychology: power and domination drives. He examines Iphigenie's role as dominant female in a male-dominated environment, tracing her reactions of destabilization, manipulation, rationalization, and role change as she encounters new situations in her relations with her gods and her men.

In Furtmüller's reading, the goal of Goethe's drama is twofold. One, similar to traditional views minus the idealizing aspect, is the production of personhood. As he shows in Iphigenie's twists and turns, this process is highly problematical. The other goal that Furtmüller ascribes to Goethe's drama is the production of community. The text of *Iphigenie* performs the achievement of community from situations of conflict and hostility between genders and nations. In Furtmüller's view, Goethe has declared truth to be the way to both personhood and community; truth is the axis on which the dramatic transaction hinges. Goethe's emphasis on truth, for Furtmüller, is part of eighteenth-century ideology. Here, then, the twentieth century has subjected a central Iphigenian value to historical relativism. The absolute validity of truth has fallen victim to skeptical modernism and to the turmoil of competing ideologies.

On the other hand, Furtmüller emphatically reclaims "reine Menschlichkeit" from its limbo of hackneyed triviality and from willful redefinitions at the hands of Gundolf, Petsch, and Korff. It means, in the most activist way possible, good will toward mankind: "keine Phrase [sondern] guter Wille gegenüber dem anderen . . . mit dem Einsatz seiner vollen Persönlichkeit [no mere phrase but good will toward the other . . . with the stake of one's total personality]" (339). With the highlight fully on Iphigenie's trials and achievements, psychologist Furtmüller has little interest to spare for that favorite topic of Iphigenian psychology: Orest's cure. His explanation of his lack of interest is nevertheless intriguing. He finds the healing process impossible to interpret psychoanalytically, because the text only offers poetic abbreviations of an enigmatic psychological event: "the inner processes have to be represented with such a degree of abbreviation that they cannot fully preserve their psychological reality" (335). Furtmüller here draws a clear line between aesthetic and psychological kinds of representation.

After a silence of thirteen years on *Iphigenie*, the *Goethe Jahrbuch* of 1937 published a substantial essay by one of the most eminent Goethe scholars, *Festausgabe* editor Robert Petsch. In view of the dearth of writing on this work, Petsch's article gained representative status for German criticism of the period. The essay is a major revision of Petsch's introduction to the *Festausgabe* of 1926. It displays a number of strategies in the effort to avoid ideological conflict. There is a search for neutral ground on ethical issues which borders on the absurd. There is a general tendency to sidestep issues altogether by promoting form over substance. More disturbingly, when central questions of the Iphigenian tradition do enter the discussion, the effects of ideological contamination surface in Petsch's thinking and terminology.

Overall, Petsch has shifted the focus on *Iphigenie* to the formal aspects. In fact, his reading is an early model of the method of (*werkimmanente*) *Interpretation* that would dominate postwar German criticism until the paradigm change of the 1970s. Classicity, Petsch declares at the outset (164), is a matter of form ("angemessene Gestaltung"), not substance ("ethisch-vorbildlich"); he consequently devotes the major portion of his text to form (thirteen pages as against four pages each on introductory· framing and substance). Concepts from his 1926 reading reappear substantially altered and clothed in a new, nationalistic vocabulary. Goethe's major innovation, we read, was the invention of a "deutsche Gottgläubigkeit [German belief in God]" for the "völkisch und rassisch [by folk and race]" (177) distinct German soul ("die deutsche Seele" is everpresent). It was the mission of this German creed to replace established and historically outdated religions: the cultic myths of Euripides as well as "the laid-back Christianity and the playful Enlightenment 'religiosity'" of Goethe's own era. Petsch propounds this new *Gottgläubigkeit* as the central message of *Iphigenie*, with unmistakable application to the ideological situation of the day:

> das eine, allbeherrschende Hauptmotiv von dem Durchbruch einer neuen Religion, die auf die . . . Wurzeln jedes Gottesglaubens zurückgeht und die, wo sie aufblüht, alle überlebten Truggebilde einer Afterreligion absterben läßt [the one all-dominating main motif is the breaking forth of a new religion, which derives from the roots of all faith in God and which, wherever it blossoms, makes wither away the outlived delusional images of any pseudoreligion] (166f.).

The point should not be belabored, but the vocabulary does link such statements to religious developments in the Nazi era. The schism of the Protestant church into *Deutsche Christen* and *Bekennende Kirche* is well known. Less well known is the fact that *gottgläubig* was the official term used for the category of religious denomination of people who for whatever reason were no longer members of any church.

Petsch's most striking innovation is his approach to the question of guilt. We have seen how Orest's culpability and its consequences had dominated *Iphigenie* criticism since the late nineteenth century. The two essays published in the *Goethe Jahrbuch* since 1918 had both dealt with this topic. Petsch now picks up a curious line of exculpation that developed during the same time period. Originally limited to Orest, who was often pronounced "innocently guilty," the argument was then extended to the entire Tantalid ancestry.

Warncke in the *Goethe Jahrbuch* (1922–24) extensively described the "force of circumstances" in order to establish Orest's innocence. Berthold Schulze, approaching the drama from genre theory in the *Zeitschrift für Ästhetik und Allgemeine Kunstwissenschaft* (1926), paradoxically argues against his own reading of Iphigenie's ancestor narrative as a struggle against shame. He finds that "heredity" from Tantalus, the "generous, highly gifted Titan," created a line of Nietzschean giants of the will, "Gewaltig-Wollende," who did their evil deeds under the mitigating circumstance of illness, but passed their "great gifts" on to their progeny (240). Ever since naturalism's discovery of heredity for literature, Tantalid family analysis had been torn between hereditary sin and hereditary curse (*Erbsünde* and *Erbfluch*), between the ethical and the biological perspective. Schulze in 1926 still emphatically asserted the biological derivation of evil.

In Petsch's 1937 universe, evil is absent due to the guarantee of a purer, gentler ("reiner und sanfter") mankind offered by Iphigenie's new gods (168f.). Concerning the Tantalids, Petsch praises Goethe's "second great invention" to present their history as merely a detour ("nach schweren Irr- und Umwegen [after serious errors and detours]") to where the generation of great-grandchildren now can prove the true worth of this great "Geschlechtsverband" (169). The latter term was one of many neologisms for *family* in the *völkisch* dictionary. Orest's own crime of matricide, the worst so far in the Tantalid heritage of "heaviest guilt and damnation," is specifically named only once in the context of source relations, where it is blamed on Euripides ("the pangs of conscience of matricide Orest" 167). Thus Petsch does not completely silence the guilt theme, but he belittles guilt and tries to exculpate.

As a matter of historical contingency it should be mentioned that the most prominent of the 1932 celebration speakers, Albert Schweitzer, who delivered the official commemorative address on the anniversary of Goethe's death in Frankfurt and who used the occasion as a pulpit to warn against the ideological and moral dangers of the ruling Zeitgeist, gave the issue of culpability a major role. In Schweitzer's speech "Schuldigwerden [becoming guilty]" is the most prominent theme of Goethe's literary writings (Mandelkow 1979 Vol. 4, 127f.).

Petsch's Orest, whose task it is finally to realize the great destiny of his noble house, needs neither a traditional "Entsühnung" nor "Heilung." He experiences instead "Heiligung," a sacral transformation of his subjectivity which Petsch places in analogy to the creative experience of the artist, Goethe. Just as Goethe had discovered the "true" meaning of the old Tantalid legend by shaping his subjectivity, "eigne Lebenssorge," into an objective work of art, so Orest with enlightened soul discovers "the 'true' meaning of the old oracle saying" (166f.). By thus elevating individual artistic production to the same level as universally valid truth, which tradition had placed at the center of Iphigenian humanity, Petsch relativizes truth at the same time as he canonizes the creative artistic subjectivity.

In a distinct difference from his earlier reading in the *Festausgabe*, which demanded a balance of individuality with community, now the supreme and only value is the outstanding individuality: "Seelengröße." It is Iphigenie's mission to model and to promote aggrandizement of the individual soul. Love is defined not as *caritas* and brotherhood, as in the traditional understanding of *Humanität*, but as a cultivation of others' souls that smacks of intrusive pedagogy and inquisition. Petsch uses religious terminology to describe this *Seelsorge*, which is itself an official clerical term for *ministry*. It consists "in der höchsten Liebe zu den Mitmenschen, nämlich in der opferbereiten Sorge um ihre Seele und um deren Heiligung, [wodurch] die Seele sich zur Größe und Reinheit entfaltet [in highest love for one's fellow humans, namely in the sacrificial care for their souls, and in the sacralization of their souls, whereby the soul will unfold into greatness and purity]" (168).

It is on this point, the care and cultivation of subjectivity, that Petsch completes the turn toward irrationalism initiated in his 1926 essay. Surprisingly in the present essay, with its strong focus on the drama's language, language yet is deemed incompetent to represent adequately the mystery of the human soul. It would take music to accomplish it, and therefore, while Petsch sees in every great poet a "Dichter des Unsagbaren [poet of the unsayable]," Wagner stands out because his opera *Tristan und Isolde* has achieved the perfection of "Seelendrama," a perfection which is denied *Iphigenie* (171). Petsch, it must be said, gives language an impossible task, for the soul, as he sees it, is a superlatively unfathomable mystery: deep, powerful, eruptive, dangerous, and potentially violent. In contrast with "rationalist" (179) French classicism, where the soul moved "in the brightness of consciousness," in German soul drama everything happens beneath the surface, in the deepest depth of the soul, dissolved in broiling chaos:

alles . . . endlich aufgelöst in das, was immer unter der Oberfläche mitschwang und was bei seinem Durchbruch . . . von dem letzten Seelengrunde her . . . die aus dem tiefsten, jetzt erst 'aufgewühlten' Seelengrunde hervorbrechenden Kräfte . . . die Gewalt der aus dem geheimsten Welt-und Seelengrunde aufdringenden Mächte [everything finally dissolved in that which always vibrated below the surface and with its eruption . . . from the last bottom of the soul . . . forces erupting from the deepest, only now 'stirred-up' bottom of the soul . . . the force of the powers surging up from the most secret bottom of world and soul] (170, 174).

Irrationalism runs wild in Petsch's rhetoric here, obsessively returning to the deepest, last, most secret bottom of the soul. But irrationalism goes beyond rhetoric when Petsch ascribes to the greatest soul, Iphigenie's, an irresistible power over her fellow humans that is entirely atmospheric: it emanates from her "Dunstkreis [aura]" (171). Unanalyzable and enigmatic, thus all the more fascinating, comparable only to the biblical example of the prophets, such power is magic, a magic that amounts to demagoguery in the conclusion of the drama. Returning to apotheosis of Iphigenie, Petsch glorifies

die große, strahlende, fast prophetische Überlegenheit der Jungfrau, die mit ihrem großen Zuge . . . Freund und Feind zu der eigenen Seele mit hinaufreißt wie mit einer magischen Gewalt [the great, resplendent, almost prophetic superiority of the virgin, who with her greatness . . . pulls friend and foe up to the height of her own soul as if with a magic force]"(176).

Greatness per se, the powerful personality overwhelms; domination is its own legitimation.

As Germany moved closer to and finally entered into war, *Iphigenie* criticism moved right along supplying legitimation, at varying levels of anguish, to be sure. In 1939, Adolf Beck in *Dichtung und Volkstum* (the venerable *Euphorion* under its new name) would like to rewrite literary history. Linking *Iphigenie* to the Sturm und Drang drama *Niobe* by Maler Müller, Beck faults Goethe for having imported a foreign ideology of decadence: the "humanist Hellenism of Classicism." What Germany needs, especially now, is to bring back the pre-Iphigenian rebels and great criminals, the Titanism that Iphigenie fights off in the *Parzenlied*; for Titanism harbors "forces which are of highest value for the self-understanding and self-formation of the Germans" (174).

A markedly different attitude informs the last German contribution during the Nazi era, an essay by Joachim Müller in the *Zeitschrift für Deutschkunde* of 1940. Müller at the time was a *Studienrat* [secondary school teacher] in Leipzig. (Twenty years later as a professor in the German Democratic Republic he would publish a substantially revised version.) His article sets out to examine the validity of Iphigenie's humane ideal, in his words: whether this ideal is "existentially" real or a mere "Bildungspostulat [pedagogical postulate]." He finds his solution by gendering. Iphigenie's values are marked as female and must be subjected to priorities set by the male world of power politics ("die männliche Machtsphäre" 282) represented by "statesman" and "Herrenmensch" Thoas. When Müller legitimates Scythian blood sacrifices as "self-defense of a threatened island nation" (275), we hear an apology for Germany at war according to the propaganda line of the time. And before a happy ending is allowed, *raison d'état* must be satisfied: Orest must read the oracle in such a way that Thoas gets to keep the statue.

Müller finally finds a compromise that would allow the teacher to send off his male students to war while saving his humanistic ideals by entrusting them to the women. To answer his initial question, he argues that the humane ideal indeed becomes "existentially real" for Iphigenie at the moment when she stakes her life on it, but that it is valid only for Iphigenie. Now that German aggression was spreading war over Europe, the horizon of "reine Menschlichkeit" had shrunk to the extent of one individual's experience at one particular moment. *Humanität* could no longer change the real world of power and politics, only mitigate the pain: "illuminate the darkness of the world and mitigate the harshness of reality" (284).

It has often been argued that such a palliative function actually helps perpetuate the status quo, most recently in the reproaches made by West German critics to East German authors who had remained in the German Democratic Republic. There is no doubt that this *Studienrat* is not happy with the world and his role in it. For him Iphigenie's question concerning the humane ideal has indeed become an existential issue. It is evident in the level of anguish that frequently surfaces in his text and in the deep contradictions that structure his argument, as Müller almost willy-nilly arrives at a compromise he had not sought.

British criticism had taken on the German tradition, we have seen, as far back as Lewes, but then fell silent as *Iphigenie* was elaborated into a national cultural icon, a tribute to specifically German *Humanität*. With the republication of *PEGS* six years after the First World War under J. G. Robertson's editorship, British critics set out to challenge the German monopoly. When German criticism during the thirties withered under the impact of ideological and soon real warfare, *Iphigenie* interpretation received its main impulses from across the Channel and, after the Second World War, from beyond the Atlantic. Robertson himself led the charge in the first issue of *PEGS's* New Series with an article on "Goethe's *Iphigenie auf Tauris*" that announced in its subtitle "Some New Points of View," in the British tradition of ironic understatement pioneered by Swift's *Modest Proposal.*

Like Hérenger protesting in 1932 against the German monopoly claim on truth for Goethe's drama, Robertson attacks traditional criticism on Goethe's alleged original invention of the humane ideal. He assembles a rich genealogy of this ubiquitous Enlightenment creed throughout eighteenth century drama, with particular emphasis on French models. Robertson's real provocation, however, is his reading of Iphigenie's prayer, as it was traditionally called: "Rettet . . . euer Bild in meiner Seele! [Save your image in my soul]" This, Robertson declares, is a challenge to the gods; it is hubris and it demands a tragic outcome, not the happy ending that Goethe engineered. In support of his heretical view Robertson cites "the distinguished Württemberg thinker, Christoph Schrempf," commending this "too little known" author to the profession as a different, Württemberg voice outside the rejected German mainstream.

With Schrempf as his guarantor, Robertson accuses Goethe of avoidance of tragedy, long before Erich Heller after the next war coined the winged word. Goethe's gods fail to punish Iphigenie's primal transgression, and the ending offers a fairy-tale solution to a real human dilemma: "It is not human that [the protagonists] will 'live happily ever after'" (36).

It is, finally, Orest's cure that gives Robertson occasion for praise of Goethe, and at the same time for more refutation of the critical tradition. The vaunted motto on "reine Menschlichkeit" is merely a Goethean afterthought; ethical and religious perspectives on the healing of Orest originated not with Goethe, but in wrongheaded German criticism. (Robertson does not cite anyone in particular.) For Robertson, Orest's recovery is a purely psychological event and should be studied with the aid of psychoanalytical science. The case of Orest as well as Iphigenie's overcoming her mental crises display Goethe's insight into the workings of the unconscious, gained from the experience of his own artistic creativity, which Robertson likewise considers a phenomenon of the unconscious. Goethe's drama thus proclaims a message of "spiritual regeneration" and it is this moral optimism, in contrast with the fallacious historical optimism of the nontragic ending, that Robertson judges "the most precious legacy to us of German classical poetry" (42).

Improbable as it seems, the publication date in the anniversary year 1932 of Barker Fairley's influential study, *Goethe as Revealed in His Poetry*, appears to be a genuine coincidence. According to the preface of the second edition (1963) the book was inspired by opposition to Robertson's Goethe monograph of 1927, which Fairley was assigned to review for a Canadian journal. With a very different approach from Robertson's, Fairley nevertheless arrives at an even more critical view of *Iphigenie*. Where Robertson's argument called on intellectual and literary history, Fairley proceeds from a Gundolfian position, asking what "experiences" and "influences" — terms corresponding roughly to Gundolf's *Ur-* and *Bildungserlebnis* — made up the creative maker, Goethe. In Fairley's frame, *Iphigenie* and *Tasso* figure as "the Charlotte [v.Stein] dramas," representing an "influence" that Goethe would have to unlearn in order to become an authentic and creative self.

In contrast to the later *Tasso* which confronts, represents, and finally defeats the Charlottean influence, Fairley sees the Charlotte power in *Iphigenie* as active but unconscious and unacknowledged. The result is a severely damaged, profoundly heterogeneous text: essentially "un-Goethean." In evidence, Fairley cites misappropriation of the Greek mythological material. Here German pietist transcendentalism as mediated and defined by Charlotte had imported the body-soul dualism from Christian orthodoxy into the alien myth to produce an "exotic humanitarianism" (28).

Fairley postulates a fundamental incompatibility of this Charlottean with Goethe's own transcendentalism, which he sees emerge in the "strangely equivocal" figure of Iphigenie herself. Neither goddess nor autonomous individual, suspended between divinity and humanity, she is wholly dependent on divine authority and utters "scarcely a breath of revolt or self-assertion." Fairley is, finally, the first to critique form in *Iphigenie* as a deceptive cover over unresolved ethical and religious dilemmas. The appearance of conflicts "beautifully reconciled" in the harmonious language is a "fallacy" that essentially serves to hide the drama's crucial flaw: the "vacuum" at its center, the absence of a sustaining moral order.

It is a far cry from Fairley's and Robertson's objections to the iconoclastic reading presented in E. M. Butler's *The Tyranny of Greece over Germany* (1935). We shall leave the presentation of Butler's fascinating and nonconformist (to put it mildly) view of the German cultural tradition to our colleagues in intellectual history, who are just now discovering her book. It seems that their discipline has kept Butler just as much under wraps as literary German studies. Goethe scholarship was certainly complicit in the endeavor from the start. Given the progressive silence of the Germans in the thirties and forties, the effort to hide Butler was carried on by English criticism; the only critic even to allude to her reading of *Iphigenie* was Boyd in his book of 1942.

What was it then in Butler's views that so traumatized the profession? To begin with, Butler's authentic Goethe is the Goethe of "Prometheus" and *Faust*: autonomous creator, pagan, "daimonic"; a self modeled in Nietzsche's Dionysian image. The classicist Goethe deviated from his true "daimon" into a Christianized Hellenism inspired by Winckelmann's utopian Greece and Charlotte's pietist spiritualism. Like the "ironical symbol" of German classicism, that "weird, distressing" Laocoön sculpture, *Iphigenie* is emblematic of the repression of tragedy. Analogous to the painful contortions visualized in Laocoön, Goethe's text like a neurosis displays the traces of repression: it strikes the reader as "strangely arresting, bizarre, piteous" (81).

Moreover, since Goethe in writing *Iphigenie* went against his own "daimonic" nature the drama is a failure in every respect. It fails in the dramatic genre; the pre-established harmony excludes conflicts and limits the action to a sequence of monologues (102f.). It fails to represent an authentic world. Instead it projects a modern humanitarian fantasy, Winckelmann's utopia of Golden Age Greece, which reveals its inauthenticity in the status of its gods. The gods are dead, the Titans vanish; Iphigenie's Greece is peopled by fleeing ghosts (96–100). The human characters of the drama are no more real, they are Christianized figments of Charlotte-inspired abstraction and asceticism: Orest an icon of purified spirit; Iphigenie a Virgin Mary, and, like Faust's Helena, a phantom created at others' command (102f., 142).

Butler sees, finally, a failure in the creative power of poetic language. This text failed to realize, to represent satisfactorily, the land of Goethe's dream; he had to go to Italy to find it. There he experienced "a violent reaction against the unreality" of his drama (109). The *Roman Elegies* represent a "flat denial of 'Iphigenie'," Butler argues in a variety of contrastive readings (116ff.). In Butler's view, *Iphigenie* has played a disastrous role in the history of German literature. Accepted as a model by the emerging authors of the modern era, Goethe's false creation, this changeling *Iphigenie*, has misled the major tradition into a direction of self-destructive alienation, beginning with poor Schiller (124).

Oxford Professor James Boyd was the last *Iphigenie* critic to take account of Butler's reading. Her criticism was too recent and too radical to be completely ignored in Boyd's own book seven years later, particularly since he had made discussion of critical opinions a major part of his project. Yet he clearly prefers discussing just about anyone else (except recent Germans), and instead of Butler, with whom he clearly disagrees most strikingly, selects Robertson as his favorite antagonist. Four years before the publication of his book, in a contribution to the *Festschrift* for H. G. Fiedler (1938), Boyd had laid out a position within *Iphigenie* criticism that went way back into the nineteenth century but excluded recent German scholarship, substituting instead Robertson, Fairley, and Butler.

In 1942 he returned to *Iphigenie* with the first book-length study (not counting dissertations) of the twentieth century. His ostensible purpose, as stated in the preface, is quite pragmatic: the education of Oxford undergraduates to whom he dedicates this book. The unstated rationale emerges in the course of the text. It is to rescue Goethe's masterpiece from its recent German appropriators and perverters as well as from its English detractors: Robertson above all, with whom he conducts a running war; secondarily Fairley and Butler, whom he occasionally mentions in the notes.

In fact, he explicitly rejects twentieth century German Goethe scholarship as useless, with the sole exceptions of comparatist Steinweg (1912) and theologian Schrempf (1907. Boyd mistakenly gives 1932 as Schrempf's publication date). A report on the critical debate constitutes an essential part of his book, which aims to generate discussion among his students on the major issues of the drama. The result is a severely distorted picture of *Iphigenie* criticism. Boyd goes back as far as 1875 for the religious views of a certain Schlosser, but eerily blacks out the last thirty years of scholarship. In method, too, he returns to the nineteenth century. He objects to the issue-oriented approach of the more recent tradition for its tendency toward bias. Explicitly rejecting the twentieth for the nineteenth century perspective, he chooses the text-based commentary practiced by Heinrich Düntzer for his own model.

Issues, however, are primary for Boyd, too. Again in contrast with recent criticism (Korff, Petsch, Robertson, Fairley, Butler) the aesthetic aspect does not interest him: for him, *Iphigenie* is an "organically well-nigh perfect" work of art (5). What drives him is the relevance of the drama's ethic to actuality, the issue of "reine Menschlichkeit" in the war-torn world of his day. In the preface he quotes the "much-abused" motto, juxtaposing it with a quotation from the poet Robert Burns on "man's inhumanity to man." The conclusion of the preface indicates Boyd's own position on the ethical question and shows that the gist of his reading of *Iphigenie* is the spirit of hope. He thanks the publisher, Basil Blackwell, for "issuing, at a time like the present, an interpretation of a work whose chief import is faith, hope, and idealism."

In line with the English pragmatist tradition of philosophy, Boyd considers truth and cognition not values in themselves. In his vocabulary they are quasi-synonyms of *conscience*, that is, the necessary but not sufficient means to achieve the end of right conduct. Right conduct, ethical action, is the key term for value judgments in Boyd's Iphigenian universe. In a similar spirit he asserts the primacy of the word *Herz* in Goethe's text against the emphasis German critics have placed on *Seele*. For Boyd the former designates feeling, emotion, the moral organ, whereas the latter stands for the intellect, identity, the thing marked *die deutsche Seele*.

His extensive analysis of the text encompasses the major critical topics. On Boyd's view the Tantalid curse is a parable of original sin, with the promise of redemption through grace. The healing of Orest is a mystery of a spiritual nature, not, as Robertson had claimed, a rationally explicable event pertaining to psychology. Equally mysterious is the working of Iphigenie's appeal to truth and humanity. Boyd declares it a property of poetic language not to be completely explicable in rational discourse, since poetry itself is a creation of the unconscious. Thus Iphigenie's famous words, that everyone hears the voice of truth and humanity: "Es hört sie jeder," allow of at least two contradictory interpretations.

Two points among the topics Boyd addresses are of particular interest. One is his reading of Iphigenie's much-debated appeal to the gods:

"Rettet . . . euer Bild in meiner Seele! [save your image in my soul!]" Where Robertson had seen a clear case of hubris demanding punishment, Boyd proposes an early version of signifier theory (without the specialized terminology, of course). The "Bild" in Iphigenie's words initiates a process of moving signifiers which ends up with Orest's new understanding of the oracle. Orest's new reading has "a spiritual image [Iphigenie's personal image of Diana] replace the plastic [a statue of Diana]" (123f.).

Boyd's second intriguing point is his making Thoas the true hero of the play. Thoas, no brutal barbarian but "noble by nature" and a wise ruler who does his duty and follows the dictates of his religion, is the truly "tragic figure" of the ending, which leaves us contemplating the "magnitude of the sacrifice he has voluntarily made." Here perhaps is where Boyd's British pedagogical perspective shines through most distinctly. He deems the public good of higher import than an individual's sanity or a family's curse. According to Boyd's interpretation, Iphigenie's real mission was not to save her brother or her family from disaster, but to bring about the conversion of King Thoas to the humane religion, and thus to ensure the happiness of the Scythian nation.

Apart from its merits on textual analysis and critical debate, the major significance of Boyd's book should be sought in its mere existence at its particular time and place in history. It would be sentimentalizing to repeat, in retrospect, Boyd's own view of the importance of hope in a disastrous historical situation. What needs emphasizing, however, is the fact that it was this particular Goethean work that offered the scene on which to stage a discussion of the most pressing moral questions of the day. The appearance of Boyd's book in 1942, then, signals the singular nature and function of *Iphigenie*, which has been, again and again, to engage criticism at a truly existential level.

SINCE 1945

"Bewundert viel und viel gescholten, Iphigenie [much admired and much denigrated]": with this variation on Helena's self-characterization, as she steps on stage in *Faust II*, Arthur Henkel opens his essay in Benno von Wiese's canonical anthology, *Das deutsche Drama* (1958), as he discusses the postwar controversy that engulfed the erstwhile masterpiece. In fact, *Iphigenie* came under attack in two phases. The first time, sparked by the anniversary year 1949, the drama served as exemplar of Goethe's alleged "avoidance of tragedy" (Erich Heller 1949). The second attack, during the anti-establishment movement of the sixties and seventies, targeted the exemplary school classic and model of affirmative literature.

As background for *Iphigenie* criticism, the situation after the Second World War can be compared to the situation after 1918 only in a limited way, for contrast more than similarity. To understand why this should be so, one need only point to the *Historikerstreit* of the late eighties. This controversy among German historians arose from the question whether the Holocaust, the event which had come to represent the essence of Third Reich history, was unique or historically comparable. There are certain events in history, it has been argued, that are quite simply unique and therefore have to be considered from a perspective of singularity.

In both postwar eras the impact of war horrors and the dejection of defeat were similar experiences for Germans, and we saw how the earlier period in consequence had rejected the Iphigenian ideal as a false idol. It is well documented how Weimar Germany settled the question of guilt: by victimology. Shifting the blame for losing the war produced the *Dolchstoßlegende* [myth of the stab in the back], and it went without saying that the enemies had forced the war on an unwilling Germany. Historiography today records the beginning of a new epoch when in 1961 Fritz Fischer advanced his thesis on the German guilt in the First World War.

In *Iphigenie* criticism we saw the issue of guilt or innocence emerge in the exculpation of Orest and the Tantalids. But after 1945 the problem was not guilt, it was shame. There was no way German guilt could be denied; it was a question of settling degrees of guilt, which was formally accomplished through the denazification procedure with its grades and corresponding penalties of *Hauptschuldiger*, *Mitläufer*, and *Entlastet* [chief guilty, fellow traveler, exonerated]. Postwar Germany provided an extensive structure for dealing with guilt. In addition to denazification, there were *Lastenausgleich*, *Wiedergutmachung* [equalization of burdens, restitution], and the generous provisions for (German) war victims. An additional tool for atonement was the continued imprisonment of the entire Eastern army in Soviet camps under extremely harsh conditions until 1955. Guilt was acknowledged, if ever so reluctantly; atoned, if ever so forcibly, and was thus undone in a familiar process that had long been institutionalized in religious and judicial culture.

No such mechanism existed for shame. And yet it is unimaginable that shame could not have been felt when the truth about extermination camps was publicized at home and abroad, when Nazi atrocities became part of German identity. The shame effect was all the more acute in the context of communitarian German culture with its social code based to a high degree on respect, honor, image, and shame. Dueling, for example, was still a formal requirement for settling insults among academics in those days. A number of Hitler's generals committed suicide rather than be shamed by defeat. The immediate past era had heavily exploited the German culture of pride, as the talk of *deutsche Seele, deutsches Wesen, deutscher Geist* [the

German soul, essence, spirit] had evolved into the ideology of the master race.

The postwar situation offered the average German (male) a lot of anchors for shame: the humiliation of defeat; the indignities suffered as a prisoner of war; and, with the heavy impact of immediate reality, the humiliation implicit in the utter destruction of the country, the inability to protect *die Heimat* [the homeland]. The most powerful source of shame at once entered the area of taboo: the men's inability to protect their women from rape.˙ For German *Iphigenie* critics it would be much harder to find substitutes for the shame of inhumanity. First of all, they did not share the wartime fate and the fallout of defeat of the average male; academics were not expected to defend the country. At any rate, as the educated elite they knew they should have known better; as professors of the humanities they had placed themselves, after all, in charge of teaching *Humanität*.

And the word *Menschlichkeit* was not to be avoided. *Verbrechen gegen die Menschlichkeit* [crimes against humanity] were the substance of the Nuremberg trials; for the first time in history the hitherto vague and malleable abstraction *Menschlichkeit* was given a precise definition and, more significantly, an awesome existence in reality. *Menschlichkeit* now wielded the judicial power over life and death. In its negative form the concept created new metaphors. *Wörterbuch des Unmenschen* connoted the pollution of the German language through Third Reich usage; Dolf Sternberger's book of 1957[†] documented the professors' own participation in the corruption.

Less conspicuously but perhaps more pointedly, the Iphigenian ideal of truth would haunt the academy. Most academics had not really sinned against humanity, but all of them had lived with untruth; they had not known, refused to know, or actively fought against the truth. Not having known the truth was now, in fact, their defense. So wherever they turned, *Iphigenie* held up the banner of shame. We propose to address postwar *Iphigenie* criticism as a discourse of shame, a body of texts that from various perspectives and with varying individual interests attempted to come to grips with what we might call, analogous to the Oedipus complex, Freud's model for the experience of guilt: the Iphigenie complex of shame.

In the context of an almost complete lack of context, reading *Iphigenie* criticism as a discourse of shame is, obviously, a risky venture. The ta-

---

˙ In this context, we may think of the uproar that arose in Germany in the early nineties over a film on that tabooed topic, *Befreier und Befreite*.

† Dolf Sternberger, Gerhard Storz, and Wilhelm Emmanuel Süskind. *Aus dem Wörterbuch des Unmenschen*. Hamburg: Claassen, 1957. The book contains contributions published in the monthly journal *Die Wandlung*, which appeared under Sternberger's editorship from November 1945 to December 1949.

boo aspect of shame entails some caveats for the study of its discourse. One is the necessarily distorted nature of such texts. Under shame's command of silence, a command which any text breaks, there is simply no straightforward way of talking about the tabooed object. Avoidance, contradiction, substitution, tautology, and other rhetorical characteristics of circumlocution are to be expected, of varying frequency according to the degree of shame the writer is wrestling with. The second point complicates matters even more. Reactions to the Iphigenie complex will vary substantially depending on a particular writer's location in Third Reich history — his or her positionality, as it is called nowadays. It matters where a writer had passed the time from 1933 to 1945: in what country, position, function, occupation. Exiles and emigrants in particular became very active in *Iphigenie* criticism. While they were emphatically exonerated from guilt, they yet had to share in the shame that was attached to the German identity.

And there is, of course, a vast difference in attitudes to the Iphigenie complex if it is someone else's problem altogether. British criticism, which had involved itself deeply in the controversy of the thirties, displays a wide spectrum of approaches from decorous moral didacticism to fierce aggressivity and cool innovation. American critics occupy the most distant position in the tangled postwar situation, which may have something to do with their taking the lead during this time.

Iphigenie criticism after 1945 is not only a huge mass of texts — the most by far of any period on any Goethean drama, always excepting the special case of *Faust* — it is also a veritable heteroglossia. The Iphigenie complex generated a multiplicity of voices, the very paradigm, one might say only half facetiously, of discursive diversity. The third point, finally, will help explain the sheer deluge of postwar writing on *Iphigenie*. A taboo is not only something forbidden, inspiring horror and confusion (a *horrendum*); like forbidden things generally the taboo is irresistibly attractive, exciting extreme interest and curiosity (a *fascinosum*): the fateful tree in Paradise. The essential ambivalence of the taboo, offering opposite aspects to critical approaches, will further complicate the picture that we are about to examine.

A first striking fact, if not surprising in view of the shame factor, is the complete absence of *Iphigenie* studies in German journals until the mid-fifties, when the new journal, *Wirkendes Wort*, offered three entries on *Iphigenie*. Writing on the drama in essay collections or monographs in the early postwar years registers the raw impact of the shame complex. Major critics appear tongue-tied: repetitive, incoherent, contradictory, recycling old clichés. Strong opinions and emphatic rhetoric overwhelmingly prevail over analysis. When it does occur, analysis is propelled and directed by the need to find excuses for having failed the ideal.

There is one passage that practically waves the flag of shame *Iphigenie* had come to signify, even if upside down. In his monograph *Goethe the Poet*, published simultaneously in English and German in the anniversary year 1949, Karl Viëtor heaps highest honors on *Iphigenie* ("will always remain one of the purest manifestations of European morality and art") in order to use the work to redeem damaged German self-respect: "The German above all may point to this work as the noblest expression of his highest essence and success whenever his essence and his worth are questioned by himself and by the world" (67). A more self-conscious and explicit expression of the Iphigenie complex of shame is hard to imagine. Viëtor's confession appears less surprising if one considers the fact that this author of a severely contaminated study, *Der junge Goethe*, of 1930 (an expurgated second edition was published in 1951), was teaching in the United States at the time and thus found himself deprived of the communal support in the avoidance of shame that life in Germany afforded.

For critics writing in Germany, a major escape route was to direct attention away from the human and humane factor and once again focus on the divine angle. Return to Mother Church was much in vogue in Germany generally, for a variety of reasons that do not concern us here. What matters for our argument is the fact that both establishment churches, catholic and protestant, were considered among the few institutions unsullied by shameful conduct. Their record included resistance against euthanasia, and both now began to claim martyrs such as the Geschwister Scholl, Pastor Gollwitzer, and theologian Dietrich Bonhoeffer. This situation goes far to explain the scandal of Rolf Hochhuth's 1963 play, *Der Stellvertreter*, which accused the catholic church of complicity in the Holocaust.

After a brief burst of activity in *Wirkendes Wort* in the fifties, German criticism fell silent again until the second wave of *Iphigenie* rejection hit in the late sixties. It is significant in this silence that mainstream journals did occasionally publish articles on *Iphigenie*, but these were authored by emigrant or British scholars. The situation in East Germany was notably different for reasons that have found much attention in the post-Berlin Wall era. The official GDR assumption of an antifascist identity had successfully repressed feelings of Nazi guilt or shame. *Iphigenie* articles were regularly published in the organs assigned to administer classical literature: the *Goethe Jahrbuch*, *Weimarer Beiträge*, and *Wissenschaftliche Zeitschriften* of various universities, beginning in 1960 with the republication of Joachim Müller's (revised) essay of 1940. But the bulk of *Iphigenie* criticism was happening abroad: in Britain and America.

In striking contrast to the German focus on divinity in the early postwar years, scholars abroad turned to scrutinize the Iphigenian concept of humanity from a new, existentialist perspective. The differences of their viewpoints mark their differing positions relative to the Iphigenie complex of German shame. Exiles in England and America arrive at diametrically opposite views. One turns aggressively against the shaming ideal to bring a charge of easy optimism against Goethe (Heller in Britain), whereas the other deems the ideal too demanding, making the human and humane mission almost impossible (Seidlin in America). With their eyes on contemporary existentialism, French, Swiss, and American scholars (Leibrich, Staiger, Seidlin) relate the drama to competing philosophies. As they carve out three distinct positions in the philosophical allocation, two of them pronounce their widely differing messages with unusual intensity of feeling. As a discourse of shame the debate on *Iphigenie* is marked by occasionally touching the edge of scholarly decorum.

British critics faced a twofold problem. Within their own tradition they had to reconcile the Fairley-Butler rejection with the Boyd canonization of the thirties and forties, a conflict which derived directly, as we have seen, from the events of German history. On the other hand they had to cope with the intensity of emotions at play in postwar criticism: Erich Heller's trashing of Goethe (and *Iphigenie*) on British radio in 1949 compounded the dilemma.

Two markedly different lines developed in response. One, carried forth in widely disseminated books by Ronald Peacock (1959), Ernest Stahl (1961a), and Ronald Gray (1967), continued the British tradition of aesthetic appreciation combined with moral criticism. What these three books accomplished , however, within less than ten years, was the de facto dismantling of that tradition. Wide divergence of opinion and evaluation erased any trace of consensus. The revolt of the sons against the fathers in Britain under the banner of the angry young men preceded its parallel in Germany by about a decade, inside and outside of the academy.

The second line of *Iphigenie* criticism developed in the pages of *PEGS*, based on the approach from imagery patterns nurtured by editors Willoughby and Wilkinson. It should be noted that the master scholars themselves, who wrote pathbreaking essays on *Egmont* and *Tasso*, eschewed *Iphigenie*. But the fact that Iphigenie's cause was taken up by women scholars may account in no small degree for the difference of the *PEGS* line from the tradition followed by Peacock, Stahl, and Gray. The daughters, it seems, did not feel the urge to rebel against the fathers; they could consider themselves, as it were, a new breed not to be held responsible for the male tradition that had preceded them.

Bursting on the scene in the anniversary year 1949 with three special studies, American criticism remained the most vocal on *Iphigenie* into the sixties, whereupon, as likewise in Britain, a noticeable hiatus ensued during the intra-German Classicism strife of the seventies. Applying the close reading of New Criticism, the American approach differed from German *Geistesgeschichte* as well as from British moralism or imagery appreciation.

In the wide field of viewpoints we can nevertheless identify a topic of major interest: in three essays the focus was truth and the speaking subject.

It was paradoxically the iconoclastic blow delivered at a *Germanistentag* in 1964 (Martin Walser 1965) that restarted dormant German criticism. Beginning with Adorno's sophisticated study in *Die Neue Rundschau* of 1967, writing on *Iphigenie* mounted to a tidal wave in the seventies and early eighties. In the classics war that preoccupied the German academic and educational scene, *Iphigenie* once more assumed paradigmatic status. At issue in the strident controversy was not so much the drama itself as its representative role of archetypal school classic and icon of an "affirmative" culture.

A case could be made that *Iphigenie* rejection in turn served a representative function in the anti-authoritarian tumult of the late sixties and seventies culminating in the traumatic year of terrorism, 1977. *Iphigenie* criticism was a stand-in for the urgent question the younger generation dared not yet ask of their elders directly, namely how a society raised on Iphigenian ideals could have produced the abhorrent past that now somehow had to be *bewältigt* [overcome]. The shame complex had returned but with a difference, as is characteristic of historical repetition. The problem now was that the children had to wrestle with the fathers' shame.*

The decade of the 1980s brought a marked change to *Iphigenie* criticism overall, whose starting point can be set in the anniversary year 1982. Shame, like pain, fades over time, and the time-span needed to resolve the postwar Iphigenie complex appears to have reached its term after about two academic generations. Two features of this change stand out: (1) criticism was becoming more and more international, or in the fashionable word: global. Peripatetic academics carried the discourse back and forth over the Channel and the Atlantic. The *Goethe Jahrbuch* undertook to get out of its provincial niche in the GDR and published authors from France, Switzerland, Italy, America, and, as always, West Germany. A new *Goethe Yearbook* started up in America with a piece on *Iphigenie* in its second volume. (2) *Iphigenie* criticism experienced a new boom as the drama became once again a test case for an entire spectrum of approaches, from the ideological to the formalist extreme, inspired by the massive entry of literary theory into German studies.

If Viëtor offers the most open statement of shame, Benno von Wiese's exposé of *Iphigenie* in his monumental *Die deutsche Tragödie von Lessing bis*

---

* The Mitscherlichs' *Inability to Mourn* was published contemporaneously, in 1967. On the parental connection in terrorism see the shatteringly eloquent piece on Gudrun Ensslin in Christine Brückner's *Wenn du geredet hättest Desdemona* (1983). On *Iphigenie* and terrorism of 1977 see Hobson 1980.

Hebbel presents a perfect example of the distortions that mark a discourse of shame. Published in 1948, the book was conceived, von Wiese tells in the preface, from 1938 to 1947. Here we have, then, a product of precisely the years that witnessed the traumatic history at the root of German shame. Von Wiese's argument is flawed by incongruities and paradoxes, tautologies, lacunae, and omissions. In stark contrast with his interpretation of *Tasso*, which immediately precedes the *Iphigenie* segment, the style is not analytical but ritual. Von Wiese's *Iphigenie* discussion is not the interpretation of a literary work; it is instead part exegesis of a theological text and part liturgical performance of a *mysterium tremendum*, the worship service before a sublime spiritual object.

Instead of speaking about the text, von Wiese lets the text itself speak, quoting liberally and indiscriminately, with or without quotation marks, so that in many passages we read a prose paraphrase of Goethe's text that parades as von Wiese's text. He even quotes, with quotation marks but without source identification, another text (not by Goethe) so as to make it appear as if it were part of the *Iphigenie* text; and this after just having praised "das stille Leuchten der Goetheschen Verse [the quiet luminosity of Goethe's verses]": "'Denn immerfort, bei allem, was geschah, blieb uns ein Gott im Innersten so nah.' [For all the time, no matter what happened, a god stayed so close to us in our innermost soul]" (104). In terms of the shame discourse, this quotation secretly imported into the *Iphigenie* text reads like a variation on Viëtor's confession, like the apology of the sinner caught in flagranti, who, moreover, takes refuge in the collective *we:* No matter what happened (what we may have done) in the past, in our innermost soul we were always OK.

In von Wiese's argument on *Iphigenie,* the quotation supports the immediate nature of Iphigenie's faith despite its basically "more allegorical than mythological substance." Oblique approaches to allegory, which still stood discredited in the critical discourse of the period, occur at other places, too. Von Wiese remakes *Iphigenie* into an allegory of German history, a history which he sees constituted in the "religious problem of 'secularization'" (1948 preface). Within this history Goethe's drama figures as an allegory of redemption. It plays out a crisis of faith and holds forth the promise of salvation, where man and world will have regained their God-ordained original state of goodness ("Heilszustand, ursprüngliche und gottgewollte Ordnung des Seins" 108). Von Wiese's religious reading thus participates emphatically in the postwar return to Mother Church.

The argument to support this reading suffers from many ills, perhaps revealing, besides the tergiversations of shame, bad faith. Placing *Iphigenie* after *Tasso* in a study that is structured chronologically, examining German tragedy from Lessing to Hebbel, is a first oddity, another is the disparity in length: less than six pages on *Iphigenie* after fourteen on *Tasso*. We are reminded of *Berührungsangst* [fear of touch] as a primary reaction to the taboo. Of the many flaws in argumentation, for example, the paradoxical elaboration of the figure of the heroine, let us focus on the problems clustered around two concepts: tragedy and humanity (*Menschlichkeit*).

The first question that needs to be asked is by what right von Wiese includes *Iphigenie* in a history of tragedy. Mostly, it seems, it is in order to show the limitation of Goethe's tragic vision. According to von Wiese's conclusion, *Iphigenie* is not a tragedy since the order of the world itself is not at risk here, merely the fate of an individual. True tragedy would require apocalyptic dimensions and could only be envisioned on the basis of nihilism, a philosophy which according to von Wiese does not emerge until Büchner's tragedies. Von Wiese's definition of *Iphigenie* as tragedy of the individual contradicts his view that the curse on the house of Tantalus represents the tragic potential. The curse strikes a ruling dynasty and thus an entire people, not merely selective individuals.

In its collective function, the "Geschlechterfluch" [family curse] receives a lot of von Wiese's attention and unveils more problems in his text. The fateful phenomenon has its origin inside the confused human soul ("verworrener Sinn"), but is also caused by outside forces ("heillose Mächte"). Man is afflicted by guilt, but at the same time he is not responsible since he is victim of a curse that inheres in his bloodline: "a circle of guilt and curse which is held together by the same blood" (106). In lieu of finally explaining the paradox of guilt and victimization, von Wiese takes recourse in Goethe's idea of "das Dämonische," a mysterious agency if ever there was one. "*The family curse is the real carrier of the demonic in 'Iphigenie'*" (von Wiese's italics 106). The issue of collective guilt, much in the public discourse of the time, registers in this tortuous discussion of the Tantalid curse.

Menschlichkeit organizes another cluster of problems in von Wiese's argumentation. Let it be noted at the outset that the word itself does not once appear in all of the six pages on *Iphigenie*. The text literally writes circles around this most sensitive spot in the postwar shame complex. At one point — and that is as close as it ever gets to using the term — the text evokes it by creating a whirlpool of rejection around its antonymic derivative *unmenschlich*. The procedure, called *mise en abîme* in deconstructive parlance, is a signal of subtextual trouble, indicating unconscious defense reactions. In contrast with Goethe, according to von Wiese, Euripides embodied in the Tantalid curse "das unausweichliche, despotische, unmenschliche Sollen des Schicksals [the ineluctable, despotic, inhuman Ought of fate]" (106). But von Wiese does not state what, by contrast, Goethe did to overturn Euripides' inhuman fate.

The concept of *Menschlichkeit*, then, while not eliminated from the text, appears in the negative. More often still, *Menschlichkeit* appears in alienated form. When the concept is used, it is always clothed in the

Fremdwort [foreign word] "Humanität" and, with only one exception, highlighted by italics or quotation marks. At the very outset of his argument, von Wiese calls the role of *Humanität* in the drama into question by referring to "Goethe's very own words 'quite devilishly humane'" (103).

Right from the start, too, von Wiese attacks the traditional view of *Iphigenie* as "Drama der 'Humanität.'" His attack targets the traditional concept of *Humanität* as an ethos prescribing general laws of behavior based on a consensual view of human rights. Against this ethical perspective von Wiese asserts that *Humanität* in *Iphigenie* means "*Humanität der Person*" (his italics) but not "a doctrine or idea separable from the individual person" (104). This view blatantly negates the most quoted lines of Goethe's text, Iphigenie's appeal to Thoas on the basis of the universal validity of *Menschlichkeit*: "Es hört sie jeder . . . [Everyone hears them]" In the gravest elision of *Menschlichkeit* from *Iphigenie's* text, von Wiese has his heroine appeal only to "Wahrheit" [truth] when he discusses this passage in the drama (108).

The erasure from the text is backed up by philosophical argument as von Wiese displaces *Menschlichkeit* by divinity. In his argument, only someone who is in harmony with the divine can be humane. The collapse of the binary terms human, or humane, and divine, which for a century had circumscribed the cultural and spiritual dilemmas of *Iphigenie* criticism, forms the very basis of von Wiese's argument. The argument, however, gets entangled in major problems. One is circularity. The divine is supposed to anchor and to explain the humane but is itself not defined. Instead, von Wiese borrows the term "Welt-Frömmigkeit [world-religiosity]" from Eduard Spranger's book with this title (1941). Yet the only way he can apply the concept to Goethe's text is by constructing a contradictory figure, Iphigenie. She, "irdische Heilige [earthly saint]," devoted to the paradox of "free service," locus of a host of other paradoxes, is the exceptional Other who alone can do what is humanly — for the average human — impossible. It is consistent with this view that von Wiese pays no heed to Thoas, who is after all the figure on whom the validity of Iphigenie's humane belief is tested.

The real "Mensch" in von Wiese's reading, representative of essential humanity, is Orest. His figure and fate constitute a universal experience of the human soul: "the soul of man has become a fury to himself, existence means both doom and disease." The last of the Tantalids serves as figure of identification; von Wiese's Orest narrative registers, too, the experience of shame. In this narrative Orest enters the stage as an ostracized leper, "der 'verpestete Vertriebene'," who suffers most of all from being shunned ("Qual der Vereinzelung [torment of isolation]" used twice). The pollution of shame can only be cleansed through acceptance by an other: "eine Reinigung der Seele durch Liebe . . . die Orest erfahren darf . . . die den Menschen aus der Qual seiner Vereinzelung und seiner Schuld löst [a purification of the soul through love . . . which is granted Orest . . . which frees man from the torment of his isolation and his guilt]" (106f.).

Von Wiese's tale of Orest's shame and cleansing is woven into the traditional Tantalid guilt narrative, from which it powerfully emerges in vocabulary and imagery. There is perhaps no clearer indicator of the troubling potency of the subtext beneath von Wiese's Orest account than the groping phrase he seizes to describe the essential incomprehensibility of an experience he is trying to tell and hide at the same time: "die unverstandene schreckliche Götterwirkung [the uncomprehended terrible effect of the gods]" (106).

Von Wiese was not alone in striving to sublate the quandaries of *Menschlichkeit* in the mystery of the divine. The religious perspective remained the prevailing German approach through the fifties, the most prominent example being Kurt May's introduction to the *Gedenkausgabe* (1954). An essay by Franz Stegmeyer in the volume *Europäische Profile* (1947) presents an anti-Nietzschean claim on *Iphigenie* for "Die Geburt der Humanität des Abendlandes [The Birth of Humanity in Western Civilization]" (title) in the name of Catholic ideology. Hans M. Wolff's monograph, *Goethes Weg zur Humanität* (1951) and essays by Gerhard Storz (1953) and Herbert Lindenau (1956) focus on the concept of the hidden God, *deus absconditus*, in the context of religious history from Greek mythology and Saint Augustine's *praxis pietatis* (using the liturgical Latin terminology) to the German pietist concept of *Heilsschema* [schema of salvation].

Iphigenie as "Glaubensdrama [drama of faith]" of essentially Christian denomination is the subject of articles in a good number of journals, including British and American ones. Writing in this vein are Ernst Moritz Manasse (*Modern Language Quarterly* 1952), Günther Müller (*PEGS* 1953; republished in von Wiese's anthology *Die deutsche Lyrik* 1959), Erich Hock (*Wirkendes Wort* 1954), Robert M. Browning (*German Quarterly* 1957), Heinz Otto Burger and Werner Hodler (*Germanisch-Romanische Monatsschrift* 1959/60). Even Arthur Henkel in von Wiese's *Das deutsche Drama* (1958), who attempts a new beginning in many ways, still insists that "the true theme" is the correct understanding of the divine will in order to lead man to his proper place: neither in Christian dependence nor in secular humanistic autonomy, but in a position of compromise, in partnership with God or gods..

It is almost impossible not to sound denunciatory when reporting on Kurt May's introduction to *Iphigenie* in the *Gedenkausgabe* (1954), as he celebrates in gushing rhetoric "the *Festspiel* of religious humanism" (1164). The formula, "religious humanism," returns obsessively throughout the text, hammering home the abuse perpetrated here on the concept of humanism. According to the accepted meaning of the term, *humanism* is the opposite of religious bonding, yet May's humans are utterly dependent on divine power. Contrary to Enlightenment humanism, where Goethe's drama had been traditionally situated, these humans need divine help to be rescued from moral crisis and to be returned to a state of perfection, which May sees in entirely religious terms. Orest is rescued from hubris and alienation from "the good gods," Iphigenie is saved from religious doubt and the danger of "Gottesverlust [loss of God]," in order for both to reach the goal of "closeness to God, religiosity."

Going beyond the abdication of human autonomy, May's religious humanism recants the essential ingredient of Enlightenment anthropology, which with Schiller and Kant insisted that man must always be a purpose in himself, never a means to achieve some other end. May's universe is the work of gods who use man as medium to achieve their ends. The Tantalids serve as exemplars of revolt against this divine world order; May denounces them in negativized Nietzschean terms as "Menschlich-Allzumenschlich" and "Übermenschen [human-all-too-human, supermen]." From Tantalid-Nietzschean rebellion, humankind as represented in Orest and Iphigenie converts back to submission under the divine law. Nearly a decade after the war, when the unbroken silence on the past had left academic reputations and careers undamaged, the discourse of shame has produced a conversion narrative in May's text. The traditional model for such a narrative is the biblical parable of the prodigal son, where the returning sinner is welcomed back into the harmony of his spurned home with high honors.

May's text shows how the pain of shame has faded with time and yielded to a feeling of relief, even euphoria. His praise of *Iphigenie's* aesthetic value knows nothing but superlatives. The work is flawless, it proclaims the harmony of form and content — "Harmonie" is another leitmotiv in May's text — of the perfect world mirrored in the perfect work of art. There is no need to dwell on the analogy of May's conversion narrative with the mass conversions ("sudden transformation" in the Mitscherlichs' words 1967) among German intellectuals from the hubris of Nazi ideology to a new version of religiosity, which one might call, in memory of Petsch's 1937 term: *Gottgläubigkeit* [belief in a divinity].

In May's account, Goethe serves as model here, too. The author of *Iphigenie*, May assures us, did have religion but not of the ordinary Christian variety; Goethe's religiosity was unique, as "einmalig" as Goethe himself (1163). May's own implication in Nazi ideology is documented in his essay on *Die natürliche Tochter*, published in the *Goethe Jahrbuch* of 1939, which he had dedicated to his teacher, Robert Petsch. May's conversion performed on *Iphigenie* now would undo the embarrassing — in present circumstances: shame-inducing — interpretation of the same drama presented by the revered teacher in the *Goethe Jahrbuch* essay of 1937.

The anniversary year 1949 was the epicenter of a quake in Goethe revision that ranged over the entire evaluative spectrum but on balance came
down on the negative side. Confronted with the disastrous course of
German history, the intellectual community found it easier to blame Goethe for lacking some qualities that might have prevented the disaster than
to examine the profession's involvement in shaping precisely the image of
their superhero which was now declared suspect.

The disparity of visions and voices appears nowhere as clearly, perhaps,
as in the two pre-eminent essays on *Iphigenie* published in that year by
scholars whose positions relative to the Iphigenie complex were yet strikingly similar: Erich Heller in Britain and Oskar Seidlin in the United
States. Both exiles and therefore absolutely exempt from guilt, yet with
their identity inextricably bound up with Germanness; both also professors
of German at a moment when German culture had fallen into disrepute as
never before, to the point where one hardly dared conjoin the words *German* and *culture* (see Heller's preface in the 1952 volume of his essays,
The Disinherited Mind).

It is this dilemma of the individual whose identity ties him to something he abhors, of the scholar professing a culture which has to hide its
face in shame, that is at the root of Heller's fierce aggression in his essay
"Goethe and the Avoidance of Tragedy" (1949). Heller makes *Faust* and
Iphigenie, the most venerated works of German literature in Britain, represent the lack of a "civilized tradition" in Germany. Following in the tracks
laid by E. M. Butler, Heller blames this lack for what went wrong with
German history. The Age of Goethe, glorified by Korff as the epitome of
German *Geistesgeschichte*, is for Heller the "spiritless time" deplored by
Hölderlin. He sees the chaotic split of that era between rationalism and
romanticism reproduced in a fundamental "defect in [Goethe's] sensibility," that is, Goethe's inability to face evil and sin (39).

Within Goethe's oeuvre, *Iphigenie* "stands for" precisely this defect
and therefore displays a basic structure of dichotomy and incongruity.
What used to be vaunted as idealization is for Heller a lack of reality, a basic untruthfulness. Iphigenie's world is not real because there is no evil in
her world. Goethe unsuccessfully attempted to dissolve the hard, inexorable Greek myth into a soft human kindness. In consequence of Goethe's
failure, the drama's radical moral law is incompatible with the heroine's
gentle and lovable spirituality; the really tough issues flowing from the
tragic substratum of the Atridic myth therefore must be repressed: "such
questions will not be asked" (45).

Most significantly for Heller, the drama represses tragedy in its central
action, the healing of Orestes. Heller accuses criticism of having conspired
in the Goethean deception by creating the misnomer of Orest's *cure*:
"there is no cure for the murder of a mother" (42). Heller's reading of
guilt denied, secreted away under the name of curable illness, translates

into Goethe's text the postwar preoccupation with assigning and denying guilt.

A few related points need to be addressed here. In Heller's schema, the quintessential guilt is murder of the mother, not of the father or brother. Parricide and fratricide are founding myths in Western culture. From Cain and Abel to Freud's primal horde, these myths have served to legitimate violence in war and in generational succession. Murder of the mother belongs in a different dimension. It stands for violence that civilization has marked as taboo, the taboo that Germany in the Third Reich had so flagrantly broken: the killing of women and children, of noncombatants, prisoners, Jews; of precisely those who were not fathers and brothers.

According to his preface of 1952, Heller would further associate murder of the mother with killing that which has given life, nurture, and sustenance, that is, German culture, the Germany of the true spirit, in which the exiles had so desperately believed, and which now seemed irretrievably lost. Finally, Heller's singling out Orest's crime is yet another instance of transferring the unspeakable trauma of shame over onto guilt. For guilt, if not cured, can be atoned, made good, and forgiven; Western civilization had learned to deal with it, at least to speak of it.

It is the hope of guilt and shame overcome that undergirds Oskar Seidlin's approach to "*Iphigenie* and the humane ideal" in an article of this title published in the *Modern Language Quarterly* in 1949, which today stands as the central interpretation of the postwar period. The essay reads like a point-by-point rebuttal of Heller's indictment. Originally presented as a lecture, like Heller's, and published without the standard equipment of critical warfare in footnotes, the attack is not direct. Seidlin purports to defend Goethe and his drama against unnamed nineteenth century detractors who faulted the Olympian Goethe and the easy optimism of his most idealistic work. As we have seen, such objections did not appear until far into the twentieth century. In fact, however, Seidlin takes aim at his contemporaries, "the criticism of a new era," which seems to share Goethe's 1802 judgment that *Iphigenie* is "quite damnably humane" (307). His conclusion identifies the addressee of his criticism as the ideology of despair that had found a home in existentialism and a patron saint in Kafka, a recent arrival on the academic scene. (Seidlin, it should be noted, commemorates Kafka, too, whose twenty-fifth death anniversary coincided with the Goethe Year.)

In Seidlin's position, we observe European pessimism opposed by the American ideology not of easy optimism — Seidlin is careful to refute this attitude — but of refusing to accept despair as the final word. Seidlin chooses "an American author, Nathaniel Hawthorne," not exactly known for his optimism, as spokesman against the European message, borne by Kafka, that there is no hope. He bases the hope to be found in *Iphigenie* on another axiom of existentialist philosophy: *l'acte gratuit*, which Seidlin reads to mean *free deed*, an action undetermined by anything outside of free human will. For Seidlin, Goethe's drama stands for a declaration of freedom pronounced and validated by Iphigenie in her decision to speak the truth.

From this platform Seidlin proposes alternative views to Heller's major propositions. His detailed exploration of Goethe's text produced a wealth of suggestions and insights to stimulate future critics. Following Seidlin's lead, scrutiny of the Iphigenian ideal under the denomination "quite damnably humane" would dominate *Iphigenie* criticism for decades to come. Concerning the role of myth, Seidlin argues that Goethe reinterpreted the dehumanizing myth of his classical source in such a way as to create the possibility of free human action. The modern *Iphigenie* rehearses human emancipation from the captivity in deterministic doctrines of religious, moral, or political provenance.

For Seidlin the tragic core in Goethe's play is not the unforgivable crime of matricide. (He slips in the point that Orest's mother was not merely a victim, but a perpetrator herself: "his murderous mother" 308.) Taking Heller's argument from culture and tradition into psychology and individual ethic, Seidlin states that "in terms of modern psychology . . . the hideous misdeed" was committed against "the source of life," for which "the mother" serves as metaphor. Orest's real crime is the assault on life itself, an assault that finds expression on stage in his longing for death and in his "blissful vision" of the underworld, of "the nothingness" that promises relief from the burden of living. Thus Seidlin makes his Orest bearer of another German wrong: the love of death so prominently displayed, for instance, in Thomas Mann's twentieth century classic, *Der Zauberberg*.

It is a wrong, however, that can be righted. Here "modern psychology" allows Seidlin to appoint Iphigenie the "healer" of Orest's "diseased mind." In this function Iphigenie stands as symbol of the "cosmic" forces of life that enable human regeneration even from the deepest decay and despair of death. Seidlin does not repeat the nineteenth century's sublimation of Goethe's woman-ideal into a romanticized saint. In a decisive turn away from idealizing identification, he historicizes the figure of Iphigenie as a new image of womanhood evolving in the eighteenth century that aimed to bridge the body-soul dualism embedded in German Protestant tradition. As its "loftiest" product, he declares, the image of Iphigenie best embodied "German humane idealism." Having thus redeemed, on the one hand, the besmirched historical concept of German idealism, Seidlin's approach on the other hand overcomes the despair over German real history reflected in Heller's reading, by setting a new frame for Goethe's drama: the cosmic horizon, within which history and myth are mere aspects of the larger phenomena of life and death.

The year 1952 saw two authoritative interpretations of *Iphigenie*, Emil Staiger's in the first volume of his *Goethe* monograph and Josef Kunz's in the fifth volume of the *Hamburger Ausgabe*. Both reaffirm the drama's stature as model classic imparting "Mitte und Maß [mean and measure]" (Kunz), and both respond to the current debate on "the problem of tragedy" (Kunz's subtitle), but beyond that they offer widely divergent readings. Kunz seeks to detach the drama from its entanglement in current history by framing Goethe's text philosophically and by closing in on details of the verbal texture. By contrast Staiger makes *Iphigenie* the centerpiece of his crusade against modernism. While he singles out Schopenhauer, Kierkegaard, and especially Nietzsche as the destructive opposition to Goethe's healthy world view, his stern sermon is intended as a warning for contemporary literature, the gloom and doom writers of the *Stunde Null*, who have chosen Kleist and Kafka over Goethe as their model.

Staiger's distaste for modern literature has been too easily dismissed as a matter of ideology. Yet here the issue is clearly the intellectuals' responsibility in history; more specifically Staiger asks the postwar question about the role of German intellectuals during the Hitler era. It is for this reason that he makes the concept of truth the center of his interpretation. "It supplies the key to the understanding of the entire work" (363). We recall Korff in his 1921 essay giving the same key function to the right understanding of *Menschlichkeit*. A radical shift of emphasis has occurred between the two postwar moments. Where after the First World War *Menschlichkeit* came under interrogation, now it is Truth that needs to be questioned. As Staiger reads history, the "Copernican turn" performed by Kant and shared by *Iphigenie* replaced the belief in absolute truth with a concept of truth constituted in the relation between man and his world. Here the human mind codetermines what we call reality; our thinking about the world gives that world its shape.

A detailed examination of the ways in which Goethe changed the ancestor narrative in successive versions of the drama helps to make Staiger's point that history is a human perception and valuation of events, not an autonomous, *true* event. Thinkers and writers, then, can spread responsible or irresponsible *truths* about man and the world. The course of history, Staiger concedes, has proved Nietzsche's pessimism right. "It is impossible to contradict. But the supposition is permitted that Nietzsche himself, through his doctrine, has codetermined the course of events." At the time of Staiger's writing, a reference to Nietzsche's doctrine of "the will to power" would unmistakably point to the promoters of Third Reich ideas among German intellectuals as "his disciples" (367).

If Staiger assigns historical guilt he finds, on the other hand, in Goethe's work a way to relieve guilt. "Heilschlaf [healing sleep]" and "Gnade des Vergessens [grace of forgetfulness]" as practiced by Orest, Egmont, and Faust, come with Staiger's highest recommendation on Goethe's authority. If this suggestion on how to deal with guilt encountered vehement opposition in later criticism it was not primarily for theoretical inconsistency — Staiger will grant "Vergessen" only if accompanied by inner change ("Verwandlung") but never explains how this metamorphosis in the act of forgetting is supposed to work. The later critics' objections were based on moral grounds flowing from the postwar debate on *Vergangenheitsbewältigung* [overcoming the past].

To understand Staiger's *Heilschlaf* prescription, his position relative to the discourse of shame has to be kept in mind. As Viëtor's confession statement so clearly demonstrates, the experience of shame is predicated on being seen by an other, on the knowledge that one is being judged by the other. From his position of Swiss outsider and arbiter, Staiger could offer the shamed German insiders *Vergessen* on condition of *Verwandlung*. The condition imposed would mean that German intellectuals would change their ways from the wrong path of participation in Nietzsche's version of historical pessimism in order to embrace instead a more promising philosophy. In particular, Staiger is warning against existentialism, which for him embodied nothing but negativity, nihilism, and despair.

Finally, on the issue of *reine Menschlichkeit* Staiger retreads old ground in Goethe's biography, but here, too, the current situation registers. "The problem of German inwardness [Innerlichkeit]" prompts him to require that action must result from the ideally "pure" mindset (373). On the other hand, he limits such action in the spirit of "Goethesche Humanität" to the private sphere. Political action is specifically excluded and explicitly downgraded as demagoguery. "The masses can be persuaded; only the neighbor [der Nächste] can be changed. Thus the kingdom of *Humanität* forms only in the smallest circles" (379f.). No wonder the political activists among intellectuals of the late sixties and seventies picked Staiger as one of their favorite targets to attack.

Where Staiger in emphatic opposition to Heller approves of Goethe's denial of evil and tragedy, asserting that Goethe mitigated the original sin committed by Tantalus ("So wäre denn die Sage doch beschönigt und das Urböse . . . geleugnet? Es ist so." [So the legend would seem to be palliated and original evil denied? It is so] 366), Josef Kunz's commentary in the *Hamburger Ausgabe* contradicts Heller from a different position. For Kunz, far from epitomizing "avoidance of tragedy," *Iphigenie* represents Goethe's debate on tragedy. Aiming both to rescue the drama from embroilment in the ideological conflicts of the day, and German culture from its discredited state, Kunz takes two seemingly contradictory approaches.

In a first move he repatriates German intellectual history into the European tradition. This approach accords perfectly with the dominant German ideology of the time, which, led by catholic conservatism under the auspices of Adenauer's reign, strove to reclaim the *Erbe des Abendlan-*

des [heritage of occidental culture]. Kunz points to the twin foundations of Western civilization in classical Greek culture and Christianity as origins of the debate on tragedy that he sees carried on in *Iphigenie*. In a second move, he devises a German *Sonderweg* [third way] within the European tradition, leading from mediaeval mysticism to a philosophy of existence inspired by Karl Jaspers.

From his new perspective of existentialist Christianity, Kunz views *Iphigenie* as a parable of German history. On this view, Goethe's text presents three basic attitudes toward life, which correlate with different epochs of German historical experience and identity, and which, since the drama is a parable, are laid out as distinct options from which to choose. Kunz's commentary wants to explicate the implications of the three options and to guide the reader toward making the right choice. Readers — Germans and foreigners alike — would be helped in correcting their image of German identity of the past and to orient their future actions according to their corrected view of German history. It is significant that of the three typical attitudes to life that Kunz sees presented in *Iphigenie* — "Schicksalslosigkeit," "Schicksalhaftigkeit," "Mitte und Maß [fatelessness, fatefulness, mean and measure]" — he explicitly correlates only the first with historical experience.

Represented in the figure of Pylades, "Schicksalslosigkeit" is the existence embraced by autonomous man, proponent of secular Enlightenment rationalism, of belief in progress and politics. Locating Pylades' choice of existence in the context of Goethe's biography in the eighteenth century, Kunz gives much consideration, all of it negative, to the one-dimensional spirit of an epoch that produced absolutism and the French Revolution. He moreover assigns the Enlightenment epoch to an alien, Romance tradition in a spirit and vocabulary recalling Goethe's essay in the Sturm und Drang manifesto *Von deutscher Art und Kunst* (1773), but reminiscent also of the chauvinistic critics before 1918. Stepping back from the period of *Iphigenie* to young Goethe's rejection of classicism and Enlightenment under the influence of Herder in Strasbourg, Kunz contrasts "rationale Rechenschaftsablage der welschen Architektur [rational rendering of accounts of Romance (denigrating term) architecture]" with "das Bildnertum [shaping creativity of] Erwin von Steinbachs," the builder of Goethe's paradigmatic anticlassicist Strasbourg cathedral.

Kunz's second existential type, represented by Orest and the Tantalid ancestors, is ineluctably tragic. Oriented toward the demands of totality and the absolute, this is the male world of unconditional response to the challenge of fate: *Schicksalhaftigkeit*. Home of the genius and the hero, we recognize here the ideals of titanism, of the fight to death that had shaped German destiny in Kunz's own lifetime.

The third type of existence, "Mitte und Maß [mean and measure]," holds the middle ground between Promethean transgression and Pyladian lack of destiny. Kunz assigns this sphere of balance to the woman, Iphigenie, for her closeness to organic essence, for her ability to bridge the gap between transcendence and the physical world. Kunz finds the model for his female ideal in medieval mysticism. Like the women mystics of that epoch, Iphigenie is the interpreter of the divine, demonstrating in her character "die letzte Geborgenheit im Göttlichen [the final shelteredness in the divine" (415).

For Kunz the language of German mysticism pervades the text, and he highlights a different category of key words than those emphasized by earlier German critics. Their master words *Menschlichkeit, Wahrheit, Seele* are notably absent from his list. Kunz's theme word is *Segen* [blessing]: divine communication to the human *Herz* [heart], to which he adds epithets describing the appropriate attitude of receptivity: *still, gelassen, fromm* [calm, composed, religious]. Iphigenie's humane ideal in this view rests on the foundation of Christianity. It is an ethic of love of fellow man (Kunz uses the Greek *agape* from theological terminology), based on an anthropology that aims to keep man in the place assigned to him in the divine order. The task of *Humanität* is "the realization of that order which is assigned to man in the whole of creation" (414).

The debate on tragedy that Kunz sees undertaken in Goethe's drama confronts two major variations of the genre, both contingent on the two pillars of European spirit: classical Greek culture and Christianity. For Kunz, classical Greek tragedy postulated an absolute division between man and gods, which was displayed in a plot of man's stepping over the line and being necessarily punished for his transgression. Greek tragedy therefore is "ontisch," tragedy of Being. By contrast, tragedy since the advent of Christianity is moral ("ethisch"). Here transgression involves a wrong decision taken by man, which must allow for the possibility of correction, of "balance and reconciliation," whereby things can be put back in order. In *Iphigenie*, Goethe contrasts the two traditional concepts of tragedy, but then goes beyond both to found a new kind of tragedy as paradigmatically performed in the action of his mythic-mystical redemption drama.

Kunz's reading strives to combine two untainted strands of German thought and tradition to rescue *Iphigenie* from the avoidance-of-tragedy charge, without on the other hand falling into Zeitgeist-engendered pessimism. For his two strands, classicism and mysticism, Kunz finds a modern anchoring point in the writings of philosopher Karl Jaspers who, unlike his more famous colleague Heidegger, had openly opposed nazism and consequently been dismissed from his Heidelberg chair in 1937. In the 1947 book *Von der Wahrheit*, his first since his political disgrace, Jaspers had set out his view of tragedy as based on the will to existential failure (*Scheitern-wollen*). Here is the source of Kunz's "Schicksalhaftigkeit [fatefulness]" as embodied in the Tantalids. But Kunz mitigates Jaspers's existential pessimism by introducing the concrete spirituality of Christian mysticism into the concept of transcendence, which in Jaspers's system had remained no more than an empty possibility of getting out of the world.

The year of Staiger's and Kunz's interpretations, 1952, also saw the restart of English criticism with an article in *Publications of the English Goethe Society* by Sylvia P. Jenkins. (In the same year, Erich Heller's critique of 1949 was made available to a wider audience in the volume *The Disinherited Mind.*) Similar to the German situation, if for different reasons, English *Iphigenie* criticism is marked by discontinuity. After the intense activity of the thirties, when British scholars made up for the failings, through silence and ideological contamination, of their German colleagues, there was first a long postwar pause. Within the flourishing of Goethe scholarship in England, evident in the field of drama in path-breaking essays on *Egmont* and *Tasso* by *PEGS* editors Leonard A. Willoughby and Elizabeth M. Wilkinson as early as 1946, *Iphigenie* was conspicuously absent.

Prewar and wartime critics had created rather a quandary. Current events and passions had reverberated in the work of Butler and Boyd, disrupting traditional scholarly controversy of the kind practiced by Robertson and Fairley. Fairley, by the way, saw no reason to change his low opinion of *Iphigenie* in his widely disseminated 1947 *Study of Goethe*. Two years later Heller did his best to discourage the study of this drama by declaring it the paradigm of avoidance of tragedy and worse. Thus, even though Jenkins wrote only ten years after Boyd's book, her article stands as a distinct mark of a rupture in tradition. Boyd, in fact, is the only critic she mentions. While she does not write exactly in a vacuum, Jenkins openly distances herself from postwar German and American criticism, dismissing its soul-searching concerns as "the current fashion of humanitarianism" (70). She proposes instead, in a sort of autogenesis of a woman critic, to go back to origins.

Following the model given in Wilkinson's essay on *Tasso* and *Steigerung* [enhancement] (1949), Jenkins's reading of the controversial concepts *reine Menschlichkeit* and *verteufelt human* [damnably humane] goes back to theoretical texts by Goethe, not to the usual battery of biographical statements. Her focus is outside the traditional horizon, too. Again following the Wilkinsonian method of relating imagery patterns to what used to be called content, Jenkins examines the image complex *Bild* as operational symbol in *Iphigenie*, structuring plot, figures, themes of moral and philosophical import, and revealing psychological processes. Jenkins signals a radical turn in postwar *Iphigenie* criticism away from the dominance of ideas, when she declares that more than any other Goethean work this drama embodies the poetic quality of a literary text as defined in Wilkinson's school: the fusion of the spiritual and the material dimensions.

A German import, Günther Müller's *PEGS* essay of the following year (in German) reverts back to tradition in participating vigorously in the controversy over ideas. Müller undertakes an uneasy defense of the German affirmation of *Iphigenie*'s tragic potential, but offers in evidence only a very close reading of the "Parzenlied" (title of essay).

In 1965 Ursula J. Colby concluded the *PEGS* line before a new period of silence in English criticism accompanied the German clamor over the classics during the seventies. Colby places herself at the opposite extreme of Jenkins's autonomous stance. Thirteen years after Jenkins, and acutely aware of the controversies during the two postwar decades, she discovers a way out of criticism's impasse by introducing a new genre for *Iphigenie*: feminist tragedy. In explicit response to Heller, Colby constitutes her new genre in the sacrifice of essential humanity by the woman. The verbal motif of *Band* or *Bindung* [bond] circumscribes Iphigenie as woman limited, bound, in bondage. Thus, for Colby, the heroine is moved by the emotional strings that tie her to the men in her life, through a sequence of sacrificial roles: from abandoned woman to asexual sister and, finally, isolated goddess.

In contrast with the cool innovation of these women critics, and with a considerable delay, we find the (male) professorial establishment wrestling with the major tradition in English *Iphigenie* criticism, which had, under the impact of German history, broken into two warring camps. Robertson and Boyd were holding the high ground of moral and aesthetic appreciation, with Fairley and Butler, from their vastly different positions, on the attack. Now, between 1959 and 1967 three studies in book format attempted to come to terms with the conflicted native *Iphigenie* tradition.

The effort to carve out a new stance on *Iphigenie* was further complicated by the question of how to deal with the German discourse of shame that had developed in the aftermath of the war. A decade and a half after the end of the war, Ronald Peacock in his standard-setting study of *Goethe's Major Plays* (1959) pursues a twofold goal. For one, in order to undo the canonization of *Iphigenie* performed by Boyd, he substitutes historical and conceptual diversity for Boyd's absolute categories. Historicization within a wider conceptual horizon would help to achieve his second goal, too, namely to free Goethe's text from the obsessions and limitations entangling the drama in contemporary ideological debates.

As a result, however, Peacock himself is caught up in the binaries and polarities he constructs; his reading displays the ambivalence characteristic of reaction to a subject of embarrassment, the monument of shame that *Iphigenie* had become. The British attitude to postwar Germany, it should be remembered, was far more cautious and less forgiving than the French advance under the leadership of de Gaulle. So Peacock, in reclaiming *Iphigenie*, hedges his bets. While he proclaims the work to be Goethe's greatest poetic drama, he yet deems it seriously flawed in plot, characters, and dramatic structure. He declares Thoas, whom Boyd had chosen for his true hero, a mere puppet. He censures Orest's "punning" reinterpretation of the oracle as a "trivial and slightly absurd" solution (69). He straddles the conflicting views on religious versus humanistic import by means of terminological jugglery. Goethe, he suggests, wrote the modern equivalent of a morality play, a "ritual . . . of a philosophical faith which appropriates [religious] feelings" (93).

Similarly, his attempt to historicize the figure of Iphigenie maintains a dual vision. Without qualification, Peacock merges two opposite lines of tradition. On the one hand, he derives Goethe's heroine from the aesthetic paganism of Winckelmann's classical ideal (see Hatfield 1964), but also from German pietism's idea of the beautiful soul. No timeless ideal of humanity, Peacock's Iphigenie is "an icon for late eighteenth century moral sensibility" (80).

According to the British critical tradition, which demands significant moral substance in literature, Peacock ranks *Iphigenie* right at the top. In the plethora of moral themes he assigns to the drama, we see him commingle the highly topical such as exile and feminine ambition with the timeless and conventional, the secular with the religious: guilt and evil, truth and innocence, goodness and spiritual redemption. He does not, however, select a focus. His summary characterization, "a monumental drama of moral emotion," is as laudatory as it is vague, with the exception of "monumental." The epithet points to *Iphigenie*'s outstanding function in the mind of contemporary critics: this drama had been appointed the mark of moral achievement to be either attained — in the humane tradition — or missed: in the inhumane failures of German history that had engendered shame.

Peacock had left *Iphigenie* suspended in a web of polarities, postulating unfounded or impossible syntheses. Two years later, Ernest L. Stahl, James Boyd's successor at Oxford, took another step towards the dissolution of certainties as they had been set down in Boyd's book twenty years ago. Stahl's own book of 1961, a slim study of less than sixty pages, is obviously intended to replace (Stahl calls it "update") Boyd's now antiquated guide to *Iphigenie*. Stahl's new guidelines, however, supply questions, not answers. In consequence, the purportedly absolute Iphigenian law of humanity, which had served to establish postwar norms of shame, is *aufgehoben* in the sense of annulled. According to Stahl, criticism must go back to basics and begin again to discuss issues which had long been considered settled. More than that, instead of stating certainties, Stahl announces a principle of undecidability for interpreting *Iphigenie*. Taking up three age-old problems that generations of scholars had loved to debate, he pronounces them out of bounds. In Stahl's view, criticism simply lacks the tools to explain satisfactorily (1) the healing of Orest, (2) the reinterpretation of the oracle, and (3) the drama's conclusion, where obedience to the humane law boomerangs on Thoas. (Six years later Adorno would zero in on the latter point.)

Stahl opened entirely new issues for debate, finding problems in Goethe's text where previous critics had seen nothing. Scholars need to address the fact, he informs them, that there are two curses, not one; that the mythical curse on the Tantalid family is of an essentially different nature than the curse on Orest originating in the spilled blood of the mother. Further, the meaning of *entsühnen* [expiate], describing Iphigenie's mission to do away with the curse on her family, is far from clear; Stahl was the first to point out that the word appears to be a Goethean neologism. And finally Stahl identifies Pylades as the originator of Iphigenie's mission of *Entsühnung*. This point resets the frame of debate on the relation between idealized Iphigenie and her brother's friend, whom critical tradition of the last forty years had loved to scorn for his pragmatism.

Iphigenie's German detractors of the second postwar phase of rejection could not have wished for more timely support than that provided in Ronald Gray's *Goethe. A Critical Introduction* (1967). Gray's own agenda are clearly based on English developments in criticism. Against the new line of appreciative interpretation of individual texts promoted in *PEGS*, he calls upon the critical tradition of Goethe studies established by George H. Lewes in the nineteenth century, linking life and works and insisting on evaluative judgments that include, particularly, the moral perspective (preface, vii). While Gray explicitly mentions only "Goethe's foremost admirer today, Emil Staiger," among those whom he intends to challenge, we may also read his project in a spirit of rivalry between British centers of Goethe scholarship. His is the Cambridge entry in the competition with Oxford (Boyd and Stahl) and London (Willoughby, Wilkinson, *PEGS*).

Following the Lewes-Robertson tradition, Gray pays high tribute to the excellence of Goethe's verse in *Iphigenie* and the perfection of the classicist form, but it is ambivalent praise at best. The excellent poetry engages in deception since it tries to pass off dreams for reality, "the dream of a human race redeemed by sheer human virtue" (72). Moreover, while Goethe may have dreamt this utopian dream of mankind, his text puts forth a different dream: the private dream of individual happiness. Gray sees Goethe deluded by the eudaimonistic spirit of his age into identifying the private desire for happiness with the common weal. At issue in the drama is not a public ethos — justice and retribution, good and evil, good or bad government; Iphigenie merely wants everyone to be happy, herself most of all, for she is the most selfish of the self-seeking characters in this play.

If Gray seems harsh on the heroine, his treatment of Thoas is still more severe. This alleged hero of humane behavior is in truth a duplicitous hypocrite, a blackmailing, calculating, unreliable, ruthless blackguard. Since in Gray's view Iphigenie's moral pronouncements are just that, lip service hiding self-interest, the disqualification of Thoas as her prize pupil is a necessary consequence. As a further consequence, if the exemplary student of humane idealism reveals himself to be nothing of the sort, the entire moral structure on which the drama is founded must collapse. Thus after fifteen years of postwar criticism, from 1952 to 1967, English Goethe scholarship ended up deeply divided on *Iphigenie*. The stage seemed set for a lively discussion. But silence ensued, while Germany entered the acrimonious debates of the classics war in the seventies.

With eleven articles published in fifteen years (1946–62), American scholars showed by far the highest level of interest in *Iphigenie* during the early postwar era. In view of the composition of German departments at the time, it is not surprising that most of the authors were of German extraction, including a majority of emigrants. All the more remarkable is the clear distinction between American approaches and their British and German counterparts. With very few exceptions, criticism in America remained coolly academic, refusing at least at the conscious level to join in the linkage of *Iphigenie* with German history. There was neither the high moral tone of British criticism nor the pathos of German soul-searching. Criticism on this side of the Atlantic did not participate in the discourse of shame for reasons that would lead too far to explore here, but which can summarily be attributed to the phenomenon of positionality outlined in the introduction to this chapter. America's historical position relative to the events of the Hitler era and especially to the war was vastly different from that of the European nations.

From an academic perspective, the New Critical methodology of focusing exclusively on the text helped with maintaining a certain distance from postwar Zeitgeist. It is nevertheless a remarkable coincidence that three of the studies concerned with aspects of content rather than form should place the concept of truth in the center of their arguments. Neither in German nor in British criticism of the time was truth an issue. (As a Swiss exception Staiger confirms the rule.) As we have seen, of the two Iphigenian key ideals, truth and humanity, the latter fairly monopolized the interest there. It seems, then, that American scholarship was reacting to recent German history after all. The questions asked here were, firstly, about true or false belief, concerning the collective issue of ideology; and secondly, questions about the individual's true or false speech.

In his contribution to a bicentennial symposium held at Indiana University in 1949 (papers published 1950), Otto J. Brendel, professor of fine arts, ranges widely across disciplinary boundaries, with his main focus on the Euripidean source. On the road from ancient Greece to modernity, Brendel discovers Goethe as precursor of George Bernard Shaw, shifting his focus to the social role of woman: "The social status of women and their full participation in the exploits of society . . . which in the play of

Euripides was found a mere side-issue, becomes a capital theme in Goethe's *Iphigenie*" (37).

In Brendel's view Goethe's text promises human progress in a future society with active female participation, progress beyond the state achieved under male rule and thought. What qualifies Iphigenie for her leadership role is precisely truth. For Brendel, Iphigenie's function is to incarnate truth, to give truth the attraction of mystery and thus the power of conviction needed to establish the modern belief in the therapeutic value of truth. Brendel emphatically shares this belief that truth's healing power is the sole antidote to the tragic condition of the world represented in Greek myth. "One act of frankness will break [the curse of the Tantalids], will restore the sane climate and wholesome action of truth in which, alone, the soul thrives" (6).

From Brendel's level of magic and religion the question of truth is raised to the complexity of an epistemological inquiry in Sigurd Burckhardt's *Monatshefte* essay of 1956. What emerges is a deeply skeptical view of the vaunted slogan about truth and humanity, that is, truth in the human dimension. Not only is absolute truth, "*logos*" in Burckhardt's term, not available to humans; even the measure of truth that man or woman can reach is accessible only at a price. It is this high cost of human truth that Goethe's *Iphigenie* states in dramatic form. For she, Iphigenie, has to walk the difficult path to truth, demonstrating that human truth is always only a becoming, never a being. Burckhardt traces Iphigenie's path from egotism and fear, through a losing struggle against untruth into amoral action, and finally to catastrophe. Iphigenie has become a murderess, when as unconscious bearer of the (divine) truth of the oracle she delivers her brother up to be killed.

On Burckhardt's terms human truth can only be found through enactment. Action is the only human way to discover and establish truth, even though the way of action may lead through disastrous error. Surely here, in the denunciation of lip service, is echoed the catastrophe of recent German professorial history. At the same time, and on a more conscious level, Burckhardt offers a Faustian apology, an opening for redemption of those (Germans) who may have done the wrong thing while seeking the path to truth. His comment on the ending confirms the link to the historical context: "[Iphigenie] teaches Thoas at last what the work was to teach the German nation. Having travelled the path of dangerous error, she achieves and establishes the truth" (55).

Detlev W. Schumann's brief and pragmatic article, an imported publication in the *Jahrbuch der Deutschen Schiller-Gesellschaft* (1960), points up precisely the act of professing in "Die Bekenntnisszenen [scenes of confession]" of his title. He establishes truth-speaking versus lying as the very foundation of dramatic structure. The "amazing symmetry" of the work is most obvious in the phenomenon "that between the 'truth acts' the explicit 'untruth acts' [Lügenakte] (II, IV) are interposed" (230).

Unfortunately he relegates to an afterthought his most intriguing discovery: structural *Steigerung* [enhancement, intensification] occurs through performing three different versions of truth emerging. The first is speech following silence: Iphigenie revealing the secret of her ancestry. The second is the lie displaced by true speech in the gradual recognition of brother and sister. The third and highest kind is deception and sacral abuse giving way to purification, pollution turned into catharsis when Iphigenie tells Thoas about the Greeks' planned sacrilege (245).

Heinz Politzer's contentious conclusion of the American contribution to the early postwar debate on *Iphigenie* (*Germanic Review* 1962) is a throwback to Seidlin's and Staiger's cultural criticism. For Politzer's world view *Iphigenie* is needed to save the "paradise lost" of *Menschlichkeit* at a time when "devaluation of everything human(e) has progressed to the level of the absurd." But beyond the topical lament, he introduces two substantial innovations to reading *Iphigenie*. One is his extensive use of psychoanalytical perspectives for the study of imagery, where he relies to a great extent on Kurt Eissler's recent psychobiography of Goethe.

The other is his insistence on the dialogic nature of all dramatic speech, including the numerous monologues which had given *Iphigenie* criticism so much cause to disagree. Combining psychoanalytical technique with a philosophy of communication, Politzer reads the symbol of the island as a symptom both of Thoas's "inhuman isolation" and of Iphigenie's aloofness in abstract (read "masculine") thought and in her self-image as virgin-priestess. Politzer shows how dialogue, modeled on Martin Buber's philosophy of the *thou*, can overcome the symptom and the disease of inhuman isolation. Community, for Politzer, is based on communicative action, and Goethe's *Iphigenie* demonstrates the necessity of both for the constitution of sane selves and for the salvation of mankind from self-destruction.

Politzer's use of psychoanalysis is somewhat problematic. On the one hand he limits his method to a rather arbitrary chase of associations. On the other hand, he uses the Freudian concept of the unconscious as an escape hatch from the really thorny issues of *Iphigenie* interpretation. Iphigenie's relation to the gods, Orest's insight on the oracle, and Thoas's conversion are relegated to the unreadable domain of an unconscious deep structure inaccessible to reason: "irrational depths, mystical."

American and British criticism had taken over *Iphigenie* discussion during the two postwar decades of conspicuous silence in Germany, where the immediate impact of the shame complex had produced fear of touch. The silence on this effect of the shame taboo was explained in turn by shifting blame. It was not worth writing about classicist literature now because classicism was irrelevant to the issues of modernity that Germany, after being cut off during the Hitler era, was trying to catch up with. *Iphigenie* in particular was considered irrelevant to the catastrophic experiences of the day. Heller's avoidance-of-tragedy argument supplied welcome ammunition to an age that sought a Goethe for the shipwrecked.

Thus, while Arthur Henkel in the critical anthology *Das deutsche Drama* (1958) attempted to address the avoidance problem itself under the motto: "Bewundert viel und viel gescholten, Iphigenie [Admired much and much scolded, Iphigenie]," and suggested a number of new approaches and themes inspired largely by English criticism, German critics did not respond; at least not until 1967, when Theodor W. Adorno, outsider to the profession in many respects, explicitly picked up from Henkel's effort. A slightly earlier article by Herbert Lindenau in the *Zeitschrift für deutsche Philologie* (1956) was severely castigated for its *geistesgeschichtliche* method by Sigurd Burckhardt in the next volume of the journal (1957). Two years later *Iphigenie* was the site of another dogfight over the competing approaches, *Geistesgeschichte* and *Interpretation*, between Heinz Otto Burger and Werner Hodler on the pages of the *Germanisch-Romanische Monatsschrift* (1959/60). The drama of universal reconciliation now functioned as the apple of discord in German Studies.

The subtext of the controversy over method should be sought in the recent history of the profession. Proponents of *Geistesgeschichte* had led the way into German ideology. *Interpretation* had recommended itself initially as a way to keep out of real history, and had ridden on to success in the postwar German academy on its promise of ignoring what had happened in the real world, and on the comforting reassurance of safe ground for critical discourse outside of historical contingency. *Interpretation* could offer a pure foundation in intellectual objectivity as represented in the literary text on the one hand, and, on the other hand, in the precision instruments developed for methodical scholarly use by the master teachers, Emil Staiger and Wolfgang Kayser.

Symptomatic of the disregard for *Iphigenie* was Käte Hamburger's study of classical drama figures, *Von Sophokles zu Sartre* (1962), where Gerhart Hauptmann's Iphigenie far outweighs Goethe's in significance. Hamburger's explanation of this phenomenon anticipates the next phase of Goethe rejection that was to dominate the seventies in Germany: "worn" through overuse in "school essay topics," Goethe's drama has sunk from the higher sphere of scholarly culture to the level of *Gymnasium* material. A decade later the progressives among German scholars would formalize this observation in their condemnation of *Iphigenie* as paradigm of affirmative literature, fit only for uncritical consumption.

The first shot across the bow in this direction was delivered significantly at a *Germanistentag*, and not by a narrowly academic member of the discipline at that. It was Martin Walser, novelist of rising reputation, who in Essen in 1964 fired his iconoclastic blast in a provocative rhetoric that was sure to incite the profession. At the same time, Walser's attack was precisely the starting noise that reawakened *Iphigenie* discussion in Germany. In Walser's argument, *Iphigenie* serves as model for everything that is wrong with the German attitude toward (German) classical literature. He blames the educational use of the classics for the persistent misuse of *Iphigenie* in the academy and on stage. The history of German education, for Walser, has downgraded the universal aspect of the classical text into literature for Everyman.

Walser's protest against this tradition: "the sum of all interpretations has been to make Iphigenie a human being like you and me," smacks of elitism (69). But there is, too, protest against current *Iphigenie* criticism. Walser's polemic is directed at the function of the drama within the postwar discourse of shame. The "Paradestück für Humanität [parade piece for humanity]," Walser scoffs, is supposed to teach the Germans "how to deal with the burdening echo [lastender Nachhall] of the Third Reich. The German is supposed to feel as a humanizable Tantalid" (77, 72). Walser protests against being imbricated in the shame discourse by the voices of others. In this statement it is the other's view that imposes the Tantalid identity on the self. The self responds with resentment of this imposition of shameful conduct, and with resentment of the arrogance of the self-righteous outsider who presumes to re-educate the sinner, in historical analogy to the Allied policy of re-education in early postwar Germany.

Finally, the crucial adjective "humanizable" contains a new variant of the old concept of *Menschlichkeit*. Tradition had discussed Iphigenian *Humanität* on the level of divine versus human, of sin versus crime or disease, of grace and redemption versus cure and justice. Walser's "humanizable" has outside judges place the German on the borderline between animal and human, between bestiality and atrocity, on the literal level of *Unmensch*, who first must undergo a metamorphosis to become human.

The position of the German born in 1927 (Walser's birth year) within the shame structure carries particular complexities of rejection and identification. This generation found itself between the stations of father and son or daughter with blurred lines of responsibility and guilt in consequence. Generalization along generational lines risks massive misinterpretation and will therefore not be undertaken here. The only observation one might venture is that of great psychological turbulence, a phenomenon to which postwar German literature owes some of its major writers: Walser, Günter Grass, and Christa Wolf (born 1927 and 1929).

Walser develops a second line of defense against postwar use of *Iphigenie* in the service of humanizing the Germans. The drama must be read within its historical context and from a critical perspective on ideology. Walser's sample of critical distancing and historical relativization was to become a battle cry for the rising generation of German scholars in their war against the classics. In a radical reversal of values, *Weimar* now is loaded with negative connotations. Walser defines German Classicism as "Weimarer Reduktion," to be understood as the idealist aesthetic of the two Weimar giants, Goethe and Schiller, who made a considered decision to ignore the real world of social and political history.

Walser's choice for the role of arch-Weimar classic, *Iphigenie*, suffers severe damage in this revaluation. His final blast against the heroine of pure truth and humanity is no mere anticlassicist rhetoric. There is more than an echo ("Nachhall") of the issue of responsibility and ethics concerning Third Reich history in his fierce accusation of unrealism, of deceptive optimism, of essential inhumanity:

> Iphigenies Salto ins pure Wahrhaftige, mit dem sie immerhin auch das Leben von zwei weiteren, sagen wir einmal, Menschen riskiert, dieser Salto wäre in jedem anderen Raum schlimmster leutnantshafter Leichtsinn. Aber Thoas ist Weimaraner. Darauf kann Iphigenie zählen. Insofern ist es dann doch kein so großes Risiko [Iphigenie's somersault into pure truthfulness, whereby she also puts at risk the lives of two other, let's say humans, this somersault in any other context would be the worst kind of lieutenantesque carelessness. But Thoas is a Weimarer. Iphigenie can count on that. In that sense it is after all not such a great risk] (77).

In the eyes of the angry heir of Nazi history, Goethe's ahistorical negation of reality has perverted from the outset the so-called Iphigenian ideals into their opposites: humanity into inhumanity, truthfulness into ego trip, courage into calculated risk at others' expense.

Walser's denunciation carried enormous weight. During the coming decades *Weimarer Klassik*, itself a reductive term, would be the denigrating name chosen by the Left of what used to be called (*Deutsche) Klassik*. The first volume of a new Reclam series for use in classrooms, *Erläuterungen und Dokumente* (Angst and Hackert 1969), which was devoted to *Iphigenie*, concludes its selection of critical documents with Walser's polemic. The background for the study of this classic in the German educational process had been irrevocably altered.

Signally missing from the *Erläuterungen* volume is the most important critical document on *Iphigenie* not just of the postwar era but, I would venture to say, altogether: Theodor W. Adorno's essay, "Zum Klassizismus von Goethes *Iphigenie*," published in the *Neue Rundschau* of 1967. This omission, at first glance astonishing, is nevertheless symptomatic of the essay's reception history. After a late start in Hans Robert Jauß's critical response of 1973, Adorno reception proved enormously productive but also eminently one-sided. From the rich and complex argument critics picked bits and pieces they agreed or disagreed with and ignored the rest.

Instances of *Ideologiekritik* and sociopolitical actuality achieved high currency among the leftist camp, for example, Thoas representing the Third World wronged by civilization; the failure of Enlightenment reason and ideals; beautiful language hiding and harmonizing a contradictory substance. The conservative wing in its turn, whose strength waxed as the progressive wing's waned under the antiterrorist backlash of the late seventies, took pains to save the uplifting Enlightenment message from Adorno's dialectical destabilization. The first sustained development of Adorno's central concern with the conflict between myth and *Humanität*, in fact, did not occur until 1988, in a *Schiller Jahrbuch* essay by Kathryn Brown and Anthony Stephens.

It is impossible in this format to do justice to Adorno's multilayered and sophisticated meditation on *Iphigenie*, Goethe, and classicism. Any summarizing rendition must needs simplify and distort this text, where dialectical thought structures not just the method but the very substance. The only proper approach for any critic who proposes to write on *Iphigenie* is first to read and think through Adorno's essay. By couching his reflections in a decidedly reader-unfriendly style, Adorno has taken care to ensure the requisite slow speed of such a reading. What follows will therefore be limited to pointing out the major issues Adorno addresses.

From his position of a Jewish German professor forced out of his university chair into exile and returning to a successful career, now at the height of fame and influence — and coming under heavy attack from the radical student left precisely because of his eminent stature — Adorno did not share Walser's burden of Third Reich heritage. He could take a sober look, within the wide horizon of his philosophy of culture and aesthetic theory, at the embattled masterwork, which over its century-long afterlife had come to stand for central values of German culture and identity.

From the perspective of his revolutionary *Dialectic of Enlightenment* (1947), Adorno redefines fundamental concepts of *Iphigenie* criticism: Goethe's classicism, *reine Menschlichkeit (Humanität)*, and the dramatic infrastructure (sub-stance) of myth. No longer the achievement of perfection, maturity, and harmony celebrated in German literary history, classicism for Adorno is the "fragile stance" of a moment in the dialectic of Enlightenment, itself a history of complexity and contradiction. Goethe's *Iphigenie* is the paradigmatic representation of that moment where the fundamental dichotomy of Nature and Culture expressed itself in the bourgeois enthusiasm for emancipation and progress, coupled with deep-seated and suppressed doubt and anxiety about that progress.

Adorno similarly historicizes the supposedly universal value of *Humanität*. This idea of the late eighteenth century masks, for Adorno, an implicit impossibility since it constructs an antinomy between humans and nature. Historically the fallacy of this exclusionary concept of humanity revealed itself in the failure of the (bourgeois) French Revolution. In *Iphi-*

genie, Adorno sees the failure of the concept in the exclusion of Thoas from the restrictive world of the Greeks.

At a deeper level and pervading the drama in its entirety, the problematic Enlightenment concept of humanity is the root of the conflict transacted at the level of myth. With a phrase that has meanwhile become a critical commonplace, Adorno highlighted in Goethe's drama "the historico-philosophical accent on the process between subject and myth" (587). Myth for Adorno stands for a substratum of physical nature that humans are inescapably tied to; this substratum enables us to understand for example man's or woman's physical dimension, the body and its limitations, the unconscious, and of course death. The Greek siblings, but Orest more emphatically than Iphigenie, in Adorno's reading stage attempts of escaping, all of them doomed, from that irreducibly resistant aspect of human existence, the mythical. Orest in his insanity scene, "in that most advanced passage of the play," demonstrates Adorno's central Iphigenian truth: that the fight against mythic power entails man's falling prey to it. "This text prophesies the (dialectical) turn of Enlightenment into mythology."

Adorno's analysis probes still deeper than a philosophy of history in order to engage the metaphysical implications of the conflict with the mythical. His focus is again the insanity scene, "the centerpiece of *Iphigenie.*" A "metaphysical critique" would discover in Orest's vision the utopian image of unlimited reconciliation, where "humanism is raised to the level of blasphemous mysticism." Goethe's text, however, denigrates such chiliastic belief as madness.

The real Iphigenian message, for Adorno, emerges elsewhere. The message is not, of course, *Humanität,* nor the eschatological "Apokatastasis" [redemption of radical evil] of Orest's vision; it is hope for the overcoming of precisely the anthropocentricity that has driven the progress of civilization. The hoped-for future would reconcile modern man with his roots in nature, mind with body ("das Tierische"), and would finally lead to all-inclusive justice instead of a network of power relations.

Adorno finds this hope expressed in Iphigenie's desire that the curse on her family might eventually fade: "ermatten." This verb bears profound meaning for Adorno, all of it positive. He finds here the promise of a nonaggressive stance of humans in the world, the prospect for "Sänftigung [relaxation]" to replace tension and "sture Beherrschung [rigid domination]" of nature in the historical course of progress (597f.).

A striking convergence opens here between Adorno and the central work of philosopher Ernst Bloch, *Das Prinzip Hoffnung,* published in its entirety for the first time in 1959. The convergence appears less coincidental if one recalls the similarities in the historical and biographical positions of the two Jewish-German exiles, a similarity that extends to the time and place of composition of their major texts. Both Adorno's *Dialektik der*

Aufklärung and Bloch's *Prinzip Hoffnung* were written in exile in America, both finished in 1947.

If this rendition has focused on Adorno's reflections on substance rather than form, it is because that was what subsequent critics responded to. Not surprisingly for a theorist of aesthetics and musicology, the essay offers a wealth of stimulating thoughts on *Iphigenie*'s language and the aesthetic traditions underlying Goethean classicism. Beyond the inspiration of critical points in content and form, however, the most important effect of Adorno's essay was the radical change it wrought in *Iphigenie*'s stature. With one stroke the embattled drama was reestablished as an eminent text: multifaceted, rich and deep enough to reward the most demanding inquiry into philosophical, historical, political, aesthetic issues.

For Adorno's essay is far more than a literary-historical investigation of classicism. It is a critique of human existence in history, a question that asks what it means to be human. Adorno reverses the early postwar existentialist attitude of suicidal pathos over the ineluctable tragedy of the human condition. His historical turn throws the alleged tragic fate ("myth") of mankind back onto Western civilized man at mid-twentieth century, asserting that he has sinned more than been sinned against. So, while his essay is indeed a philosophy of history, a metaphysic of the individual spirit, a Marxian critique of ideology and much more that found a fashionable echo in the late sixties, the text is most urgently an ethics that originates from a metaphysics. Adorno proposes to read in *Iphigenie* a healing method for the human spirit, which has wounded itself in the fight against its own connectedness with the whole of life. Anyone familiar with the pervasive presence of Hölderlin in Adorno's texts will not be surprised at the resemblance of this position to Hölderlin's *Hyperion*, where the original sin, from which all historical and individual wrongs and misfortunes derive, is individuation.

The void in academic *Iphigenie* criticism during the sixties was marked by the voices of outsiders. Besides the novelist Walser and the philosopher Adorno, theater critic Siegfried Melchinger stepped forth with an article in the *Schiller Jahrbuch* of the same year as Adorno's *Neue Rundschau* essay. Melchinger's is an explicit attempt to defend Goethe's drama against the attack carried forward by Käte Hamburger. Like Walser and Adorno from their divergent perspectives, he aims to historicize the classic. From his own theatrical perspective and with support from a hitherto neglected Goethean text, the *Regeln für Schauspieler*, Melchinger argues for a historically specific role of theater, insisting on the importance of practical theater work at Weimar for Goethe's dramatic writing. On this view there can be no universally valid, timeless concept of theater. Melchinger casts the Euripidean and the Goethean drama in diametrically opposite functions. Greek theater, "gewaltiges Theater der Öffentlichkeit [monumental theater of public life]," is a scene of public pathos, "Pranger der Ausstellung [pillory of exhibition]," for the transaction of political, historical, and social issues. Goethe in Weimar created a theater of privacy, "family theater." *Iphigenie* epitomized this effort to present the value of intimacy itself, "Vertraulichkeit [confidentiality]," by making it generate "Vertrauen, Wahrhaftigkeit [confidence, truthfulness]" as the climate in which alone beautiful souls and courtly sociability could thrive.

Melchinger's privatization of *Iphigenie* did nothing to commend the drama to the politically oriented Zeitgeist; thus, despite publication in a mainstream organ his essay found no resonance. Walser had called for the unmaking of the classic through historicization. Adorno's philosophical approach likewise pointed the way to historical contextualization. But the politicized profession of the seventies heard a call to actualize, not to historicize. *Iphigenie* became a demonstration piece in the debate over canon and critical theory, which spread from the universities to the stage and, with the strongest political overtones, to the educational reform movement at the Gymnasium level.

Another outstanding feature of German criticism in the seventies was a pronounced isolationism which completely ignored the Anglo-American debate. *Iphigenie* became part of the German question as West and East Germany engaged in *Erbediskussion*, the heated discussion of what to do about German classical literature. In West Germany the drama figured prominently in a three-pronged controversy over educational policy, reception theory, and socioliterary history.

Concerns of secondary education reform drove the debate in a new journal, *Diskussion Deutsch*, alternately saving and condemning *Iphigenie* for being politically (ir)relevant, (non)elitist, emancipatory or utopian, affirmative, that is, bad, or provocative, that is, good. Articles by Hubert Ivo (1973), Rolf Lorenz (1974), and Erika Fischer-Lichte (1975) carry on a vigorous argument, which remains, however, inconclusive.

A major change nevertheless is evident. The practice of *Interpretation* of the Staiger school has been displaced by new approaches from cultural and critical theory under the patronage of Gadamer and Habermas. The controversy that had erupted between these two patron saints, particularly concerning the correct attitude toward tradition, helped to intensify the turmoil within the *Iphigenie* debate.

One of the newcomers on the methodological scene, reception theory, likewise sprang from the Gadamerian source. Its growth was nourished in the competitive climate between West and East Germany. A major reception theorist, Robert Weimann, was developing a special, Marxist variety in the German Democratic Republic. In the West, Hans Robert Jauß in the new journal *Neue Hefte für Philosophie* used *Iphigenie* (1973) in the contest with Weimann to demonstrate the application of his brand of reception theory. Looking back over *Iphigenie* criticism, Jauß detects in the bourgeois culture of the nineteenth century the establishment of a new myth: the secular myth of salvation through human power. It should be noted that Jauß reads the history of criticism through the documents supplied in the Reclam volume *Erläuterungen und Dokumente*. His source material is thus preselected and prejudiced.

To illustrate the use of reception theory in literary history, Jauß explores the links between Goethe's and Racine's Iphigenie dramas within their significantly different yet related cultural-historical contexts. Jauß's window on Europe, on Enlightenment as a European, not solely German phenomenon, went unnoticed until the eighties, when Dieter Borchmeyer picked up on *Iphigenie's* French connection. Jauß's second focus is a critical response to Adorno, after six years the first reaction to the *Neue Rundschau* essay. Against the philosopher's skeptical view of Enlightenment belief in human emancipation from the bo(u)nds of nature, Jauß wants to uphold a Hegelian faith in reason. Whereas Adorno had placed Orest and the collapse of reason in the center of the drama, Jauß reclaims the central spot for Iphigenie. The heroine herself, not just Pylades, represents Enlightenment rationality: "die List der aufklärerischen Vernunft [the ruse of enlightenment reason]." Her appeal for divine help before her decisive deed, however, defeats the victory of reason that Goethe had intended to present.

In Jauß's reading, Goethe proposed an unworkable compromise between religion-based subjectivity and Enlightenment autonomy; the outcome was a new myth of the eternal feminine as savior. Jauß's critique had the unfortunate effect of conveying a simplified reading of Adorno combined with a strong negative cast to subsequent critics, who on his authority could continue to reject *Iphigenie* as exemplar of bad classicism.

Another new arrival in methodological practice, sociohistorical criticism, found a prominent spot in the revisionist volume of essays edited by Karl Otto Conrady, *Literatur der Klassik* (1977), where *Iphigenie* serves Erika Fischer-Lichte in championing sociological principles based on Habermas and Adorno against Jauß's approach from reception theory. Testimony to the inadequate reception of Adorno's *Iphigenie* essay, Fischer-Lichte argues instead with Adorno's fashionable aesthetic of negativity, never even mentioning the essay. Fischer-Lichte's interest is in method, where she engages in strident polemics. Her demonstration sample, *Iphigenie*, receives less attention (20 percent less), yet finds her final approval as a text with "Aufforderungscharakter [appeal structure]," a text that is also politically correct in promoting "authentic interhuman relations."

Though less in tune with socioliterary jargon, Christa Bürger in her book of the same year, *Der Ursprung der bürgerlichen Institution Kunst im höfischen Weimar*, likewise uses *Iphigenie*, besides her main example *Tasso*, as evidence in an argument for socio-history: to demonstrate the sociohistorical origin of artistic autonomy (that is, elitist art) in Goethe's

Weimar. Bürger makes her case on *Iphigenie* primarily through an examination of formal features, especially language. Here she finds a split developing within language as communication, whereby language serves to install division in two dimensions. One is a division into insiders and outsiders, the familiar and the foreign, Greeks and Barbarians. The other line would follow power structures, dividing masters from servants, those who are free to take risks and speak the truth from those who serve as their utilized instruments.

The later seventies saw German *Iphigenie* criticism slowly returning to normalcy. There was room once more for essays outside the topical war over methodology and the classics, for attempts to apply again the standard approaches to the embattled drama. It is nevertheless remarkable that for all their differences in perspective, these critics were united in ignoring British and American criticism. The sole exception is Konrad Schaum, who does address Burckhardt's and Seidlin's work of twenty and twenty-five years before, an exception which finds its explanation in the fact that Schaum is in heavily non-German company as a *Festschrift* contributor for Erich Heller (1976).

The isolationist attitude is most striking in Gerwin Marahrens's essay on imagery of the same year, where the ignorance of British work in the field (Jenkins, Colby, Fowler, Weiss) effects confusion, indecision, and much retreading of old ground. By contrast, an essay by Peter Pfaff (*Euphorion* 1978) stands out for its intellectual sophistication and for pointing the way toward the prevailing approach of the next decade: philosophical and historical contextualization. Pfaff models a return to *Geistesgeschichte*, but with a difference: his perspective has more in common with the Anglo-American praxis of intellectual history.

Pfaff's effort to relocate *Iphigenie* in history, next to Kant and away from Hegel, is motivated by strong opposition to the modernizing attempts of Jauß and (misunderstood) Adorno. Here *Germanistik* reclaims one of its basic texts from supposed misappropriation by the interdisciplinary raiders Jauß (a Romanist) and philosopher Adorno. Pfaff declares *Iphigenie* to be Goethe's treatise on empirical ethics: "foundation for a metaphysics of morals — and perhaps better: for a physics of morals." But this genesis of moral consciousness does not establish an autonomous subject as postulated by the Hegelian Enlightenment partisans of the new academic Left. For the voice of conscience in *Iphigenie*, according to Pfaff, is the voice of the other; the subject is not her own moral arbiter. Neither has the human freed herself from divine interference. Myth remains in power; in Pfaff's reading, the drama enacts "in the Kantian sense an *authentic theodicy*" (26f.)

Pfaff's reorientation along neoconservative lines must be seen before the turbulent background of the late seventies. Particularly in the universities a backlash had set in against reformist zeal, which had led to the worst episode of civil violence in Germany since the Weimar Republic. The terrorist acts of the Red Brigades since 1972 had quickly disillusioned reformist enthusiasm. With the peak of violence in the "year of terrorism" 1977, the last vestiges of public support for the Left movement vanished. For the intellectual class it was time to rethink and revise. In academic circles the ideological turnabout, *Tendenzwende* in the parlance of the time, can be pinpointed at the middle of the decade. We can trace this retrenchment in *Iphigenie* criticism through the antiquarian reading of Schaum, the rhetorical desubstantiation of Marahrens, and the neoconservative repositioning of Pfaff.

At the end of the decade the conservative reclamation of *Iphigenie* received its seal in a book-length study by senior scholar Wolfdietrich Rasch (1979). Rasch's motivating desire is to rescue the drama from the humiliation it suffered at the hands of Adorno and Jauß disciples. If critics find fault with *Iphigenie*, he tells us in the preface, it is to be blamed on their misreadings, not on Goethe's text. To counter the fragile moment *Iphigenie* marked in Adorno's Enlightenment dialectic, Rasch anchors the drama in the French prehistory of German Enlightenment, a move that allows him at the same time to widen the frame of reception history beyond Jauß's focus on Racine.

Goethe's drama thus becomes part of a progressive history from Racine's Jansenist theology to Voltaire's autonomy of human reason, for which Rasch invents the name "Aufklärungstheologie [Enlightenment theology]." The term, however, asserts a synthesis between historically antagonistic movements. The effort to construct syntheses from contradictions marks Rasch's reading throughout; it is his way to escape the problematizing movement of Adorno's dialectical thought. Rasch's Enlightenment theology is a reissue of the fifties' reading of the "*Festspiel* of religious humanism" (May), which in turn had its forerunner in Kuno Fischer's famous interpretation of 1888. *Iphigenie* criticism has taken a decisive step backwards in Rasch's book.

Another contradiction inhabits Rasch's concept of individualism, an essential ideal of his Enlightenment theology. He glorifies individual autonomy, "Selbstbestimmung" and especially "Selbsthelfertum [self-helping, a term borrowed from criticism of *Götz von Berlichingen*]," in Iphigenie and Orest, who heals himself without Iphigenie's assistance. On the other hand, he sides throughout with Thoas as representative of the state, defender of law and order: "Rechtsordnung [order of law]" asserting itself above and against the claims of individualism. It is in Rasch's statist ethic that the contemporary background emerges from subtextual to surface level.

The word *Rechtsordnung* itself points outside the field of literary studies to a leitmotiv in the public discourse of the time: *freiheitlich-demokratische Rechtsordnung* (*FDO* in the language of liberal critics) [order of law based on freedom and democracy], which had to be defended against the assault of radical individuals by means of such controversial edicts as the *Radikalenerlaß* [decree against radicals]. Rasch's transference of values from political life onto Goethe's drama generates the strongest condemnation ever pronounced on the three Greeks and their mission to obey the oracle: they are "temple robbers, worthy of punishment, criminals."

At this point, too, the second crucial ideal of Rasch's Enlightenment theology, the humane ideal, cracks open under the weight of conceptual contradictions. If previous critics were bothered by Thoas's apparent exclusion from the blessings of Iphigenian humanity, Rasch asserts that "Humanitätsmoral [ethic of humanity]" need not be extended toward the Greek criminals; Thoas, in other words, would be right to have them all killed (168ff.).

The most obviously contradictory result of Rasch's reading is the figure of Iphigenie. He has, in essence, relieved her of all her beneficial functions in the dramatic development. She has no role in healing Orest; she is guilty of betrayal towards Thoas; her truth decision is at first disastrous and then irrelevant, since only the oracle corrected by Orest saves the Greeks; her leave-taking does not reconcile Thoas, nor open a future for a common mankind. Her exercise of free will, which in Rasch's view makes her represent self-determination, individual autonomy, is thus restricted within the limits of a mere self-image. And indeed Rasch does offer a new image for Iphigenie. Showing her as driven by the selfish desire to emulate a male heroic ideal, as a "Virago" (Rasch uses this neologism) rather than the holy virgin of tradition, Rasch's deeply negative image of Iphigenie recalls the conservative reaction to women terrorists of the time, many of whom had taken leadership roles. It is well documented that the reaction of the German professoriat to the youth revolution of the time was extremely strong, essentially fearful, and overwhelmingly negative. Many features of Rasch's study of *Iphigenie* exemplify this reaction. Such a motivation would help to explain the essentially epigonic nature of the book and its incomparably lesser quality than Rasch's book on *Tasso*, written fifteen years earlier, an achievement of rich complexity and destined to reorient *Tasso* interpretation in an immensely fruitful direction.

Later critics would oppose Rasch on individual points, particularly on the negative figure of the heroine and on the meaning of the ending. But on the whole, as Hartmut Reinhardt observed in the *Münchener Ausgabe* (1990), Rasch's new dogmatism effectively blocked German criticism in the next decade, a phenomenon that is most evident perhaps in Dieter Borchmeyer's successive Rasch adaptations from 1980 to 1988. In his widely used study, *Die Weimarer Klassik: Eine Einführung* (1980), and in *Deutsche Dramen* (1981), a volume of interpretations intended primarily for secondary school teachers, Borchmeyer attempts, one is tempted to say, the impossible: to synthesize Rasch with the Adorno-Jauß line. (His introduction to the Goethe edition of the Deutscher Klassiker Verlag of 1988 is a slightly revised version of the 1981 essay.)

Following Jauß and Rasch, Borchmeyer extends the drama's European political and cultural frame from Racine and Voltaire to Gluck and Mozart, who in this view translated political discourse into their literary and operatic texts. Here Borchmeyer discovers portraits of the gods intended as *Fürstenspiegel;* tales of human sacrifice as code for inalienable human rights versus the priority of the state; Iphigenie's ethos of human brotherhood as correlate of the Kantian utopia "Vom ewigen Frieden [Of Eternal Peace]."

Borchmeyer differs from Rasch most significantly on the figure of Iphigenie. He adjusts Rasch's negative view of the virago to an image more in keeping with progressive German opinions on feminism. Iphigenie embodies "Viraginität [viraginity]," a decidedly positive concept, which harbors the essential utopian moment of Goethe's drama. The promise here is of a new model of social relations, matriarchy displacing the violent patriarchy of the Tantalid kind. *Iphigenie* would then move, in a quotation from Herbert Marcuse, "very close to the peace utopia of a feminine society" (114).

Other casualties of the stalemate in the ideological struggle over *Iphigenie* are essays by Fritz Hackert in the Reclam volume edited by Walter Hinderer, *Goethes Dramen. Neue Interpretationen* (1980) and by Herbert Kraft in a contribution to Australian anniversary celebrations of 1982. Karl Otto Conrady in the first volume of his monograph on *Goethe* (1982), is profoundly ambivalent as he hovers between Adorno-inspired objections and Rasch-induced grudging appreciation. A fear of interpretation had taken hold, explicitly stated by Hackert, who refrains from voicing any interpretive opinion in order to avoid "eigene Wunschziele als Wirkungsintentionen . . . zu unterstellen [insinuating one's own desired aims as intended effects]" (157).

The blockage did dissolve in the course of the eighties, aided by the burst of renewed interest in Goethe on the occasion of the anniversary year 1982. Anniversary celebrations were typically international in scope. Swiss, French, British, and American voices in symposia and published proceedings, special journal issues, and essay volumes introduced and encouraged a multitude of new approaches. The eighties thus saw the German focus on *Iphigenie* widen, with a pronounced emphasis on approaches from intellectual history.

Dieter Kimpel's essay on ethics from Plato via *Iphigenie* to Hegel, in a *Germanisch-Romanische Monatsschrift* issue dedicated to Heinz Otto Burger (1983), who had been a stalwart defender of this traditional German method, signaled the reemergence of *Geistesgeschichte* in its new, interdisciplinary and international shape. In a distinct break with the ideological preoccupation of the seventies, the decade of the eighties examined Goethe's drama in contexts of philosophical, moral, theological, legal, aesthetic, and genre history; frequently the historical context commands the primary interest in these studies. Historicization had displaced the actualization of the seventies with a vengeance.

The American scholar Wolfgang Wittkowski's running battle with Borchmeyer and Rasch, in two symposia of 1982 and the (Weimar) *Goethe Jahrbuch* (1984), did much to mediate outside views and to undo the Rasch fixation of German criticism. By publishing contributions from Swiss (Pestalozzi 1981), French (Grappin 1982), and American authors (Wittkowski), the *Goethe Jahrbuch* likewise widened the critical horizon. Twenty years after Martin Walser had initiated the Germanization of *Iphigenie* in this particular venue, the *Germanistentag* 1984 featured a British view of the drama (Reed 1985).

The contextualizations of the eighties gave concrete shape to the abstract ideal of *reine Menschlichkeit* in genealogies of historical concepts, such as "substantielle Sittlichkeit [substantial morality]," the dialectic of gender, natural man, or natural and international law (Kimpel 1983; Grappin 1982; [Swiss scholar] Weimar 1984; Wierlacher 1983). The human-divine relation was made to turn on eighteenth century Protestantism or on the history of theological rhetoric (Pütz 1984; Villwock 1987). New approaches from literary theory combined production and reception aesthetic (Pestalozzi on Lavater's *Iphigenie* manuscript, 1981) or, as part of book-length projects, involved a reconsideration of genre (Brandmeyer 1987; Schanze 1989).

In view of the diversity and innovation of *Iphigenie* studies in the last decade in Germany alone, Hartmut Reinhardt's pessimistic reticence in the *Münchener_Ausgabe* (1990) is hard to explain, except perhaps as a result of the inevitable time lag in critical reception. Avoiding interpretation altogether, except for rejecting Rasch-[Borchmeyer]'s dogmatism, Reinhardt resorts to the safety of a new philology: uncanny return, twenty years later, of the *Erläuterungen und Dokumente* complex. The historian of criticism is reminded of a far more remote past: Heinrich Düntzer's approach to *Iphigenie*, more than a century earlier, within the safe confines of etymology and classical philology in his similarly entitled study-guide, *Goethes "Iphigenie auf Tauris." Erläutert* (1859), one of the volumes in his series *Erläuterungen zu den deutschen Klassikern*. Forty years of impassioned *Iphigenie* interpretation, when criticism in Germany tried to solve problems of political and social life by literary means, seem to have engendered a fear of interpretation.

While Germany recovered *Iphigenie* through a rebirth of intellectual history, English and American scholarship in the eighties displayed a multiplicity of approaches that developed with the entry of literary theory into critical discourse, after a noticeable hiatus in *Iphigenie* studies during the preceding decade of intra-German strife. British critics in the seventies had maintained traditional stances in Age of Goethe-type books (Prudhoe 1973, Menhennet 1973, Reed 1980). America was silent on *Iphigenie* until 1979, when Clark Muenzer's essay in *Monatshefte* explored the theme of virginity in *Emilia Galotti* and *Iphigenie*. In the same year, Benjamin Bennett's study *Modern Drama and German Classicism* assigned Goethe's drama pride of place as self-reflexive theater.

Psychoanalytical approaches entered the field with Ilse Graham's Goethe monograph of 1977, placing a new emphasis on the word as bearer of essentially humanizing processes such as transference and countertransference. *PEGS* editor Frank M. Fowler (1981), in vehement opposition to Rasch, reads Orest's story as a case study after Melanie Klein. Questions of power and marginalization in relation with gender evolve in readings by Horsley (1982), Reed (1985), and Wagner (1988/90), while Geyer-Ryan addresses patriarchal and racial othering (1985).

The problematic status of language and truth in literature is at issue in essays by Salm (1981), combined with Lacanian concepts of subjectivity by Hobson (1984), and focused on a redefinition of myth by Brown and Stephens (1988). As comparative literature reconstituted itself in the wake of theories of discourse and intertextuality, *Iphigenie* gained new relevance in articles by Furst (1984) and Reynolds (1988), who contextualizes Euripides in the Greek canon and Goethe in eighteenth-century classical scholarship. In Jean Wilson's frame of *Belatedness* (1991) the drama explores the problematical status of history, genealogy, tradition.

Finally, Nicholas Boyle in the first volume of his massive *Goethe* biography (1991) continues the British approach of high appreciation for *Iphigenie*'s verse ("poetry of the young Goethe is reborn") and critical evaluation of substance, mediating, in a manner of speaking, Fairley with Adorno. Boyle gains his critical perspective from a radical distinction between the first and last versions of the drama. In his view the "extreme subjectivity" of the "apparently classical ... new *Iphigenia*" culminates in the fallacy of Thoas's conversion, where pure subjectivity pretends to be objectivity (453–56).

2: *Torquato Tasso*

UNTIL 1918

IT IS A shock to come to *Tasso* criticism of the nineteenth century from the obsessive absorption and praise lavished on *Iphigenie*. We get an overwhelming impression of embarrassment, defensiveness, and controversy. There are severely negative and stridently positive judgments on characters and themes; there are wild fluctuations among favorite characters; there are bold statements that regrettably, with *Tasso* Goethe made a mistake. Critics like to emphasize the closeness between this problematic drama and its perfect predecessor, *Iphigenie*, so that the earlier drama might redeem *Tasso* in linkages such as: *Iphigenie* and *Tasso*, Greece and Ferrara, Antiquity and the Renaissance. As the early twentieth century noted, scholarship took up *Tasso* only late, and then reluctantly. Moreover, if there was agreement on anything, it was that *Tasso* could be appreciated only by a select few even among the highly educated classes, and certainly not by the general public. In the elitist culture of the nineteenth century this was not necessarily a drawback. The reader of our time will more likely see an attempt to account for the lack of *Tasso*'s popularity. The post-Romantic nineteenth century, including the scholarly profession, was quite obviously not interested in the unfortunate poet-hero. This reader's overall impression was that nineteenth century critics did not know what to make of the drama. They would rather not have to deal with it, but they could not avoid it because it was, of course, part of the Goethe canon and because they felt called upon to defend *Tasso* against harsh attacks by prominent critics such as Lewes and Hettner. The embarrassment over *Tasso* is reflected in the most general way in an avoidance strategy: critics discuss characters rather than issues or themes. While character analysis is a prominent feature of nineteenth century criticism generally, it dominates *Tasso* criticism to a well-nigh exclusive degree.

Again to the amazement of today's reader, the nineteenth century was far more interested in Antonio than in Tasso. Evaluation of Antonio's character is the focus of *Tasso* criticism until the 1880s. The well-known division over the tragic or nontragic ending is a secondary issue and depends essentially on how Antonio is judged: as helpful friend or envious courtier. As early as 1847 Rosencranz finds the Antonio controversy an astounding phenomenon for its extreme positions; over the rest of the century, the ayes far outweigh the nays. Critics *want* to approve of Antonio, they write about him with genuine empathy and emotional involvement, he is their figure of identification. He is assigned the ideal roles that the German bourgeois would have liked to see himself play in the history of his country: always the realist, who successively acts as a superior "Hofmann, Weltmann, Staatsmann [courtier, man of the world, statesman]," and, first in Goedeke's introduction to the Cotta edition of 1866, "Geschäftsmann [businessman]." Only after Antonio's character was securely saved in the late eighties did the Princess arouse critical interest, and she, too, at once engendered controversy. Idealized in philosopher Kuno Fischer's much-acclaimed book of 1890, denigrated immediately afterwards by Fischer's main opponent (otherwise forgettable Franz Kern 1892), Hugo von Hofmannsthal raised her to a new level of literary ambiguity in his "Unterhaltung über den *Tasso* von Goethe" (1906).

A similar pattern of avoidance as in the Antonio-Tasso constellation operated around the Princess. It was the other Leonore, Countess Sanvitale, who frequently moved to the center of attention. Opinions on her fluctuate widely but the majority of judgments are in her favor, supported by arguments that strike the modern reader as strangely contrived and exceedingly forgiving. It would be of interest for feminist criticism to examine the special moral code applied to this elegant and charming lady of the court, who was seen to reconcile manipulative self-interest with tender loving care for friends, husbands, sons, and lovers in "truly feminine" fashion. We might find it surprising that Duke Alfons was a nontopic for an age focused on character analysis. However, since he was generally assumed to be modeled after Goethe's own Duke, Karl August of Weimar, and since the Haus Weimar was endowed with absolute value for nineteenth century Goethe scholars, Tasso's patron was not up for discussion.

To complicate matters further, *Tasso* presented a distinct dilemma for a profession oriented toward biographism and engaged in the Goethe cult. Goethe's own statements concerning the confession character of this work could not be ignored. The problem therefore was how to reconcile the desired Goethe image with the dramatic figure of a deviate poet. Critics found three ways out of the dilemma. The first uses Goethe's much-quoted acknowledgment of the (French) critic Ampère's view that Tasso was "ein gesteigerter Werther," to declare Tasso a luckier Werther who no longer had to commit suicide. Since Tasso survives he must be mentally far more stable than Werther; he is thus not insane, merely a young Sturm und Drang radical enthusiast, who is willing to learn the hard lessons of life. It could then be claimed that in addition to his model Bildungsroman, *Wilhelm Meister*, Goethe had created a *Bildungsdrama*, a genre after the heart of the education-obsessed nineteenth century. This version, by the way, included the possibility of a tragic ending. *Tasso* would be a tragedy of renunciation: of the loss of youthful dreams, reflecting Goethe's changing experience from early Weimar enthusiasm to frustration and disillusionment in later Weimar reality, with Italy as turning point in Goethe's life and central metaphor in the drama.

The second approach sees Goethe as Antonio, and Tasso as a troublesome other poet, more precisely an alter (or former) ego, from whom the matured man of worldly wisdom distances himself. In some readings Antonio-Goethe will play mentor and adopt the youthful rival as his disciple and friend. The favorite originals for this Tasso are Lenz, Rousseau, Herder, and especially Schiller, whom the estranged Goethe-Antonio returning from Rome had found the darling of his erstwhile friends in Weimar.

The third approach, finally, produced the most fascinating, even amusing variations. Here Goethe is both Tasso and Antonio; in the unique individual Goethe, Nature has overcome the dichotomy that causes all the problems of the problematic drama. And critics quote insightful Leonore Sanvitale: " . . . *einen* Mann aus ihnen beiden formte [shaped *one* man out of these two]" (line 1706). This view was particularly attractive to Hegelians and others who took a more theoretical approach. They could transfer the Tasso-Antonio dialectic to the sphere of aesthetics, leading up to the synthesis of the autonomous poet. This perspective developed and grew to dominance alongside the *art pour l'art* movement at the turn of the century.

The metamorphoses of the Tasso figure express the desire of German nineteenth century providers of *Bildung* to see poetry as a *Bildungsgut* [educational property]: in order to be educational, poetry had to be sane. Crazy poets were rejected or — on Goethe's authority — assigned to the "sick" Romantic species, of whom Goethe, of course, must be the opposite.

If the nineteenth century found *Tasso*'s themes and characters awkward, the formal aspects of the drama were no less of a problem. For the classical vision demanding organic form: *aus einem Guß*, the lack of unity of action and theme was sorely obvious. More bothersome still was the inconclusive ending, which made it impossible to assign the work to a traditional genre. The issue of unity did not get much play, even from the severest critics; instead, a sort of compromise took shape. Positivist philology found it quite wonderful to assume an *Ur-Tasso*, unfortunately not yet unearthed, but all hope was not lost. Like the recently discovered *Urfaust*, the original text could well have been quite different from the completed work. The latter would of course, to the delight of the philologist commentators, bear the traces of the first version, and this assumption could serve to explain a host of the alleged inconsistencies. The first two acts, this theory held, were essentially the work of young, post-Sturm und Drang Goethe. To the last three acts, post-Italian Goethe brought a different outlook on life, similar to Schiller's change of mind as reflected in

Don Carlos. Eduard Scheidemantel's decisive work on the genesis of *Tasso* (1897) blew these speculations out of the water, as he revealed an extremely complex and unconventional process of composition.

The ending of *Tasso*, on the other hand, remained a favorite playground for cleverness, line-by-line exegesis, speculation, hypothesis, and scholastic dogfights. Positivism could not admit undecidability; the scholar had to make up his mind about the ending. In fact, critics seemed to welcome the challenge of *Tasso* to show off their acuity and resourcefulness. And they came up with a number of solutions. For the proponents of the tragic ending, *Tasso* defined a new, higher kind of tragedy: the tragedy of the broken spirit which does not need the crude loss of life. The tragic hero could be Tasso or the Princess or, of course, both. Nontragic solutions proffered endings which included a prospectus of the future: a Tasso-Antonio synthesis, or Tasso as the autonomous poet. The paradigm change in criticism around the turn of the century away from positivism toward a focus on aesthetics finally welcomed the open ending as stimulating for the recipient's own imagination and creativity.

In *Tasso* criticism, one might say, the nineteenth century cured itself of the idealism of its Romantic beginnings. The poet-hero, bearer of the (Hegelian) creative spirit as he still appeared in Rosencranz, was gradually shifted off-sides, into the corner of utopian dreams and fantasyland. He wants to turn life into poetry, his critics accused him in a rephrasing of Friedrich Schlegel's definition of Romanticism with strong negative connotations. The age that invented realpolitik had no use for that. Realpolitiker Antonio became their standard-bearer and finally succeeded in converting, in "healing" even the misguided idealist Tasso who had been in danger of self-destruction.

At the same time, by having Tasso learn the Antonio lesson, Goethe had created a new genre, the *Bildungsdrama*. His exquisite drama of education had the additional advantage for the critics that it was accessible only to the highly cultivated, not to the masses reached by general education. The drama could thus serve as a test for elite culture. Appreciating *Tasso* bore the pleasures of self-congratulation for those who passed the test "höchsten Bildungsadels und Bildungsgenusses [of highest educational nobility and enjoyment of education]" (Schöll 1882).

The most significant development of nineteenth century *Tasso* criticism took off in the nineties, when scholars discovered yet another new genre in German literary history: the *Künstlerdrama*. The emergence of this new genre took shape in a peculiar dialectic associated with, and most likely inspired by, the Nietzsche phenomenon. In a first move, driven by the first, highly positive phase of Nietzsche impact, Goethe's poet-hero modeled the new superman. Sane artist whose work ethic makes him a superachiever, whose work is every bit as important as that of statesman-businessman Antonio, Tasso toward the end of the century was groomed to serve as self-image of the professional wordsmith, the emerging intellectual class, in which the literary critic, of course, included himself. A negative countermove around the turn of the century next read *Tasso* as a deterrent parable of the (Nietzschean) nemesis awaiting artistic hubris. In another turn, beginning with an initially obscure, but eventually highly influential insertion of Richard Wagner into the *Tasso* debate early in the twentieth century (Castle 1907), a positive image of the artist reappeared. Throughout the interwar period (1918–1939), the dialectic of the artist shaped in the Nietzsche-Wagner image continued to dominate German *Tasso* criticism in an impassioned pro and con, reflecting the self-doubts of the new and still insecure intellectual class, and even more fervently the culture wars over modernism in the arts that raged during the Weimar era.

Until the Lewes-Hettner shock of 1855 and 1870, *Tasso* criticism is marked by a low-interest attitude and unproblematic acceptance of both antagonists, Tasso and Antonio. Critics downplay the conflict between the two characters and prefer instead to talk of duality, which they see rooted in Goethe's successful integration of the Tasso and Antonio aspects in his own personality. Of the two characters, Antonio holds far more interest. In an early example of later developments, two minor lights of Königsberg and Halle engaged in a heated fight over seeing him as a "gemeiner Höfling [common courtier]" versus an "edler Hofmann [noble court attendant]." Early mainstream criticism as exemplified by Rosencranz, however, tended to reject the controversy as aberrational.

Our two authors of the 1840s, Gervinus and Rosencranz, both focus on the Tasso-Antonio duality to the exclusion of everything else, most notably the love issue. Gervinus aligns himself with Antonio, while Rosencranz strives to remain neutral in theory at least, but in practice he supports Tasso with uncharacteristic dedication. Gervinus endorses Antonio in terms that would become a nineteenth century convention: defined by "Ernst, Maß, Pflicht, Amt [seriousness, moderation, duty, office]," Antonio is the Prussian *Beamten*-ideal. Rosencranz rises above the emerging Antonio controversy by way of Hegelian abstraction. *Tasso*, for him, is a demonstration piece to exemplify the "idealistische Bildungsweg": the idealist's dialectical path to self-consciousness. His schematic philosophical approach escapes the problems of plot and ideology addressed by his contemporaries and reported in his account. He abandons abstraction, however, for a fascinating exploration of the "absolute idealist," the poet. His focus on poetic production as essentially a process anticipates mid-twentieth century criticism (see Wilkinson 1946), just as his view of the poet as existential paradox foreshadows discussions of *Tasso* as the tragedy of the poet a century later. He leaves abstraction far behind when he finds illustrative *Tasso* examples in the precarious economic existence of contemporary poets.

Seven years later, Düntzer could pick up Rosencranz's exalted 1847 idea of *Bildung*, and in his line-by-line comment on the final scene between Antonio and Tasso, develop a pedestrian educational program which would become typical of subsequent Tasso views: how to become a happy, well-adjusted, even though poetical person through self-discipline. If self-discipline was a general educational ideal of the time, Düntzer's materialist image of the poet is equally time-bound. His poet will recycle real life, "die Wirklichkeit verwerten"; he will accept his poetic talent as God-given compensation for the losses he suffers in life and will thus achieve the average sum of human happiness. Poetry is a job like others, a poet is a man like any other, who has to learn "das Leben ertragen [to tolerate life]."

The comfortable assurance evidenced by Düntzer, that *Tasso* was a Goethe play like any other, collapsed under the one-two punch of Lewes (1855) and Hettner (1870). Lewes's summary dismissal of core assumptions — he deals with *Tasso* on less than one page, compared to fourteen pages on *Iphigenie* — provoked destabilization. Fifteen years later, Hettner's carefully reasoned argument in critical philology decisively altered the baseline of *Tasso* interpretation. Goedeke in the Cotta edition (1866) is a perfect example of Lewes-induced destabilization. In an effort to please all sides, he declares the conflict between Tasso and Antonio a tie: both are good and bad. The ending is inconclusive, but not tragic. He feels vastly more at ease with Antonio, whom he is the first to characterize as "Geschäftsmann [business man]," than with Tasso's "vacillating character." Clearly affected by Lewes's most summary condemnation — that the piece was to be disqualified from any poetic genre because we were made to witness "a disease, not a story" — Goedeke goes so far as to question Goethe's art. In his concluding sentence he reproaches Goethe for having made Tasso appear more insane than he needed to be. With its convoluted syntax, with its rhetoric signaling overcaution and apology, the never ending, barely intelligible sentence demonstrates, instead of closure and conclusion, the profound destabilization in the wake of Lewes:

> Viele Züge im Charakter Tassos werden verständlicher, wenn man sich erinnert, daß Tasso, wie ihn die Geschichte kennt, späterhin einem tiefen Trübsinn verfiel, und daß unser Dichter, der dieses spätere Schicksal allerdings nicht anzudeuten und vorzubereiten brauchte, da er ihn auf dem Platz verläßt, wo er sich an der weltklugen Erfahrenheit [Antonios] mit dem Leben in Einklang zu bringen scheint, vielleicht unabsichtlich mehr als nötig erscheinen mag, sich von der Kenntnis, die er von Tassos späterem Leben hatte, bestimmen ließ, die Keime seines Unglücks schon in dieser Epoche seines Lebens kenntlich zu machen. [Many features of Tasso's charac-

ter become more comprehensible if one remembers that Tasso, as history knows him, in later time sank into a deep melancholy, and that our poet, who nevertheless did not need to anticipate and prepare this later fate, since he leaves him at the place where he seems to bring himself into harmony with life aided by [Antonio's] worldly-wise experience, perhaps unintentionally may appear more than necessary to let himself be determined by the knowledge he had of Tasso's later life, to make perceptible the seeds of his misfortune already in this epoch of his life.] (The German original is just as unintelligible as the translation.)

Hettner in his history of eighteenth century literature (1870) cuts through such troubling ambiguities with his hypothesis of a split drama. The first two acts would belong to the Sturm und Drang Goethe who sides with genius, represented by Tasso, against convention, represented by Antonio. Acts 3 to 5, written after Italy, by contrast reflect Goethe's change of mind toward Weimar court ideology and his affirmative acceptance of "undurchbrechbare Weltverhältnisse [conditions of the world impossible to break through]." Hettner's theory of the split conception and two-phase composition found wide acceptance, but the critical community went into shock over his severe reading of Antonio. Hettner makes Antonio's character the focus of his analysis; Antonio's "Zwiespältigkeit [split personality]" is the crack along which the drama breaks apart. In the last three acts, when Antonio is seen as ostensibly right and Tasso flagrantly in the wrong, the "leidige Verzeichnung [regrettable caricature]" of the courtier produces the miscarriage of the ending. Goethe intended to have Antonio stand for "Sophrosyne" [the central Greek virtue of *Besonnenheit,* wisdom], but what the drama represents is "the victory of court manners over human rights."

Over the next twenty years, critics either explicitly endorsed Hettner (often with an approving nod to Lewes) or they evaded the stumbling block by placing their focus outside the drama proper. The seventies offer instances of such evasion. Grimm in his Goethe lectures (1877) evades Hettner by instead attacking Lewes, who had contested the prevailing German reading of *Tasso* as an Italian play, calling it entirely the product of Weimar, whose very "tone" was German. Strehlke in the Hempel edition (1879) takes recourse in history: his topics are Ferrara, the Este family, the real Tasso — and amazingly confesses that Goethe's drama is "incomprehensible." To help himself out of his quandary, he is the first to lean on the Werther crutch supplied by Goethe and Ampère ("gesteigerter Werther"); *Tasso,* he decides, is *Werther* overcome. Quite the contrary, asserts an article in the *Preußische Jahrbücher* by Julian Schmidt (1880): *Tasso* is *Werther* consummated. Mostly, however, Schmidt practices Hettner evasion by means of rank biographism as he equates Tasso with Schiller and Antonio with Goethe returning from Italy. Concerning the insanity issue looming over *Tasso* criticism ever since Lewes, Schmidt offers an interesting solution. Similar to Molière's *Misanthrope*, the supposed insanity is a matter of perception, of "Weltekel [world nausea]." Not Tasso is sick, but rather "das ganze Leben sieht wie eine Krankheit aus [all of life looks like a disease]."

The eighties were strikingly unanimous in their support for Hettner. *Tasso* came in for some heavy criticism, and not just, as was to be expected, from Goethe's Jesuit biographer, Baumgartner (1882), who by the way proposed a view that would reappear as the most shocking of post-World War II interpretations: Tasso is a bourgeois parvenu who performs for the court as Werther-clown. Two other critics of the same year sharpened the barbs thrown by Hettner and Lewes. Both theatre scholar Bulthaupt and mainstream academic Adolf Schöll insist on Tasso's insanity; neither is interested in Antonio. We see the beginning of the shift of focus to the figure of the poet, to the working of the poetic mind. Schöll's fascination with the poetic mind, however, does not mean approval; in tune with the new Zeitgeist he sees a clinical case of decadence. Both he and Bulthaupt find the conciliatory ending incompatible with their diagnosis of insanity: "ein Mißgriff [mistake]."

In the following year, both Scherer's history of German literature and Geiger in the Grote edition of Goethe's works state their support for Hettner's view of a substantially flawed drama. In an effort to escape the Antonio trap, Scherer is the first to propose Leonore Sanvitale as substitute character of interest. Finally, the late eighties saw an end to the paralyzing Hettner trauma, as the focus of criticism generally shifted to aesthetic issues. The poet, the creative process, the work of art, artistic form emerged as new *Tasso* themes.

This was the approach taken by philosopher Kuno Fischer in his immensely popular study of 1890, after the path was broken by Schröer in the *Nationallitteratur* edition and in a published *Festvortrag* by Karl Reinhardt on Goethe's birthday before the *Freie Deutsche Hochstift* (1889). Both Schröer and Reinhardt read *Tasso* as an aesthetic of pain. In their view, suffering and loss are prerequisites for artistic creation. The true artist has no need of the world — Antonio and the Princess are irrelevant — all he needs is the consciousness of his lack, the realization that poetic existence ("Traumwelt") is an exile from the real world. Thus *Tasso* criticism took a decisive turn alongside the emerging view of art as autonomous — *l'art pour l'art* — foreshadowing the neoromantic view of the poet as supersensitive man of the Rilke-Hofmannsthal type.

Besides the innovative approach from aesthetics, the old line of biographic positivism continued, but attention in this camp shifted more and more from Antonio to the Princess. She and to a lesser extent Leonore Sanvitale now generated controversies of their own, with direct reference to the ambivalent role of Charlotte von Stein in Goethe's *Tasso* period. As

Goethe scholars gradually emancipated themselves from the House of Weimar, their view of the Ferrara-Weimar court took on more sombre hues. Tasso's Duke is still taboo, but the Duke's sister, Tasso's Princess, now gets to represent the court, and she, read as Goethe's portrayal of Charlotte von Stein, is fair game.

The first to turn his attention to her was the doyen of Goethe scholars, Herman Grimm. His essay, "Leonore von Este," was published in *Deutsche Rundschau* as a "Gabe [offering]" to the House of Weimar (1892). Emphatically, Ferrara is not Weimar, for Grimm senses in Alfons and his court a depressing and melancholy atmosphere, "ein Gefühl von Vergeblichkeit, als sei die Welt im Aussterben [a feeling of futility, as if the world was dying out]," similar to the "historical rot" felt in present-day Italy by a forward-looking, Empire-building German visitor (187). The Princess is the symbol of such decadence. With her egoism typical of the sick, Grimm's Princess seems to come straight out of Nietzsche's gallery of *verarmtes Leben* [impoverished life]. Deprived of life herself, she aims to pull Tasso into her own deprivation. In order to survive as poet therefore, Tasso has to liberate himself from his unnatural dependence on this siren — he is quite right in calling her "Sirene!" — and on the depressive Italian court.

With his initiative of blaming the woman, Grimm struck out on a path that would soon resemble a roller coaster. Critics now saw Tasso's main problem to be the Princess, whose evaluation alternately soared or nose-dived for no apparent reason except for each writer's subjectivity. The other woman meanwhile, Leonore Sanvitale, became the understudy for main temptress who occasionally, especially in criticism at *Gymnasium* level, might take over center stage (see especially Willenbücher 1910). To give a brief sketch of the ups and downs of the Princess: Karl Heinemann in the edition of the Bibliographisches Institut (1900) — up; Adolf Metz in the *Preußische Jahrbücher* (1905) — down; Hugo von Hofmannsthal (1906) — down and up; Erich Schmidt in the *Insel-Goethe* (1910) — down but with some blame on Tasso; Carl Steinweg in his *Seelendramen* study (1912) — up.

Of special interest among these views is, besides Hofmannsthal's of course, the essay by Adolf Metz. A rich study that explores the enabling and disabling conditions for poetic creativity, its focus is on the Princess as the center of tragedy in *Tasso* and on the symbolic function of the love issue. Metz interprets the gender relation according to the *Geist-Leben* [spirit vs. life] opposition current in contemporary thought coupled with emergent racialism. Thus the "unnatural" love conflict represents the natural antagonism between the spiritual orientation of Romance peoples and the sensual character of the Teutonic race, with the Princess embodying the Romance-catholic ideal of sanctity, which Tasso's "Schmutz der Begierde [dirt of desire]" defiles.

It is against this background of racial symbolism that Hofmannsthal's sophisticated essay (1906) must be read. From a consciously gendered perspective — it matters whether a woman or a man authored the essay within the essay on the Princess — Hofmannsthal, with echoes of Freud in the wings, constructs a multiple paradox of literary representation. In the same way as the Tasso-Antonio dynamic represents the paradox of living-in-the-world, and in the same way as the artist himself incarnates the paradox of individual existence, so the Princess embodies the basic moral and emotional ambivalence of a taboo. In Hofmannsthal's reading, Goethe's *Tasso* is a self-reflexive text on the enigmatic nature of literature itself.

To solve the literary enigma created by Hofmannsthal, Carl Steinweg's study of *Goethes Seelendramen* (1912) offers a scholarly explication, which links content with formal aspects in the current academic style. The Princess is "the heart of the tragedy" in a new subgenre of tragedy that Steinweg names "Qualdrama [drama of torment]" and which is structured so as to cause the maximum pain possible. Antonio and Leonore Sanvitale are deliberately overdrawn ("verzeichnet") in order to make them better torture instruments. The purpose of this sadomasochistic *Qualdrama* in the baroque manner is to educate the poet — who also suffers but not as much as the Princess — toward the goal of mastery and fame in his craft: "per aspera ad astra [through bitter experience to the stars]."

Notwithstanding the fascination of the ambivalent Princess, the main focus of criticism from the 1890s to the First World War was the figure of the poet, center of the newly discovered genre *Künstlerdrama*. Following Kuno Fischer's initiative, the poet Tasso emerged as a new human paradigm to rival the successful bourgeois, Antonio. He was Tonio Kröger in Thomas Mann's novella who must learn to see himself as autonomous producer of a unique achievement: the work of art. Soon, however, a new twist appeared in the view of the poet, for which the sensational tragedy of Nietzsche's life supplied the background. *Tasso* was read as a Nietzsche parable, as a warning against the self-destructive potential of the artistic existence. Yet a further development brought about a Wagner-contra-Nietzsche turn. In defense against fin de siècle decadence, the Nietzsche model of the artist disappeared from view; the new interpretive mold for *Tasso* became Wagner, epitome of successful integration of life and art.

Philosopher Kuno Fischer approaches *Tasso* as a drama of ideas. In his view, the progressive thought of the late eighteenth century inspired Goethe's idealized Renaissance world at the court of Ferrara. More important for Fischer, Goethe has crafted, modeled on himself, a new image of man, Renaissance man, and it is Tasso's task in the course of the drama to recognize and realize in himself this higher man. To reach this goal he has to renounce his pathogenic existence as a court artist and devote himself instead entirely to producing great art. For in Fischer's view, the true work of art can only be produced by an autonomous creator who knows that the power of his genius is stronger than any other secular (the ruler's) or spiritual (love's) power. The true Tasso postulated by Fischer does not yet exist in the drama. He will only come into existence in the future, after he has freed himself from the shackles of Ferrara and lives as a free-lance artist ("freischaffender Künstler") in Rome.

Fischer's ethical optimism with its futuristic perspective, which essentially sidesteps the problems of the text, found great resonance with the general public engaged in Goethe cult and Renaissance enthusiasm, but in academic criticism there was no discernible echo. The sole exception is a review essay on three recent *Tasso* interpretations in the *Preußische Jahrbücher* by Constantin Rößler, entitled "Das Tassoräthsel" (1896). Rößler prefers Fischer to Grimm and Goethe biographer Bielschowsky precisely for his optimist ethics. Self-salvation, however, according to Rößler, rests not on raising oneself up by one's own spiritual bootstraps. What saves man is his work ethic, an ethic of achievement that is available to all men, not just artists; an ethic that founds man's individuality and distinguishes the individual from the masses. In support of his antidemocratic ethos Rößler offers an interpretation of the famous *Tasso* simile of the galley slaves (act 5, scene 5).

In Rößler's confused philosophy of work resonates the threat to individuality in the age of industrialization that had belatedly arrived in Germany. What man needs according to Rößler is "erneute Arbeit, erneute Leistung, der erneute Ehrerbietung zu Teil werden kann. In der eintönigen Gleichförmigkeit einer täglich erneuten niedrigen Leistung erstirbt die Menschenseele [renewed work, renewed achievement, which can earn renewed respect. In the monotonous sameness of a daily renewed low achievement the human soul expires]." Rößler's is a unique instance in nineteenth century Tasso criticism where, thanks to establishment philosophy's efforts on behalf of optimism, Goethe's controversial literary enigma ("Tassorätsel") has been put to such eminently practical and wholesome use.

By contrast, criticism over the next decade showed clear traces of Fischer avoidance, highlighting the Princess, or in a regression born of desperation over the "Tassorätsel," Antonio; until the Nietzsche paradigm of artistic self-destruction moved in to displace Fischer's ethical superhero. The *Tasso* chapter in Bielschowsky's Goethe biography (1895) had received Rößler's lowest marks mainly for the severe judgment it passed on Antonio. Indeed, Bielschowsky reveals the profound embarrassment, even helplessness that traditional Goethe scholarship experienced with *Tasso*. In the first place, Bielschowsky refuses to accept Fischer's perspective on the drama as "Künstlers Apotheose" (one of Fischer's chapter titles). For him Tasso remains caught in "verwirrter Sinn, Wahn, Verbohrtheit [confused mind, delusion, obstinacy]." This artist is an embarrassing case and Bielschowsky would rather not talk about him. Instead he lavishes attention (a total of eight pages) on Antonio, whom he molds into the deterrent example of a bad *Beamter:* much education but no heart, envious and calculating, manipulative, ice cold, "no character but much talent."

In an almost perverse opposition to accepted opinion, Bielschowsky has nothing but praise for the Countess Sanvitale and far more text on her than on the Princess. In his summary he upbraids Goethe for not having realized his intentions, whatever these may have been. For Bielschowsky complains, too, that it is impossible to identify Goethe's intentions in the undecisive text he has left to his commentators. Trained in the school of positivist biographism and dependent on authorial intention, critics in the late nineteenth century were helpless faced with the complexities of this Goethean drama. While they did not dare expel *Tasso* outright from the canon they yet engaged to an amazing degree in *Dichterschelte* [cussing out the poet], a behavior far more characteristic of the iconoclastic twentieth century.

Goethe's other two biographers of the time, Meyer (1895) and Witkowski (1899), placed themselves in stark opposition to Bielschowsky's severe sentence on the work by reading in *Tasso* a Nietzsche-inspired parable of the self-destructive artist. Both go to great lengths to stress the superb artistry of the drama, while pointing out its elitist exclusivity: such sublime art is, they tell us, not for everyone. In an unmistakable reference to Nietzsche, Witkowski grants special rights to the genius, but only if he combines strong willpower with the basic requisite of great passion. Thus Tasso, who lacks that will, destroys himself through excess of passion; his end is exhaustion not tragedy.

Not the power of personality but the contest between realism and idealism is the perspective of Meyer, who devotes his *Tasso* chapter to a probe into the essence and dangers of poetic existence. The poet's most destructive feature is his utopianism, which Meyer sees as the ultimate stage of idealism. Idealism is fine, as long as it knows its place, namely set over against and acknowledging reality as a separate and sovereign realm. But Tasso's utopian belief commingles life and poetry; like an opium addict he needs to be on a constant high which he reaches through poetic creation, or through the substitutes of love and fame. While Witkowski and Meyer, in contrast with Bielschowsky, consider Goethe's drama of the artist an artistic success, they deem Goethe's artist an unambiguously negative hero, fit only to warn against the excesses of the modern artistic temperament and the dangerous ideas about art that begin to shape the modernist mentality.

An essay in the *Goethe Jahrbuch* of 1902 by Georges Dalmeyda would abandon the Nietzsche parable as a symptom of modernity, linking *Tasso* instead with the Romantic tradition. Alfred de Vigny's drama about the unfortunate English poet Chatterton serves as companion piece to Goethe's drama. Dalmeyda pronounces German criticism wrong in claiming

Tasso for the classical tradition; the disjunction of poetry from life makes the drama a distinctly Romantic text, reflecting the radically different conditions in which poets found themselves in the postclassical era.

In the same year Albert Köster's introduction to the *Jubiläums-Ausgabe* aims to move *Tasso* interpretation away from the Nietzschean insane artist paradigm: such an image of the artist would underwrite decadence and pessimism. Köster subscribes instead to the developing German ideology which sees the nation advancing vigorously toward world power status. Köster's reading of *Tasso* as "Die Leiden eines [jungen] Dichters [the sufferings of a {young} poet]" is the first step in the revision of the Nietzsche model. In an uncommonly explicit actualizing gesture he declares the drama to be a warning for young poets of today against the temptation of *l'art pour l'art*, against excessive subjectivism, which is "unrettbar sich selbst verfallen [irredeemably doomed by its narcissism]" and will necessarily end in "zerschellte Existenz [shipwrecked existence]."

The same Witkowski who had initiated the Nietzsche model in 1899, now took energetic action to turn *Tasso* criticism around, away from the predominance of ethics since Fischer, and following the new direction of academic studies toward aesthetic issues. Like Reinhardt before him, who also had tried to shift the focus toward formal aspects, he used the forum of a *Festvortrag* on Goethe's birthday before the *Freie Deutsche Hochstift* (1903). And again like Reinhardt, he failed. Reinhardt's topic, "der künstlerische Bau [artistic structure]," had been obliterated by the figure of the supreme artist propounded by Fischer a year later.

Witkowski's sophisticated interpretation of *Tasso* "als dramatisches Kunstwerk" (title) failed to divert attention away from the fascination of art and the artist in conflict with life, literature's version of the *Geist* vs. *Leben* [spirit vs. life] debate that was in its heyday in German intellectual circles. As we have seen, the prominent authors Metz and Hofmannsthal continued to mine the traditional vein of character analysis and symbolism. Newcomers to the field, such as Kierkegaardian theologian Christoph Schrempf (1907), and junior scholar Hans Rueff in a straightforward academic study (1910), enriched the image of the artist as "other." He is demonic, infantile, intuitive, "ein Instinktmensch" in harmony with organic life, a figure out of Ibsen (Rueff), constitutionally incompatible with the demands and strictures of social reality.

Obviously, a new image of the artist was in the making. No longer necessarily self-destructive, the artist began to take on features that increased his fascination to the point of charm, of magic. Beginning with Eduard Castle's extensive Wagner quotations in an unfocused article in the *Zeitschrift für österreichische Gymnasien* (1907), the model artist Wagner now helps explain Goethe's artist. Remarkably, the guiding image is not that of the successful artist-manager Wagner, who had proven to be spectacularly *lebenstüchtig* [successful in living] with the establishment of

Bayreuth as New German shrine, but of Wagner the antibourgeois celebrant of the artistic lifestyle. At this point an excursion would be in order into the contest over the social and political values of a buzzword of the epoch, *Bürgerlichkeit*. Let me refer the reader instead to Thomas Mann's explorations of the issue in essays and fiction of that period.

In his introduction to the Pantheon edition of Goethe's works (1908), Otto Pniower quotes approvingly Wagner's letter on *Tasso* to his (illicitly) beloved Mathilde Wesendonck, and proceeds to identify his own reading of Goethe's hero with his image of Wagner. Pniower's poet is an antibourgeois radical of sensibility and passion, whose essential condition — of life and of productivity — is ecstasy. Love therefore is the focus of the dramatic action; Antonio does not matter. If the poet fails in real life, so much the worse for real life. By the laws of genius it is real life, social and moral reality, that has failed. Pniower enlists Goethe on the side of genius against *Bürgerlichkeit* as he concludes with a Goethe quotation on the lack of bourgeois comprehension for the higher morality of art.

Eduard Engel's popular Goethe biography (1909) relies yet more extensively on Wagner's *Tasso* reading. His own interpretation makes of Tasso a hero of strong and noble will, who alone fights the good fight against the whole ignoble world united against him, led by a demonized Antonio, who is drawn with obvious relish as "Goethe's sole villain in the grand style": a power-hungry court functionary "der über Leichen geht [who walks over dead bodies]" (319). In contrast with Engel's grand villain Antonio, Tasso remains a noble abstraction, but it is interesting to see that this abstraction stands for more than specifically the poet or artist. Engel's hero represents any man of artistic temperament and idealistic inclination ("der ideal fühlende Phantasiemensch und Künstler"), who will necessarily collide with realistically inclined reality ("phantasiearme feindliche Welt" 315). The equally noble because artistically inclined reader (this is a "reading drama for the minimally few highminded" 320) is offered a figure of identification and compensation in his own hostile arena of worldly success.

Carl Steinweg in his study of *Seelendramen* (1912) does not specifically mention Wagner, yet his approach bears the Wagnerian imprint in matters of form and theme. Steinweg has chapters on the formal aspects of *Tasso*, couched in terms of Wagnerian music, with emphasis on dynamics, dissonances, motifs, allusions, and leitmotivs. His summary of the dramatic process in *Tasso* is musical as well: a passionate longing for harmony is frustrated and ends in dissonance. While Steinweg places the Princess at the heart of the tragedy she is yet not the purpose of her own tragedy. Her suffering serves the purpose of educating the poet to achieve his proper character and vocation, for he needs the torment of love to produce his art. The poet, on the other hand, is a magician who spellbinds women with his art. (compare Thomas Mann's "Wagner" stories.) If this reads like heartless educational (male) chauvinism it is precisely what Steinweg intends. Tasso's path toward his true poetic existence "führt über das Herz der Prinzessin" — meaning that Tasso has to trample on her heart — and it is the purpose of Steinweg's subgenre of *Qualdrama* "to educate the poet through great suffering and to break the Princess's heart through even greater suffering" (120).

From his non-German perspective, Georg Brandes (1915), exponent of naturalism, demystifies the Tasso-Nietzsche-Wagner myths and legends. Brandes asserts that in contrast with the historical Tasso, Goethe's hero is neither insane nor even paranoid. In fact, Brandes declares Goethe's drama a case study in psychological realism; wild dreams and morbid introspection are simply part of poetic nature. Neither is Antonio an evil genius. His actions, for Brandes, mark him as a realist, the man of deeds trying to cope rationally with the unrealistic man of words. In shaping their conflict Goethe, after his own Sturm und Drang-tossed period of life, was coming to terms with the inescapable position of the poet in the world. This aspect of the drama shows the realist Goethe of whom Brandes approves. The idealist Goethe, however, is still represented in the figure of the Princess and it is here that Brandes's debunking takes on a sarcastic note. Conceived to be as attractive as Tasso, if in a more sublime mode, "to the modern mind she seems to be writing poetry for albums." Her love in its resigned and reflective way is a typical "Deutsche Liebe [German words in Brandes's English text]"; in fact she is "thoroughly German and represents the short-lived period of [eighteenth century] humanity." Equally as fictive, in Brandes's view, as this illusionary figure of German idealist humanism is the dueling incident based on artifice and court etiquette. Here Brandes finds Goethe thoroughly out of touch with the historical context, for only a year after the completion of *Tasso* the French Revolution swept away the entire courtly civilization. With this reference to the revolutionary background, Brandes introduced a major theme of twentieth century *Tasso* criticism, to be further explored first by British critics in the twenties, but reaching its apogee much later: in German sociohistorical readings of the 1970s.

Finally, in 1916, Friedrich Gundolf in his *Goethe* monograph offered a superb summary of the critical debate, as he conceptualizes major issues discussed as far back as Rosencranz. Gundolf sees the drama exfoliating multiple aspects of the fundamental nature-culture dichotomy in human existence. Subsuming all other dichotomies is the central antithesis of Tasso and the court, where Tasso's "free humanity" confronts domesticating civilization. Gundolf's chosen term, "freie Menschlichkeit," unmistakably plays on the well-known topos from *Iphigenie* criticism, *reine Menschlichkeit*. We have seen the embattled status of that Iphigenian concept at the time of Gundolf's writing and Gundolf's own, innovative definition in terms of an aesthetic of power. Tasso's artist humanity,

claiming to be absolutely free, proves to be far more problematic in Gundolf's reading of this drama. The main figures represent the tension between the ideal (Princess) and the real (Antonio), and Tasso finds that his
ideal cannot be realized. Another tension exists between Tasso's desire of
love, and others' desire of service from Tasso. It is Tasso's tragic flaw that
he cannot bridge the gap between his own and others' desire.

From the perspective of Goethe's own development, Gundolf sees in
the drama an act of mourning ("Totenopfer") the exuberance of youth, as
adulthood demands resigned acceptance of limits. More seriously yet for
Gundolf, Goethe's drama enacts "Selbstverurteilung," pronouncing the
death sentence on the Self as a metaphysical value in the name of Law, of
values imposed by society. This is the ultimate condition of Tasso's tragedy, and Gundolf is a strong supporter of the tragic ending: "Goethe has
written nothing more shattering." The ending, however, is not the focus
of Gundolf's textual analysis. Instead, in an innovative move, Gundolf
highlights the fourth act as the germinal point of the drama. Here, and especially in Tasso's last monologue, free subjectivity rebels against the imposition on genius of mere use value ("Nutzwert"). But the poet's
rebellion finds no outlet in reality, fails to realize itself as revolution. Instead Tasso substitutes his subjective fantasies for the reality he rejects,
whence derives his delusional behavior in the final act.

Gundolf's Tasso then, who starts out celebrating the artist as free man
wrestling with the ineluctable nature-culture dichotomy, ends up in the
role of the intellectual as failed revolutionary. Culture-civilization reveals
fully its tragic potential in tempting the man of ideas to escape from the
intolerable demands of political and social reality, into the realm of his
own constructs. Art here is indeed for itself only, as *l'art pour l'art* had
claimed, but it is art as amputated life; Gundolf's artist as escape artist has
declared himself defeated.

FROM 1918 TO 1945

If the nineteenth century felt reluctant toward *Tasso*, German criticism
between the wars positively squirmed. After senior scholar Gustav Roethe's regressive kickoff in the 1922 *Goethe Jahrbuch*, there was only one
article in an academic forum, again in the *Goethe Jahrbuch* (1927), timidly
practicing Gundolf exegesis. The only other article during this time, by
Walther Linden in *Zeitschrift für Deutschkunde* (1927), addressed itself
explicitly to Gymnasium teachers. No book-length study was published,
but there are three dissertations, all by women: writing on *Tasso* was assigned to the terminal apprentices. The positivist orientation toward biog-

raphism and source philology had helped scholars of the earlier period out of facing the substantive problems of *Tasso*. The reorientation toward aesthetic and ideological issues in the early twentieth century forced critics to cope with the text itself and the still unsolved *Tassorätsel*. Also left over from the previous century was a sharp division of opinions on the substance of the drama; of this scholarly divide the interminable debate over the ending was both symptom and code. Gundolf's effect on mainstream criticism remained as good as invisible; his balancing act on the dichotomy of artistic freedom and civil society was submerged by a new wave of criticism of the artist, which turned increasingly negative. The disappearance of Gundolf from *Tasso* criticism might well have been aided by a rising vogue of anti-Semitism in the profession. When Roethe, for example, objects to Gundolf's *Tasso* interpretation he uses the critic's Jewish-sounding birthname: "auch Gundelfinger befriedigt mich nicht [neither does Gundelfinger satisfy me]" (127).* During the Weimar years Gundolf became a subtext to be altered, adapted, or fought off as critics tried to cut the *Tasso* knot in favor of one or the other side of the conflict between artistic freedom and social control.

It was not just Gundolf who entered the Weimar debate on a bias; the interwar interlude in *Tasso* criticism altogether was played out on the bias. The aspect of the artist, so long avoided, now indeed dominated, but from a negative angle, and involved in a double dialectic. Along the first line, critics took a decidedly anti-artist stance. From outright rejection of the artist in the beginning, there developed an effort to gain control, to reannex the autonomous artist — the paradigmatic "outsider" in accepted views of Weimar Culture. The second dialectic was one of gendering. Tasso the artist was shunned to a remarkable degree by the (male) ruling class of academics and editors of periodicals, while a substantial proportion of dissertations on *Tasso* were published by women.

Of the many underlying factors, two elements in the gender dialectic surfaced as explicit issues in the debate. One was a new ideal of masculinity that developed after the First World War.† This masculine ideal structures an early comparison of Tasso, indecisive artist-dreamer, with Kleist's Prinz von Homburg, decisive agent-warrior. On the other hand, the new ideal contrasts favorably Tasso's masculine education (by Antonio) with the feminine education performed in *Iphigenie* (Daffis 1919). It is important to see that the emphasis on masculinity was not primarily antifeminine: Tasso is never criticized as effeminate, but as infantile, soft. Masculinity is what separates the men from the boys, as in Gustav Roethe's admiration

---

* Of the two dissertations on *Tasso* as *Künstlerdrama*, by Goldschmidt and Levy, only Levy's lists Gundolf in her bibliography.

† On the phenomenon of *Männerbünde* after the First World War see Krockow 1990 p.160 and n.17.

for one artist who got it right: Richard Wagner whom "die Zeit und sein Dämon zum Manne schmiedeten [time and his daimon wrought into a man]" (1922, 128). The second explicit element in the gender dialectic was a stereotype concerning women and art. In her dissertation on the history of *Künstlerdrama* (1929), Erna Levy uses the generally accepted argument that women, while not creative artists, are yet the ideal consumers of art as well as the perfect artists' companions, because they possess far more aesthetic *Einfühlung* [in-feeling, empathy] than men (21). Seen the other way round, the stereotype stated that only women and other artists, "wahrhaft künstlerisch veranlagte Menschen [truly artistically inclined individuals]" such as Richard Wagner (Castle 1926, 162), could understand art, artists, and dramas about artists, and that therefore professional academics (males) had better stay away from this particular Goethe drama.

Compounding Tasso's problems arising from the new masculinity was another facet of the Zeitgeist: anti-individualism. This was the era that developed the idea of *(Volks)gemeinschaft* [(völkisch) community], and our critical texts leave no doubt that the anti-*Tasso* dialectic originated here. The battle over artistic autonomy was a powerful undercurrent of Weimar culture, a phenomenon that still waits to be explored, and which prepared the way, in political culture, for the success of the Hitler regime in taking control over artistic production. There is no better hallmark of this history of controlling by exclusion or inclusion than the 1937 twin exhibit in Munich on ostracized ("Degenerate") and integrated ("German") art. The most pervasive theme in *Tasso* criticism over the Weimar period was the opposition of individual and collective; and scholarly opinion overwhelmingly supported the collective. The artist must be and act *pro publico:* he must represent the collective and he must create for the benefit of the group. Tasso's capital sin is being "weltfremd [a stranger to the world]." The intended meanings of *Welt* here would require a long discourse on Zeitgeist. Predominantly, however, *Welt* designates the social world, the *Gemeinschaft* that claims ownership of the artist and that extends conceptually from "Volk [folk, people, nation]" (Goldschmidt 1925) to "gebildete Gesellschaft [educated society]" and "Musenhof [court of the muses]" (Korff 1930).

If by the time of Korff, who goes farthest in his denunciation of Tasso, Goethe's poet-hero had become the wrong kind of artist, there was also a right kind, bearing the stamp of approval by *Doktor-* and other academic *väter* [Ph.D. thesis supervisors]. With a commanding presence in *Tasso* dissertations, this was Hans Sachs, head of Wagner's *Meistersinger*. He embodied the ideal of communal artist who might bridge the gap between classes and generations that was threatening to rend apart the German republic. The impact of Wagner — as source of controversy, too — in Weimar culture can hardly be overestimated and has been sorely underinvestigated. Exceptions to the anti-artist movement were introductions to the Goethe editions with their longer term perspective and obligatory attitude of appreciation. Thus *Festausgabe* editor Robert Petsch was Tasso's most outspoken champion (1926), outdoing even fellow artist Ernst Hardt in the Ullstein edition of 1923.

Outside of Germany, *Tasso* evinced singularly little interest, particularly if compared to *Iphigenie*. Perhaps it was Lewes's early condemnation by silence that kept English contributions limited to comments on transla- tions or on a few lines of text.[*] English *Tasso* criticism properly began in 1928 under *PEGS* editor Robertson's leadership, who published an article on the drama in the first volume of the journal's new series. Inspired by the urge to break the German *Tasso* monopoly, Robertson remains nar- rowly focused on opposing Roethe's tragedy argument. The next step, however, Barker Fairley's opposition to Robertson (1932), widened and deepened the horizon in significant and productive ways. What distin- guished English from German *Tasso* criticism, as well as from English ap- proaches to *Iphigenie*, was the focus on the poetic text, not on ideas or message. In tune with the development of New Criticism, both Robertson and Fairley asked fundamental questions about authorial intention and the validity of interpretation.

The first voice on the German scene came from the theatrical corner and it assigned *Tasso* a negative role. Hans Daffis's essay in a new Berlin journal "for the friends of dramatic art" (1919) is one of only two on noncon- temporary drama (of a total of twenty-eight articles). This outstanding fact by itself would indicate high significance, but Goethe's hero is not there for his own sake. He is used instead to help understand Kleist better, to serve as foil for Prinz Friedrich von Homburg. Long before socialist real- ism coined the concept of the "positive hero," Goethe's poet emerged as negative hero vis-a-vis Kleist's Prussian general. Daffis shows all the marks of the interwar *Tasso* dialectic: the opposition between artist-dreamer and fighter; of aesthetic versus ethical issues; of individual versus collective in- terests. Daffis's strongest emphasis is on the defeat of feminine influence by masculine power in shaping the protagonist, in raising him from youth to manhood. He concludes: "So muß alles feminine gegenüber dem Tasso bei Kleist . . . weit zurücktreten. Die Erziehung des Mannes durch den Mann ist das wesentliche, der Einfluß der Frau gering geworden [Thus everything feminine in Tasso has to recede into the background in Kleist's drama. The education of the man through the man has become essential, the influence of the woman has become small]" (83). Four years later, theater author and director Ernst Hardt confirms the suggestion made by

[*] Four items up to the First World War, plus one positivist revision of Scheidemantel's genesis in *PMLA* 1919.

Daffis that artists ("jeder Schaffende [every creative {male} individual]"), poets especially, have come to identify with Tasso. Hardt's preface to the Ullstein edition is pure panegyric, which makes it an outstanding phenomenon in interwar criticism. All the more noteworthy is the extent to which Hardt plays down the theme of the artist. He situates the dramatic conflict between human struggles of the most universal dimension ("ringende Menschlichkeiten"). Tasso's particular role within the cast of struggling humanities is self-creation, not as a poet but as autonomous man who sets his own goals, whatever they may be: "eine zu selbst gestecktem Ziele sich unerbittlich umformende Seele [a soul which unrelentingly transforms itself to reach the goal set by this soul itself]" (13).

It is hard to imagine a greater contrast (except perhaps Korff 1930) to Hardt's panegyric than Gustav Roethe's nearly contemporaneous (1922) diatribe against the poor poet who is Goethe's Tasso. Both in method and form, Roethe's essay is a regression to nineteenth century positivism; its new feature, striking the keynote for interwar criticism, is the negative image of the artist. No less surprising is the dim view Roethe takes of Goethe's art. To be sure, scholarly decorum still demanded that such criticism remain well wrapped, but it sounds a persistently negative note underneath the rather confused surface text, which returns obsessively to the sorry figure of the artist. Roethe's problem derives from his fighting a war on two fronts, one against the prevailing opinion, up to his time, that *Tasso* was not a tragedy. The other front of Roethe's attack remains unacknowledged; his text in fact tries to hide it: he resents Richard Wagner's usurpation of Goethe's place as master artist, master of tragedy, and — ever since Castle inserted Wagner into the debate — as critical authority on *Tasso*. So Roethe needs to prove that Goethe indeed meant to write a tragedy, not a Wagnerian drama of *Mitleid* or salvation: "Wagner ist der Dichter des Mitleidens; Goethes Absichten hat er hier schwerlich erfaßt [Wagner is the poet of compassion; he has hardly grasped Goethe's intentions here]" (126; see also Roethe's Parsifal metaphor 131).

Roethe's title opens the hiding game, announcing yet another jaunt of that old war-horse, "Der Ausgang [ending] des *Tasso,*" while in reality his topic is "Goethe's (unfortunately) Botched Tragedy of the Artist." Roethe's trouble with *Tasso* is that he can find nothing great, nothing whole in it: no great passions, no nature, mere indiscretions instead of great events, "nicht Urkräfte, sondern Halbgefühle [not Ur-forces but half-feelings]." Catharsis therefore, prerequisite for tragedy, is impossible. Neither does this half-tragedy bring about a moment of insight and thus misses out on another crucial criterion of tragedy: anagnorisis. Indecisive until the end, Tasso's final image is one more self-deception. Roethe gives due praise to Goethe's language art, "the classical measured beauty of this art," but his choice of words in praise of such art sounds a note of protest against beauty as a cover-up of dark content: "Diese glatte Hofsprache . . .

breitet eine tondämpfende Atlasdecke über das Stöhnen und Aufschreien [this smooth court language spreads a muffling satin cover over the moans and screams]." Tasso's language suppresses the truth, even suppresses the poet ("the courtly speech has mastered Tasso, too"), who thus cannot truly "'sagen wie ich leide' [tell how I suffer]." (line 3433) Worst of all for Roethe in this "extreme artist drama" is the "extreme" protagonist. The sick artist whom Roethe depicts ad nauseam is an impossible tragic hero. As Roethe himself says of the Princess, opposing Steinweg (1912, see above): we feel sorry for her, but that does not make her a tragic figure, "traurig, aber nicht tragisch" (126). Rather than reproducing Roethe's litany of Tasso's shortcomings, suffice it to say that he includes all the items regularly listed by the anti-artist camp of his period: Tasso is selfish (that is, individualistic), *weltfremd* [unworldly], infantile, undisciplined, illusionary. There is one signal addition though to the conventional list. Calling for support on scientific studies linking "genius and insanity," Roethe considers Tasso unquestionably insane. The root of Roethe's diagnosis leads back to the root of the problem critics of this period had with artists: the claim to autonomy. Roethe's conclusion states it clearly: Goethe's drama *Tasso* shows "die Gefahren des reinen, sich selbst setzenden Künstlertums [the dangers of pure, self-constituting artistic existence]" (132).

To Roethe's lament over the artist's pathogenic self-centeredness, Korff's second volume of *Geist der Goethezeit* (1930) adds a foundation in cultural history, together with a startling intensification of anti-artist partisanship. Korff's vitriolic indictment of the artist is much harder to account for than Roethe's tormented discourse; it becomes all the more puzzling if one compares the denunciatory tone of Korff's *Tasso* discussion with its immediate antecedent, his adulatory *Iphigenie* sermon. Instead of engaging in out-of-historical-context speculation, let me suggest as a clue to the Korffian *Tasso* enigma Adorno's argument on Wagner's self-denunciatory practices (*Versuch über Wagner*, Chapter I. 1952). On Adorno's model, a writer on literature would reject his former identification with the creative writer and instead embrace the enemy: he would join the ruling order's effort to assert control over the wayward artist. Another explanation offers itself for the ideology propounded in Korff's surface text. We hear the voice of academic conservative resistance to the artistic avant-garde in the Weimar Republic. In Korff's reading of *Tasso* the court of Ferrara represents the German contribution to European cultural history. Here the superior humanity of German Classicism in its social aspect of "Geselligkeit [sociability]" and "Gesittung [civility]" has absorbed and improved French-inspired rococo culture. The members of this court, that is, the "gebildete Gesellschaft [educated society]," are appointed "guardians of cultural tradition"; their task is the conservative goal of preservation ("bewahren"). Another indicator of Korff's conservative ideology is the feminization of his guardians of tradition. In analogy with Dowager

Duchess Anna Amalia's rule in Goethe's Weimar, Korff's court of Ferrara is a "Musenhof" dominated by women. It would be the ideal society created by Korff's Iphigenie, where Iphigenian ideals have been distilled into "Takt [decorum]" — one of his key terms. His positive view of the feminine role in the arts and in civil society places Korff in stark opposition to the masculine ideal embraced by the Young Turks such as Daffis and the artists of the new Weimar, whose battle cry was *épatez les bourgeois*.

Since Korff counts himself among the members of the court of *Gebildeten*, he proceeds to repossess the artist, or to condemn him should he refuse to be converted. Most amazing perhaps is the degree to which he identifies his cultural ideal with genteel society. "Tact" is the supreme law, "tactlessness" — object of derision in *Tasso* criticism as far back as Hettner — is a capital crime. The sentence pronounced twice over Tasso is the ultraconventional cliché for unconventional behavior: "er hat sich unmöglich gemacht [he has compromised himself]." Moreover, Korff's genteel society assumes universal validity as he defines "truly human" successively as "truly lawful, truly cultivated, 'hoffähig [officially admissible to court society]'" (170f.). The courtly ideal, embodied in the Princess, is also Tasso's ideal. The artist is unconditionally dependent upon the culture guardians: the court of Ferrara in Korff's reading is a court of law where Woman has the decisive voice. This supreme court ("höchste Gericht") decides over the artist's life or death, his worth, his identity. Korff plays out the judicial metaphor ad infinitum. The dramatic action has the sole purpose of provoking and then executing "the sentence over the artist" (176), whose sins fill more than two of Korff's vituperative pages. Here is a sample:

> auf seine Genialität pochend, tyrannisieren zu können glaubt . . . künstlerische *Weltfremdheit*, auf die sich Künstler dieser Art so gern etwas zugute tun . . . wenig angebrachtes Überlegenheitsgefühl . . . verzogener, nicht für voll genommener Phantast . . . verantwortungslose Erzeugnisse seines 'Originalgenies' . . . sich in eine typisch künstlerische Menschenverachtung hineinredet und die in Wahrheit treue Gesinnung seiner Gönner in unverantwortlicher Weise verdächtigt. [presuming on his genius, he thinks he can play the tyrant . . . artistic *unworldliness*, which artists of this kind love to be proud of . . . quite unjustified feeling of superiority . . . spoiled fantasizer whom no one takes seriously . . . irresponsible products of his 'original genius' . . . talks himself into a disdain for mankind typical of artists, and casts suspicion in an irresponsible way on the attitude of his patrons, who in fact are completely loyal to him] (174, 180).

No wonder the sentence passed by this court (in a *Faust* allusion: "von oben her eine Stimme [a voice from above]") is: "'damnatus est' [he is damned]" (173). In the end Tasso gets away with his life ("das nackte Leben" repeated twice) but only just, for Korff's judgment deprives him in a loaded term of his human worth: "das Urteil über seine menschliche Minderwertigkeit [the sentence on his human inferiority]." The term *Minderwertigkeit,* in the biological, racial, social, or artistic dimension, became a basic category of dehumanizing Nazi doctrine. The sentence pronounced on his human inferiority likewise takes away Tasso's identity as a poet, for true "Dichtertum [poetic nature]" is tied to "höchster Menschenwert [highest human value]," a norm which in turn is set by the Court (182f.). The collective of cultured society, then, decides who is an artist and who is not, what is art and what is not; the only art is art according to the precepts of cultured society.

Among German critics, Robert Petsch in the *Festausgabe* introduction (1926) is the great exception to this bashing of the artist. Taking a clear stand against Roethe on the basis of (Gundolfian) *Lebensphilosophie* [life philosophy], he pronounces *Tasso* a work of authentic *Klassik.* In contrast with the mere classicism of *Iphigenie, Tasso* in Petsch's view represents life's *Urphänomene* [original phenomena: positive Gundolfian term], cast in greater-than-life symbols. Opposing Roethe on another crucial point, Petsch raises the artist-hero to larger-than-life stature. "Tasso ist kein Halbdichter und kein Ichdichter [Tasso is no half-poet and no ego-poet]," his poetic talent is one of life's superpowers: "dichterische Kraft . . . mit ungeheurer Mächtigkeit" (127). In an effort to get away from nineteenth century biographism as revived by Roethe ("ein langer Irrtum [a long-lasting mistake]"), Petsch calls for an approach from a real-historical context. Much of his text is devoted to the Renaissance poet Tasso in history and legend. He does, however, abide by old-style philology and indulges in extensive speculation about Goethe's use of sources and the presumable shape of the hypothetical *Urtasso.*

A major innovation is Petsch's emphasis on formal aspects. Devoting special, though brief, sections to structure and form, he finds two interweaving spirals constituting the plot, both centered on Tasso. His focus on the play character of language is a significant departure from the traditional praise for Goethe's sententious pronouncements in this drama on life's eternal truths through the mouths of his characters. The emphasis on form serves a didactic purpose. Today's reader, Petsch declares, is not commensurate with such formal sophistication as practiced by Germany's greatest poet; far more education is required to appreciate, even to understand the arch-classic. We may be excused if we see here the return of the old refrain that *Tasso* is accessible only to the elitest of the elite.

Petsch himself, by devoting so much of his interpretation to paraphernalia (fifteen pages versus six on content and form), indicates that hermeneutic problems persist in *Tasso.* His awkward treatment of the ending ("Tasso am Ende seines *Lebens* . . . " My emphasis: why should the end of the Ferrara period be the end of Tasso's life?) remains caught in the literal level of the imagery, and is, finally, an admission of hermeneutic defeat:

"Äußerlich läßt Goethe diesen Schluß absichtlich im unklaren [Seen from outside, Goethe leaves this ending intentionally unclear]" (127f.).

Petsch's approach to the thematic substance of the drama is split in two directions. The first approach narrows down Gundolf's nature-culture dichotomy to a polarity between the demonic genius and civilization, which in turn constitutes the paradox of artistic existence. Tasso and Antonio in their mutual attraction and opposition represent this polarity most starkly in Petsch's system; Tasso and the Princess replay the polar constellation in a different register. Altogether, Petsch directs attention away from Tasso as sole focus in order to emphasize groupings around Tasso, suggesting a relational structure at the bottom of the play's dynamic. His second approach, derived from this view of dynamic configuration, explores the drama's structure as an interplay of desires. It is the most innovative and fascinating feature of *Tasso* criticism up to this point. In Petsch's drama of desire, all the figures represent different "Urformen menschlicher Existenz [original forms of human life]," that is, different species of desire, all focused upon Tasso: "they all desire Tasso, each in his own way" (128). It is the interplay of these desires that drives the action: the stronger the desire, the more destructive its effect. Thus Antonio's will to power, being frustrated by the modest horizon of his master the Duke, turns aggressive. Thus Tasso's desire for recognition, when unfulfilled or rejected, turns into despair.

Unfortunately, Petsch merely appends this structure of desire to his analysis proper of the drama; his exciting idea remains just that: an exciting idea in the abstract, not worked through, not illuminating the text. Petsch shies away from following out the implications of his bold new view of *Tasso* as a drama of desire. He hints at Tasso's autoerotic lust of self-mutilation — but stops with the hint: "mit wollüstiger Selbstzerfleischung bohrt er sich hinein in das Wort [with voluptuous self-laceration he bores his way into the word]" (132). Similarly, Petsch's account of the final catastrophe remains evasive and abstract; Tasso's collapse is simply unique: "Tasso ist eben nicht mehr, was er vor kurzem noch war [Tasso is simply no longer what he was until recently]" (127). Walther Linden's essay on "Lebensprobleme" in *Tasso* (1927), published on the heels of the *Festausgabe*, tries to clarify Petsch's approach for the practical use of teachers by streamlining the multiple play of desires into a simple matter of polarities.*

Opposition to Roethe likewise inspired the first *Tasso* interpretation outside of Germany: John G. Robertson's 1928 essay in *PEGS*, which was essentially identical to the *Tasso* chapter in his popular Goethe book. Against Roethe, Robertson asserts that Goethe intended to write not a tragedy but a "Bildungsdrama" with the central idea to heal the mental

---

* The connection with Petsch is demonstrable. Linden's essay in the *Zeitschrift für Deutschkunde* immediately follows a brief review of Petsch's *Festausgabe* introduction.

imbalance of his own and his era's Sturm und Drang. *Tasso* as "the education of a poet" would raise the hero to self-consciousness and make him
recognize that his mission was to teach. Robertson finds, however, that
Goethe failed to realize this balancing intention, with the much-debated
inconsistencies of the drama as a result. Thus *Tasso* is a tragedy despite
Goethe's intention. For Robertson, the root of this tragedy lies in the
character of the hero. He is a "problematic nature" of the Hamlet type:
not necessarily a poet, but an over-sensitive soul. Robertson follows the
tradition of *Urtasso* speculation, yet transcends it by being the first to explore the connection between Goethe's work and the Tasso drama by
Goldoni, which the Italian Goethe could not have missed. Again going
beyond tradition, Robertson argues on the basis of textual not philological
evidence. In the light of Goethe's text, he asserts, "this . . . is the most
satisfying interpretation" (50). The most satisfying part of Robertson's
reading are his final remarks on the spooky atmosphere of the drama, recalling Herman Grimm's 1892 intimations of decay and rot in the Fer-
rarese court. The language of *Tasso*, he finds, without however providing
specific examples, makes unreal figures out of the courtly characters, all
except Tasso are as bloodless ghosts who live in an unreal world. With the
help of yet another predecessor, Georg Brandes (1915), Robertson finally
explains Goethe's uncanny Ferrara as an idyll walled off against the threatening reality of the French Revolution.

As a chapter in Robertson's *Goethe* (1927) this interpretation was unsatisfactory indeed: narrow and superficial due to its fundamentally philological perspective. It had, however, the singular merit of inspiring Barker
Fairley, who reviewed Robertson's book, to generate not one, but two
original and immensely productive readings of *Tasso* in his own book *Goethe as Revealed in His Poetry* (1932). Fairley's first reading views *Tasso* as
one of the "Charlotte dramas," more deeply marked by that "mistress of
Goethe's poetry" (38) than the companion *Iphigenie*. This drama is concerned not with individual or philosophical issues, but with relationships.
Fairley reads in it a pervasive transcendental subtext, which makes of the
hero a reluctant illusionist, an exile from his own nature. Since the transcendental slant remains latent, the Princess, who is its representative, is a
necessarily ambivalent figure. Fairley considers transcendentalism thoroughly un-Goethean, and *Tasso* therefore unrepresentative of the poet
whose true nature is "Nature." Thus not only the poet Tasso, Goethe
himself is alienated from his true self in this work, which leads Fairley to
his second perspective on *Tasso* in the chapter "The Self in Disguise."
Here the drama represents the quest of a split self for identity. The dramatic action shows the divided self trying to grow together again, but in
vain: the self remains conflicted. From this perspective, Fairley offers novel
solutions to the thorny problems of the *Tasso* tradition. He finds the relation between Tasso and Antonio patently absurd as a basis of dramatic

conflict; read as lyrical self-communion in a monologic dialogue, however, their interaction would make sense. The perplexing twin set of endings likewise makes sense to Fairley as the correlate of Goethe's shifting identification sometimes with Tasso and other times with Tasso-Antonio. In fact all characters should be seen as aspects of Goethe, aspects of a self that is trying to work out its identity. Fairley offers a solution to the genre question as well. Following Goethe's word on *Tasso* as "confession," he wants the work understood as a poetic-lyrical autobiography, as the poem of a self in search of consciousness. For Fairley's project of revealing the poet in his poetry, *Tasso* is indeed a master text. At the same time Fairley has finally rescued *Tasso* from its Lewes-imposed exile from the English Goethe canon. Like Lewes, Fairley rejects the work as drama, but then he reinstalls it as a central poetic text in Goethe's oeuvre. Furthermore, by exploring *Tasso* as poetry of self, Fairley has made a place for it in the company of modern literature. His vanguard interpretation from a modernist perspective prepared the soil for a rich bloom of New Critical readings after the hiatus of the Second World War.

It is remarkable, especially in comparison with *Iphigenie*, that *Tasso* produced no centennial criticism in 1932. (Surely the publication of Fairley's book in that year was coincidental.) In fact, with the exception of a voice from the distant margin of France in 1934 — René Michéa, who published two articles in French journals, hails from Périgord — nothing was written on *Tasso* until Elizabeth Wilkinson's path-breaking essay in *PEGS* 1946.[*] Michéa's two essays, on "Italianism" and on the "Pictorial Element" in *Tasso*, break the peculiar German fixation on the problematic poet by opening avenues to European horizons and to other kinds of artistic experience: from religious iconography to architecture, landscape, and the gardens of Florence. In another innovative move, Michéa emphasizes the visual dimensions of Goethe's creative mind, in contrast with the verbal and literary direction pursued by the philological tradition. Explicitly Europeanizing *Tasso*, Michéa proposes an intriguing alternative to replace Charlotte von Stein and her allegedly damaging impact in the figure of the Princess. Michéa's choice for this role deserves to be further explored, from a feminist perspective perhaps: she is Angelika Kauffmann, the Italianized German Swiss woman free-lance artist, friend and literary critic to Goethe in Rome.

---

[*] Another exception is the marginal publication, in peaceful Winterthur, Switzerland, of an essay by Emil Staiger in 1943.

SINCE 1945

The first three decades after the Second World War present a strange picture. Germany was as good as silent; *Tasso* study was initiated, propelled, and carried on at a steady pace by British and American critics. German *Tasso* criticism revived only with the paradigm change of methodology in the mid seventies from intratextual interpretation to sociohistorical perspectives. In the case of *Tasso*, this change was introduced with spectacular éclat by the 1969 Bremen stage performance. Exceptions to the pervasive silence were the obligatory chapters in monographs and the introductions to the new works editions. The strange landscape of *Tasso* criticism is marked by yet another outstanding feature. While German scholars produced no articles on *Tasso* until the mid seventies (with one timid exception in *Wirkendes Wort* 1952), two book-length studies — efforts to get out of an interpretational impasse — appeared at a ten-year interval (Rasch 1954, Neumann 1965). The absence of *Tasso* from German professional journals is no less striking than the total silence on the drama in the Goethe year 1949: not a single essay in all the special issues or symposium volumes. German scholarship seemed paralyzed by Korff's curse on Goethe's poet.

The earliest postwar writers on Goethe (von Wiese 1948, Viëtor 1949, Voser 1949, and Wolff 1951), reacted to *Tasso* with a sort of totalitarian recoil and again, as in the case of *Iphigenie*, with a strong preference for tragedy. They transferred Korff's moralistic *damnatus est* to the metaphysical dimension. Korff's spoiled-brat artist became a victim of demonic forces; of his talent and fate, which combined into "schicksalhafter Untergang [fateful perdition]." While von Wiese exculpated his hero by dint of the demonic, Voser and Wolff maintained, even intensified Korff's damnation.

Staiger (1952), too, while not part of the catastrophic school, remained in thrall to Korff. Carried away by "Dichterschelte [poet bashing]" (Heukenkamp 1976) he instead raised his Princess to new heights of Zen-like wisdom. The works editors, obliged to appreciate, obviated the Korffian curse by saving the drama, if not yet the hero, through philosophic abstraction. Both Kunz in the *Hamburger Ausgabe* (1952) and May in the *Gedenkausgabe* (1954) borrowed the "meaning" of *Tasso* from versions of existentialism. Kunz took a Heideggerian perspective on historical alienation of essence from social life; May followed the French variant popularized by Sartre and Camus with a focus on individual alienation.

The outstanding significance of Wolfdietrich Rasch's book of 1954 was to have lifted Korff's curse, to have broken the taboo on *Tasso*. Yet in order to rehabilitate *Tasso*, to reclaim the hero and the drama as topics worthy of their creator, Goethe, there was still another problem to be solved. For postwar Germany, Richard Wagner was anathema; Tasso as paradigmatic artist therefore had to be dissociated from Wagner, with whom the preceding era had so proudly linked him. Rasch achieved both goals. He was the first boldly and explicitly to reject Korff's judgmentalism. To counteract the artist's Wagner contamination, he took pains and more than half the space of his book to create for Tasso a specific image of The Poet, instead of artist-in-general, protagonist of (Wagnerian) *Künstlerdrama* and model of the now infamous producer of *Gesamtkunst*.

Unfortunately, however, Rasch's effort, because so deliberately focused on correcting the accumulated "prejudices" of his predecessors, did not provide a new impetus for *Tasso* interpretation. His work performed a transvaluation, from the negative to the positive, of the *Tasso* tradition, but did not offer a new perspective or approach. In a further move of retrenchment, Rasch, like his contemporaries in editions and monographs — von Wiese, Viëtor, Voser, Staiger, Kunz, May — used *Tasso* in order to reaffirm the classical ideal against modernity, in an effort to rebuild the solidity of tradition as a bulwark against the Zeitgeist of radical change.

The German silence on *Tasso* was broken by two signal exceptions eleven years after Rasch. A long essay by Lawrence Ryan in the *Schiller Jahrbuch* of 1965 must be accorded exceptional status in the strong sense of the term. Ryan was an outsider to the German *Tasso* tradition in two dimensions: as a Hölderlin scholar and as a foreigner to the historical consciousness that formed the root of the Korff curse. Given the departmentalization of the profession into Goethe scholars versus Hölderlin scholars, Ryan's introduction of Hölderlinian categories into *Tasso* interpretation fell on barren ground.

A similar fate befell Gerhard Neumann's downright original study, *Konfiguration* (1965), if for different reasons. His focus on formal and relational aspects and above all his base in skepticism, buttressed with quotations from Nietzsche (another anathema) and esoteric Hofmannsthal, placed him outside the dominant discourse of his era. This was the late sixties with their ethical fervor: Vietnam, the war crimes trials, student revolt, Red Army Faction terrorism, the revolutionary Paris May and Prague Spring. Relativism and formalism of Neumann's brand could not but encounter the scorn, at best the benign neglect of the academic Zeitgeist. Another decade of deep silence on *Tasso* ensued.

Note should be taken of *Tasso* study in East Germany during the fifties, even though it was limited, directly or indirectly, to the work of one scholar, Lieselotte Blumenthal. The type of work done in the fifties and the silence that reigned during the sixties and seventies (a single exception in the 1968 *Blumenthal Festschrift* proves the rule) shows that the German Democratic Republic had problems of its own with *Tasso*. Artists were not supposed to be in conflict with their society. Comments on a rare performance of "the shunned play" revealed that *Tasso*, unless radically his-

toricized and thus made irrelevant to a non-feudal culture such as the
GDR's, must remain taboo (Heukenkamp 1976).

Meanwhile, English criticism was having a field day ever since Elizabeth M. Wilkinson published her path-breaking essay on "the creative artist" in the 1946 *PEGS*. *Tasso*'s problematic energy continued to prove
itself outside of Germany as well; the field of English criticism resembled a
battlefield where strong opinions and widely divergent evaluations
emerged, sometimes at the same moment, and where the war over theories and methods was fought out in exemplary clarity. As Sigurd
Burckhardt recognized in 1958, when he refereed the fight between old-
line philology (Silz 1956) and the new text-focused readings of Rasch and,
by Silz's intention, Wilkinson, *Tasso* had become a vehicle for criticism's
self-investigation. The drama's exceptional difficulties had made it a test
case for method.

The divergence opened with Barker Fairley's astounding self-revisionist
thumbs-down on *Tasso* (1947), in opposition to Wilkinson's unadulterated admiration. Wilkinson's next essay (1949), while explicitly a belliger-
ent discourse on method, implicitly countered Fairley's tarring *Tasso* and
Werther with the same brush of disastrous introspection. Three years later
Ernest L. Stahl, by means of the Wilkinsonian method, yet improved on
Wilkinson's good *Tasso*. The two Goethe monographs of the fifties and
sixties (Peacock 1959, Gray 1967) both took the traditional British moral
stance. While Peacock found the most satisfying feature of *Tasso* in the
"moral architecture," Gray censured the drama for precisely its (a)moral
import. The two opponents did, however, meet in joint condemnation of
the final imagery, the part of *Tasso*'s text that would continue to taunt and
resist critical acumen seemingly forever.

With the ending, again, as the outstanding mark of controversy, *Tasso*'s
reputation see-sawed on in mainstream journals (*PEGS* of course, with its
Wilkinsonian agenda; *German Life and Letters, Modern Language Review,
PMLA*) and *Festschriften* (three for the period), until by the early seventies
critics were ready to throw in the towel. Surveying the chaotic history of
reading *Tasso*, two senior scholars concluded that Goethe's text had
proved too much of a challenge for literary criticism as presently constituted. Barring the discovery of major new documents such as an Ur-Tasso,
nothing could put a stop to the running in circles or teetering back and
forth of *Tasso* interpretation (Magill 1969, Atkins 1973). And indeed
English criticism took a break until the mid-eighties, after the impact of
the Bremen stage performance had taken root in German sociohistorical
approaches and provided a fresh focus of controversy.

Benno von Wiese set the stage for the strange postwar scene. Purporting
to survey the development of German tragedy from Lessing to Hebbel

(1948), he yet subverts chronology by placing *Tasso* before *Iphigenie* in his discussion of Goethe's classical dramas. For von Wiese, *Tasso* represents the climax of tragedy in Goethe's oeuvre. A deep structure of identification is unmistakable in his reading. An overwhelming melancholy pulls the critic into the text, yet there is also a pervasive sense of frustration at not comprehending, not being able to penetrate and completely analyze the "unbegreifliche [incomprehensible]" poem. Von Wiese considers *Tasso* as poem rather than drama, a monologue with mirrors, or, in his own simile in tune with his musical metaphoric throughout, a chamber concert for solo voice with accompanying voices.

Music is more than metaphor in von Wiese's reading of *Tasso;* it serves to explain analogically why this work is so hard to understand. Von Wiese declares the text essentially "mehrdeutig [having multiple meanings]," at least "doppelsinnig [ambiguous]": every meaning "could also be quite different, even exactly opposite." He insists that Goethe, at least, is not Tasso; he detects and describes an ironic distance between the author and his hero. While the subject of the drama is indeed poetic existence as a priori tragic, the poet is to be understood as symbolic of the human condition. His tragedy is the paradox and inevitable suffering of individuation itself. But the poet is not Everyman. Von Wiese defines him as "Ausnahme": he is the exceptional individual par excellence, different and separate from what is generically and generally human. We see the return of Nietzschean superman in a different guise: as hero of exceptional suffering, whose capacity to suffer constitutes his greatness.

In the poet understood as exceptional subject of tragedy, poetic imagination ("Phantasie") in von Wiese's reading represents the human spirit which pretends to essential-existential freedom. The origin of Tasso's tragedy then is the built-in contradiction between that free spirit and the limiting reality of the world. The stronger the spirit the harsher the paradox: the poet as exceptional man bears this spirit heightened to the power of the demonic. His existence is a configuration of antinomies, filled with tensions that tear him apart between extremes. Poetic man is by definition sentenced to self-destruct.

Underlying von Wiese's reading of *Tasso,* finally, is a totalitarian nihilism, where the ultimate good is identical with the ultimate bad. Poetry, Tasso's talent, is at once "Gnade und Fluch [grace and curse]." Von Wiese's eminently representative individual is unfit to live; the world who needs the poet must yet expel him. What remains for Tasso after the catastrophe, his poetic gift, is merely a "metaphysischer Trost." In a profoundly negative turn, von Wiese declares such metaphysical consolation no longer "überirdisch [supra-terrestrial, unearthly]," that is, like music a power encompassing and transcending the real. The metaphysical dimension intended here is instead "geisterhaft, übersinnlich [spectral, supra-sensual]."

Seen in these terms Tasso's poetic gift is separate from and irrelevant to the real world, in which the poet therefore cannot live (90–101).

In contrast with von Wiese's intense focus on *Tasso* — witness more than twice as much text in his chapter abstract than on any other Goethe drama (always excepting *Faust*) — Karl Viëtor's lack of interest in *Tasso* in his big Goethe monograph of 1949 is truly remarkable. How to explain his misplacing the famous silkworm simile, which yet forms the center of his view of the tragic poet, except possibly as an aspect of Korff-induced paralysis of reading the text of *Tasso?* Viëtor is careful, however, not to echo Korff, except for implicitly adjudicating the conflict between the poet's egotism and the just claims of his social environment. Instead of adopting Korff's openly judgmental stance Viëtor goes back to the Gundolf-Petsch line on the basic dichotomies of life. Here the poet's opposition to his world is redeemed in the larger frame of life, which needs conflict in order to keep up its dialectical drive. Confusing the issue of poetic existence made right in the totality of life, however, there is a demonic power driving Viëtor's poet, too, a power which interferes with the neat Hegelian solution to existential contradictions. Thus it is more than a matter of rhetoric that Viëtor's brief chapter on *Tasso* is so full of rhetorical questions without answers. *Tasso* remains a confused issue.

The matter is far simpler, almost schematic, for Hans-Ulrich Voser in his study of individuality and tragedy in Goethe's dramas (1949). Voser unquestioningly sides with Korff's support for the Court against the "unfertiger Jüngling, der . . . entartet [unfinished youth who degenerates]." While not as polemical in style as Korff, Voser's verdict against the poet is as strict and for similar reasons. He accords great significance to the "Daimon" of talent, yet this factor neither exculpates the "haltlose [unstable, reckless]" champion of the autonomous imagination, nor does it convey value on him. The true values are embodied in the legitimate world of Ferrara and they are never endangered by Tasso's failure. The drama therefore is not a tragedy even though Tasso is destroyed: his loss is no loss to the valued world. Thus Voser finds himself compelled to invent a new genre: *Tasso* is a "tragisches Schauspiel."

Severe moral judgment is also the focus of Wolff's view of *Tasso* as he explores Goethe's path to *Humanität* (1951). The drama, to follow Wolff, presents rather a roadblock on this path, throwing Goethe back to his *Werther* phase. In support of his thesis Wolff constructs a complete Ur-Tasso pertaining to the Frankfurt period, not to the early Weimar years as Ur-Tasso tradition had it. As in Viëtor's case, there is here an effort to avoid having to deal with the awkward work itself. For the Goethe-as-humanist portraitists Viëtor and Wolff, Korff's indictment had made *Tasso* an even more embarrassing topic than it had been for the Goethe worshippers and philologists of the nineteenth century. Wolff therefore summarily adopts Korff's sentence of condemnation for the poet and explains his bad Tasso by equating him with the much earlier Werther. The two heroes are identical, the only difference is that Goethe changed his mind about them: "Tasso ist ein Werther, der nicht beklagt, sondern gerichtet wird [Tasso is a Werther who is not lamented but condemned]" (237).

Emil Staiger (1952) shares with Wolff at least the place he assigns *Tasso* in Goethe's life story. He reports, though he does not endorse (but neither does he reject) Wolff's Ur-Tasso idea, and for him, too, the drama as a whole precedes Goethe's Italian experience. His picture of *Tasso* remains as narrow and fundamentally negative as a dim view of Goethe's early Weimar years would suggest: we are reminded of Barker Fairley's treatment of the "Charlotte drama" in 1932 and, with a far more disparaging slant, in 1947. Add to this Korff's dismal image of the artist and the result is Staiger's thoroughly distressing *Tasso* chapter. "Dichterschelte [poet bashing]" a later critic called it (Heukenkamp 1976). But Staiger's polemic is not addressed to all poets, only to the wrong kind, the Tasso-types, such as Hölderlin or Keats, whereas Homer, Wieland, and others of their kind prove that good poets can be happy, too.

In Staiger's view Tasso's fate has no universal significance, not even for poets: "nur einem solchen Menschen stößt das zu [this happens only to such a person]" (391). The drama is not a tragedy. Lacking universal significance and a sublime dimension, it is merely a character drama, a genre whose purpose it is to offer a deterrent example. And here Staiger, echoing Korff, weighs in with his castigation of the bad characteristics that make up the wrong kind of poet. The reader is referred to Staiger's specifics; here is a sample of his poet-bashing that shows him particularly close to Korff, including the tone of resentment: "naiv-selbstsüchtiger, eigensinniger, seine Rolle im Welttheater weit überschätzender Geist [naively self-addicted, stubborn spirit who far overestimates his role in the theater of the world]" (399).

Staiger can redeem the drama for the morally uplifting Goethean universe by placing its true center in the figure of the Princess, whom he raises to unprecedented levels of sublimity. She embodies, or rather she constitutes, Staiger's ideal of German classicity through her philosophy of *Entsagung* [renunciation] as he celebrates in her all that is worth defending against the onslaught of existentialist and other radical modern ideas: "Who yet remembers what this word [Entsagung] means?" Rooted in preclassicist "pietistischen innigen Seelenkunst [pietist soulful soul art]," the Princess is a "beautiful soul" prefiguring Schillerian "beautiful morality [Sittlichkeit]." Her version of the Golden Age anticipates (since Staiger places *Tasso* before Goethe's classicist phase) Goethean "klassisches Lebensgefühl [classical attitude to life]" (406–13). In a rhetoric approximating the absolutism of religious language, Staiger enthrones the Princess as a saint of aesthetic Zen, way above and beyond any discriminating and divisive Platonism:

Einverständnis mit dem heiligen Willen des Alls . . . [was sie] ohne
Einschränkung als das Verklärte und Entrückte verehrt und liebt . . .
die ständige Gegenwart, ein niemals unterbrochenes Gefühl des
Schönen . . . das Schöne, dessen Wesen vollendete Gegenwart und
Befriedigung ist. [Agreement with the holy will of the cosmos . . .
[what she] worships and loves without limitation as the transfigured
and inaccessibly transcendent . . . the perpetual presence, a never in-
terrupted feeling of the beautiful . . . the beautiful whose essence is
perfect presence and contentment]" (405f.).

In consequence, just as her definition of the Golden Age disqualifies
that offered by Tasso, the Princess-ideal illuminates yet more intensely the
unsatisfactory poet's shortcomings.

By the same token, Staiger's extraordinary foregrounding of the Princess shows that he really misses the point of *Tasso*. Clear evidence is his
helplessness vis-a-vis the ending. At first he warns the reader not to think
beyond the final moment about the possible future of the erstwhile antagonists Tasso and Antonio, but then he himself invents a dire future for
Tasso by seeking help outside the text. Easily the most fascinating part of
the chapter, Staiger's Tasso fiction deserves to be explored:

Tasso, the intensified Werther, could well renounce life but does not
want to renounce the pleasure of creating. He drags himself on, excluded from the society whom he loves and needs, and received with
suspicion and distrust wherever he might show up, crowded deeper
and deeper inside himself, a strange and uncanny magician, who more
and more resembles the harpist in "Wilhelm Meister" and who finally
consumes himself in himself (424).

Displacing the text by his own fiction or by other Goethe texts — *Wilhelm Meister* for the harpist and (unacknowledged) for the figure of the
beautiful soul — such strategies indicate that Staiger at bottom rejects
Tasso as a poetic text. He reveals his negative stance when he finds that, in
condemning Tasso, Goethe condemned himself as artist. By writing this
anti-poet work the author has damaged his own creative powers. In consequence, according to Staiger, Goethe's art after *Tasso* was significantly
impoverished; the later poetry lacked the whole range of the truly enchant-
ing dimension (424f.). Staiger, we must conclude, despite the praise he
lavished on its artistry, did not like *Tasso*.

But at least he wrestled with the drama itself; his interpretation amply
engages the text. Josef Kunz in the *Hamburger Ausgabe* of the same year
(1952) gives the text of *Tasso* a wide berth and instead offers a philosophical discourse in cultural criticism from the perspective of Goethe's far later,
and by critical consensus at the time, far lesser drama *Die natürliche Tochter*. Kunz uses *Tasso* as a vehicle for a historical metaphysics that combines the Nietzsche-Spenglerian cyclical myth of history with Heideg-

gerian essentialist pessimism. According to Kunz, what is wrong with his (and Goethe's) "historical moment" is "Entfremdung von Wesen und Wirklichkeit [alienation of essence and reality]." In line with this view, Goethe's drama is at once a return of Sophocles' *Oedipus Rex* and of Shakespeare's *Hamlet*. The time is out of joint — "schicksalhafte Gebrochenheit der Zeit [fateful brokenness of time]" — and Tasso-Hamlet knows but cannot realize the claim of the absolute.

Kunz's Tasso is more than poet, more than person even; he is demanding spirit, "Forderung des Geistes," who at the present moment of the historical cycle is absolutely alienated from reality ("schlechthinige Unwirklichkeit des Geistes"). Let me refrain from further reproducing Kunz's philosophical abstraction, but note that his approach leads him to reject explicitly the political and social sphere as well as the psychological dimension of the drama. While he deems psychological perspectives merely irrelevant because they are too particular, he rejects the political dimension with the totalizing *Ohne-mich* [without-me] gesture so common to postwar German intellectuals. In Kunz's view, partnership with power is to be avoided; demanding it is what makes Tasso "questionable" and indeed, pathological. The state only uses and abuses art to hide its own interests behind a "Schein der Transzendenz [appearance of transcendence]" (465), for the state's only true interest is power: "this world of the state and of the court, where the only issues are self-assertion and power" (462).

The one place where Kunz gets close to the text yields an interesting discovery. He is the first to connect the troubling ambivalence of *Tasso*, soon to be thematized by Walter Silz (1956), with the play of language. In Kunz's analysis, key terms of the spiritual sphere — *Glück, Freiheit, Maß, Bildung* [luck or happiness, freedom, moderation, education] — undergo radical changes of meaning in the course of the drama. From his essentialist perspective, Kunz has to deplore such language play as abuse and perversion, more proof of the "Zweideutigkeit von Schein und Sein [ambiguity of appearance and being]" (451) that is, in his view, the substance and theme of Goethe's *Tasso*.

Compared to Kunz, Kurt May's commentary in the *Gedenkausgabe* (1954) is downright down-to-earth and far closer to the text, especially in its attention to features of form and their import for content. A touch of essentialism shows mainly in May's terminology — an overabundance of *Wesen*-[essence]compounds — and in his tendency to totalize, as "this poet" more and more becomes "the poet" and Tasso's tiny Ferrara is equated, without further ado, with the world that Tasso's true "Wesensbild [image of essence]," Faust, desires to encompass. May borrows the meaning of *Tasso* partly from *Faust* — Tasso is only a fragment, "bruchstückhaft," of Faust's complete humanness — and partly from the existentialist view of the artist as quintessentially solitary man who is caught in the paradox of mutual desire of the social world.[*]

But May's particular innovation is his differentiation between text and author. The clue to this difference lies in the formal features, which May understands as shaped content, Gestalt. Seen in this light, *Tasso* is not immediate expression of pressing personal experience but conscious formation of past experience. In a yet more radical move of distancing, May finds in *Tasso*, in addition to shaped remnants of experience, a collage of bits and pieces from the literary tradition. The characteristic language of *Tasso*, too — sentential, strictly metered, antithetical — demonstrates for May authorial distancing. There is no lyricism, no self-representation here, no Werther rerun. This is post-Italian Goethe presenting indirectly ("mittelbar") — and here May's argument veers into an odd curve — his new poet-ideal: the synthesis of "Dichter und Weltmann [poet and man of the world]."

Following May, we are not supposed to read in *Tasso* the (Werther) kind of poet Goethe himself had rejected. We are to perceive instead, *mittelbar*, an opposite kind of poetic existence that the text does not present. The meaning of Goethe's text, then, would not be in the text; the text would mean precisely what it does not say. May is reduced to arguing an absurd case of representation *a negativo*. We must conclude that finally, despite his best intentions, May has been defeated by Goethe's problem play.

The most that could be attempted, it seems, were modest part-interpretations, as in the sole special study of *Tasso* in postwar Germany: Arno Mulot's article on four isolated scenes in *Wirkendes Wort* (1953). Mulot brims over with philosophy and ethics of the existentialist type, where Tasso experiences his zero hour of conversion from "Hof*poet* [court poet]" to "*Dichter* der Unmittelbarkeit [poet of immediacy]" (my emphasis). Yet in a novel feature Mulot emphasizes the poet's fundamental need for recognition, a need reflected in the text of *Tasso* through the importance of gesture and ritual as expressions of that recognition.

Before we come to the end of the early postwar German line in Wolfdietrich Rasch's book of 1954, we need to take account of English criticism, for Rasch was the first to work within a context that included the new English approach as modeled by Elizabeth M. Wilkinson in her two articles of 1946 and 1949.[†] The beginning of English postwar criticism can be seen as emblematic of the general history of reading *Tasso*, which is

---

[*] Compare the theme of *solitaire-solidaire* in Camus.

[†] Wilkinson's *Tasso* essay of 1946 was such a sensation that it could not be ignored. Both Staiger and Kunz acknowledge and document the article in notes and bibliography. Staiger even uses Wilkinson on particular passages of Goethe's text, in order to confirm his own points.

the continuity of divergence. Wilkinson's New Critical approach in 1946 exfoliated the text as artwork from within its own boundaries; her strong reading brought out the excellencies of the drama, raising its aesthetic value. On the opposite pole, Barker Fairley's contemporaneous rereading of *Tasso* in his *Study of Goethe* (the preface is dated 1946) revised his view of 1932 under the impact of recent history.

In his new reading, Fairley has absorbed traces of Robertson's critique (whom his 1932 book primarily opposed) and of E. M. Butler's diagnosis of the German problem. Fairley now pairs "Werther and Tasso" within "the malady of introspection" (vi) as bad models for the disastrous German culture of inwardness. His earlier view of the spiritual and transcendental world of *Tasso* has changed into the spooky "spirit-realm" that Robertson had seen (113). In Fairley's view the drama lacks all political and social reality; with extraordinary assertiveness he insists that "there can be no two opinions about *Tasso*, which is and remains the most sequestered, the most cloistered, of all Goethe's masterpieces, *Werther* not excepted" (218). Possessed and denatured by Charlotte, his Princess, in a phase of retarded maturity, Goethe wrote this "life-and-death study of the introverted poet" (259).

Fairley is no less severe on the history of *Tasso* criticism. This work of "morbid refinement" (220) has lured German critics of the last century to model Goethe on his tragic creature; they would have preferred him "to go to pieces at all costs like a good poet" (271). Fairley's two-pronged approach of 1932, via transcendentalism and the split lyrical subject, has converged in 1947 into a Tasso-Werther equation. The irrationalism and subjectivism he attributes to these two figures now could serve to explain what went wrong with the German spirit and thus with German history.

It is an irony worthy of the erratic course of *Tasso* tradition that Elizabeth M. Wilkinson's essay on the "Tragedy of the Creative Artist" (1946), the single most important study of *Tasso*, proceeded from Fairley's 1932 reading to arrive at a point diametrically opposite of his new position. Wilkinson, like Fairley, views the poet as a split or dual subject, whose definition is to "see himself and be himself." She is, however, not interested in the poet as person, but in poetic activity, in the process that turns the raw material of life into poetry.

In a pre-structuralist approach drawing on the associative method of psychoanalysis, she traces the course of verbal imagination in four "fictions" created by Tasso, through their successive phases of unconscious source, inspiration, and conception. From Wilkinson's perspective of New Criticism, poetic creation is an objectifying activity, not subjective and introspective as Fairley saw it. In New Critical terms, poetry is an "objective correlative" of personal experience. In these terms, Tasso's monologues are purely subjective and introspective speech and thus do not qualify as poetic creation, fiction or vision. The distinguishing mark of poetic versus nonpoetic language is the act of shaping: a poem is a well-wrought urn, or, as Wilkinson states quoting Rilke: the decisive poetic activity is *bilden* [shaping]. Her reading of the final imagery demonstrates this quality. Here Tasso's language shifts from the nonpoetic to the poetic mode, from "sich beklagen [complaining]" to "klagen [lament]."

The profound impact of Wilkinson's essay was due to two main factors. In the first place, her celebrating the poet, emphasized by a rhetoric of sublime encomium, encouraged German critics in their attempt to rescue him from his Korffian condemnation. And secondly, for *Tasso* criticism generally, she showed a new way to approach it. Her essay introduced into Goethe criticism the renewal of method that so spectacularly had revived English Shakespeare studies with its new focus on imagery and structure.

Wilkinson's follow-up article of 1949 on "Tasso — ein gesteigerter Werther," was the second blow in her one-two punch. She blasts the traditional use of biography in Goethe scholarship, which has led to "indiscriminate, irresponsible, primitive, stultifying chaos" (185), and she offers a methodical course on how to do it right. In the main body of her text she examines the meaning of the term *Steigerung* [heightening, intensification] throughout Goethe's work and in the scientific context of his epoch. At the same time, even if compressed on the first and last pages of her essay, she unhooks that old, unholy linkage of Tasso and Werther so recently reinvigorated in Fairley's study.

Three years later, in a *Festschrift* devoted to Wilkinson's associate Leonard A. Willoughby, Ernest L. Stahl used the Wilkinsonian method to apply another much-misunderstood Goethean pronouncement on Tasso and *Verklärung* [transfiguration] to Tasso's final speech. Following the imperative of moral progression in British criticism, Stahl corrects Wilkinson's reading of that speech. In Stahl's reading, Tasso achieves not merely the cathartic insight granted by Wilkinson, but experiences a change of essence through redemptive salvation.

The significance of Wolfdietrich Rasch's *Tasso* study of 1954 lies in its bridge function: Rasch built a bridge between the German tradition of *Geistesgeschichte* and the new text-based approach pioneered in British scholarship. The bridge was a long time a-building. Rasch tells in his preface that he began rethinking *Tasso* on the anniversary lecture circuit in 1949. His paper at the 1951 *Germanistentag* created enough of a sensation for Arno Mulot to state in a preliminary note to his 1953 essay on *Tasso* in *Wirkendes Wort* that he had arrived at his interpretation independently, without borrowing from Rasch's presentation. Over several years Rasch developed his reading further through contacts with the Wilkinsonian school at the University of London and with French audiences. The bridge he built in his book, then, linked Germany to the European context, too.

The decisive impetus for Rasch was Wilkinson's 1946 essay. Her exploration of verbal imagination had taken *Tasso* out of the artist-in-general frame, which had become a site of crucifixion and demonization in German criticism. Rasch could now focus on the concept of *Dichter* [poet] with its positive connotations, instead of the profoundly ambivalent *Künstler* [artist]. To appreciate the gap between the two concepts, one might reflect on such topoi in German culture as "Land der Dichter und Denker [country of poets and thinkers]" or: "was aber bleibet stiften die Dichter [but what remains is the poets' work]" (Hölderlin) on the one hand and, on the other, Thomas Mann's and Kafka's treatment of the artist-artificer theme.

It is in the nature of bridges to stand on the old while reaching out to the new. Rasch's book contains much of the old and much less that is new. This account then, for obvious reasons, will focus on the innovative aspects which would stimulate future readings and ultimately bring about fundamental changes in *Tasso* criticism, even if these were still far off in the future on the German side. For the immediate effect of Rasch was on English criticism. His delayed effect on German scholarship at first sight seems hard to explain until one remembers the overwhelming dominance of established critics such as von Wiese and Korff in the German academy. Rasch explicitly and repeatedly attacks both eminent critics. He stands nonetheless firmly on old ground with the image of the poet that he presents in part 1 of his book. We meet familiar categories from the German tradition — the poet is "*poeta magus* [magician]" and *vates* [prophet], mythic, originative, demonic — with strong ties to Gundolf, Hofmannsthal, Rilke, and especially to Heideggerian essentialism. Rasch's unreservedly positive valuation of the poet adheres firmly to classicist conservatism in the tradition of German *Geistesgeschichte*.

His long introductory chapter, however, breaks with that tradition in substance as well as style. (Introductions, it is useful to remember, are commonly written after the main body of the book.) Following the way shown by Wilkinson's essay on Tasso and *Steigerung* (1949), Rasch here constructs a historical concept of the poet. The historical inquiry leads to one of his most innovative suggestions. The epochal change in the status of literary production wrought by the French Revolution — "Abschied vom 'Hofdichtertum' [farewell to the 'institution of court poetry']" — would recommend sociological perspectives for *Tasso* criticism: "a sociological approach to literature, for which the Tasso drama appears altogether promising" (34).

Part 2 of Rasch's book, the analysis of the drama proper, in its odd mixture of old and new is exemplary of the bridge function. Old is above all the adversarial structure of the argument. Rasch combats the accumulated "prejudices" of his predecessors and in consequence his own argument remains too closely tied to theirs: stuck in the past. What is new appears for the most part as initiatives glimpsed, not followed through, but initiatives nevertheless suggested for possible followers. Thus Rasch promotes New Critical thinking and terminology when he rejects biographical perspectives. His insistence that the literary text is an "objektives dichterisches Sinngefüge [objective poetic structure of signification]" (68) places him squarely inside the anti-biographist camp, in opposition to mainline Goethe scholarship of his time.

Against von Wiese and Fairley he reclaims *Tasso* for the dramatic genre, but on the other hand he protests Staiger's belittling classifying it as character drama. For Rasch the generic innovation of *Tasso* is the fact that a purely poetic event, the completion of Tasso's work, should serve as the precipitating motif of dramatic action. He finds irony constitutive for the work as a whole, detecting concurrent but different dramatic processes at the surface and subtextual levels.

The most forward-looking feature of Rasch's study is, finally, his treatment of the laurel wreath in the new British way, as he traces the path of this "sich wandelnde Sinnfigur [transformational figure of signification]" (113) through the text. Rasch himself points out in the preface that it was this aspect which, in his long rethinking of Goethe's drama, appeared to him increasingly significant, eventually as "der Kern des Stückes [the nucleus of the play]." The motif of the laurel wreath counts among those of Rasch's discoveries that would prove especially fruitful in future *Tasso* interpretations.

It was, again, exceedingly fitting for *Tasso* history that Rasch's first effect should have been to provoke an adversary, not a follower in the first American intervention of the postwar period: Walter Silz's 1956 essay in *The Germanic Review* on "Ambivalences." As Sigurd Burckhardt stated in a brief article in the *Journal of English and Germanic Philology* (1958), the battle was joined over theory and method, over old-line biographical criticism versus the New Critical perspective. If his opposition to what he considered uncritical appreciation as practiced by Rasch and Wilkinson motivated Silz to protest, the driving force of his own argument is exasperation over this drama "where we get no clear answers" from the text. For Silz, only biography can unlock the final imagery in *Tasso*; only the long composition time and the different sources can explain Goethe's unsuccessful attempt to fuse three different poets into one character. The combined Rasch-Wilkinson effect at least had established the figure of the poet as the focus of the drama, with the result that in Silz's interpretation the two contradictory Antonio figures beloved by *Tasso* philology of the nineteenth century could be displaced by three incompatible Tasso characters.

The first constructive echo of Rasch came much later from the Hölderlin expert Lawrence Ryan in an article in the *Schiller Jahrbuch* of 1965 under a title that was practically identical to Rasch's: "Die Tragödie des

Dichters in Goethes *Torquato Tasso*." Notwithstanding his firm stand on Rasch's shoulders, Ryan gets mired in the disaster area of *Tasso* criticism to the point where most of his effort is spent reporting its pros and cons, including a particularly sharp polemic against Wilkinson. Thus his own original contribution, a dialectical perspective on historical change derived from the Hölderlinian concept of *Werden im Vergehen* [becoming in passing away], remains limited to a rather surprising conclusion concerning the ending of *Tasso*. According to Ryan, Goethe here shows the remaking of the poet, from a practitioner of classicism and the epic genre into a modern creator of subjective and lyrical poetry. Ryan applies his thesis of a dialectical reversal both to literary history, where he pinpoints the birth of Romanticism, and, in a move much contested by Goethe scholars, to Goethe's own poetic development.

The same year, 1965, saw, in the second book-length study of postwar times, an erratic block that stands as far outside the traditional *Tasso* discourse as Ryan was stuck inside: Gerhard Neumann's *Konfiguration*. Unlike Rasch, Neumann does not offer a conscientious account of Goethe's text. Instead, in another variation on *Tasso* as a testing site for methodology, he proposes a new method of reading literary texts in general with *Tasso* as demonstration sample.

Neumann's hermeneutic approach could be called a nonformalist kind of structuralism. It originates not in the Jacobsonian synthesis of linguistic and psychoanalytic theory that founds twentieth-century structuralism. Rather, Neumann goes back to the morphological thinking of Georg Simmel, combined with an eclectic emphasis on relationality based on Nietzsche and buttressed with Hofmannsthal and Musil. Neumann takes relationality all the way to relativity, most conspicuously with his principled refusal to evaluate, in explicit opposition to the ideological and judgmental criticism so prevalent in the *Tasso* tradition. In literature generally and particularly in a text as sententious as *Tasso*, he states, "opinions . . . are masked form." While form, as organizing principle, must have priority for the critic, for Neumann it is not empty form; form organizes and determines content.

The rich content Neumann sees organized in the configuration that is *Tasso* is another reason why he has had no followers to speak of. He uncovers a multilayered sediment of European cultural tradition, especially in its Latin variants, displaying an abundance of knowledge mastered by few of his contemporaries. Ernst Robert Curtius, Leo Spitzer, Walter Benjamin, Baudelaire, Proust, Valéry; Machiavelli's *Principe*, Castiglione's *Cortegiano*: their eclectic assembly constitutes Neumann's thesaurus of content in *Tasso*.

His inventory of forms includes spaces (for example, gardens) and times, components of language (words, phrases, sentences, metaphors), and visual elements (gestures, rituals, codes, depictions, pictures). First to have taken Goethe at his word about *Tasso* as a "konsequente Composition," Neumann reads the drama as one might a musical score — a structure of relations — or, as he concludes in a Valéry quotation: *danse verbale*. Stimulating, immensely rich, and woefully impractical (no index, meager bibliography, the theoretical argument conducted mainly in notes), Neumann's book offers an immeasurable treasury of the rich and diverse cultural material that went into Goethe's drama. Long ignored and then less understood than exploited and mined in the eighties (Borchmeyer and Hinderer), it still awaits discovery by *Tasso* criticism. Neumann's only genuine follower might be perceived in the 1969 Bremen performance, a revolutionary staging that shocked traditionalists by going backwards, forwards, and sideways in transposing pieces of text, very much in the way that Neumann had declared prerequisite for reading *Tasso*.

With German scholarship dormant for another decade after Neumann, the *Tasso* effect continued to generate extremes in English criticism. In Ronald Peacock's case the drama worked according to the principle stated by Burckhardt (1958): as a challenge for the critic to outdo himself and produce the most sophisticated chapter in his study of *Goethe's Major Plays* (1959). In Ronald Gray's *Critical Introduction* to Goethe (1967), *Tasso* functioned as provocation of another sort: the text's perceived ambivalences carried over into that reader's response to produce aggressive antagonism. In the earlier book, Ronald Peacock's reading of *Tasso* is a superb illustration of discriminating criticism. Chiding Wilkinson and Rasch for their uncritical appreciation, he insists on the need to read critically. He cites for an example the final imagery, the signal part of the drama that he cannot cope with other than by judging it, after thorough analysis, bad poetry: "the weakest part of the whole play" (112ff.). Other than that, however, in Peacock's view the drama excels by its complexity. It is precisely the complex interrelation of form and content, with form the determining factor, that is the focus of his reading.

In a revolutionary departure from British critical tradition so intent on moral substance, Peacock is the first to give form paramount importance in *Tasso*. Two formal categories, eloquence and control, constitute (together with the obligatory moral philosophy) the drama's main characteristics. Like Neumann after him (who apparently did not know Peacock), he finds his summary image for *Tasso* in a dance metaphor. The drama is the choreography of a philosophical meditation on life and thought, where the characters-dancers represent ideas, not individuals. Peacock organizes his discussion according to structural concepts. He explores the text's "philosophical architecture," dissolves ambivalences in "double foci," and distinguishes between center and periphery of perspective.

The double focus on Tasso, for instance, reveals the hero as innocent child and inadequate man at the same time. Central and peripheral perspectives highlight the moral philosophy represented by the poetic self on the one hand, but illumine with equal justness the civilizing values embodied in the court of Ferrara. If Peacock's own focus is on the latter, it is because, so he states, *Tasso* tradition has overexposed the side of the poet. In his analysis of this "drama of conflicting values," however, ideology ("*Weltanschauung*") matters greatly, and Peacock supports the social against the individual party. "The real theme of *Torquato Tasso* is the rejection of the romantic dream of simple self-fulfilment and happiness as in itself inadequate to the real problem of living in a society" (121).

If Peacock saw in *Tasso* Goethe's debate with European Romanticism since Rousseau, we might see in Peacock's reading a reflection of the heated debate between the Establishment and the Angry Young Men of his own time and place: England of the 1950s. In Peacock's analysis, Goethe's debate does not end in the defeat of one side but instead, dialectically, in a refinement of both. Thus *Tasso* is not belated Sturm und Drang, it is rather an anticipation of classical-romantic synthesis, where Nature becomes the healer of Culture. This is how Peacock reads the last two lines — the only part of Tasso's final speech he approves: "The symbol [of sailor and rock] reflects the ambiguous function of all natural events and objects, providing the cure within the poison" (136).

Peacock's ingenious, dialectical or twin-focus solution could not solve the *Tasso* problem, not even in the short run. Four years later, Henry Hatfield's *Introduction* to Goethe (1963) hovers on *Tasso*, a hung jury, between Wilkinson and Fairley. Hatfield discovers a leitmotivic "uncertainty" in vocabulary, characters, ending, genre, and above all in Goethe's intention. Concerning the genre, Hatfield follows Wilkinson but with reservations. In his view *Tasso* is a tragedy, but of a special, "durative" kind; it is about an artist, but not *the* artist. Concerning the theme, Hatfield adopts Fairley's view of Tasso as the bad pupil of an equally bad teacher: the Princess.

Another four years later, Ronald Gray's *Critical Introduction* to Goethe cut the Gordian knot of indecision by declaring *Tasso* not worth bothering with. Blaming the text for criticism's shortfall, Gray opines that the worthlessness of this Goethean work explains the difficulties critics have experienced in dealing with it. The drama "accumulates problems" because it consists of nothing but a "pusillanimous group of characters." So Gray sets forth in considerable detail the reasons why *Tasso* is such a bad piece of work. Even though he takes pride in ignoring other critics, or at least in writing against the grain of criticism, Gray's text on *Tasso* makes depressing reading for the historian of ideas and literature. We are left with some nagging questions: Did the many subtle and sophisticated critics we have so far encountered write to no avail? Or alternatively: What is wrong with Goethe's text that a naive reader could end up with such a terrible opinion of *Tasso*?

Others who attempted interpretations of *Tasso* sounded scarcely more hopeful; some voiced frustration or intimidation, most evidence the impasse that criticism had reached. One exception was a solitary voice from the German Democratic Republic. Horst Nahler in the *Blumenthal Festschrift* (1968) gives *Tasso* an optimistic Hegelian reading. Here Goethe emancipated the "court poet [Hof*poet*]" to have him enter history as a "bourgeois poet [bürgerlicher *Dichter*]" (my emphasis). With this thesis Nahler anticipated the sociohistorical approach of West German critics a decade later, as he did with his argument on the poet's playacting and on Tasso's antiauthoritarian, even democratic impulses.

But contemporary critics took no notice, they remained firmly within the Western mainstreams of textual immanence or biographical contextualization. An early attempt to call on psychoanalytical theory for help with the difficult text must be deemed a conspicuous failure: Ilse Graham's *Tasso* chapter in her book, *The Wellsprings of Creativity* (1973). Fortunately we need to consider this only as a preliminary effort to be vastly surpassed in relevance and acuity by the *Tasso* chapter in her later book, *Goethe, Portrait of the Artist* (1977). Graham's 1973 reading is driven and flawed by the urge to oppose the establishment critics, particularly Wilkinson and to a lesser extent Rasch.

Like Wilkinson, Graham's topic is the poetic process, but Graham views this process within the overly explicit Freudian concepts of libido and sublimation. In this view, post-sublimation "poetry" is not really poetry at all; it is instead the expression of self-alienation and animal libido and as such destructive, "cancerous." Graham thus disputes the poetic quality of Tasso's four "visions" canonized ever since Wilkinson. More fruitful than her contest with Wilkinson is Graham's exploration of the Platonic concept of *eros* and of imagery patterns constituted by the signifiers *web* and *spin* in *Tasso*'s text. In the light of *Tasso* history it should not surprise us that Graham's reading of the final speech is woefully inadequate: she simply ignores the closing image of the surviving sailor, in order to have the play end with unmitigated wreckage.

Articles in journals and *Festschriften* took a deliberately, even explicitly modest stance. Both C. P. Magill in *German Life and Letters* (1969) and Theodore Ziolkowski in the *Festschrift* for Walter Silz (1974) suggested a new frame for interpreting *Tasso* without themselves attempting an interpretation. Magill rather despairingly speculates that the truly competent reader of *Tasso* would have to be endowed with "unearthly percipience" and might best approach the text as if it were a musical score. After thus having ceded *Tasso* to the domain of music, he still hopes to make Goethe's text accessible to literary critics of merely earthly caliber by "domesticating" it. Read as a soap opera variation on the theme of the "hostile brothers," Tasso and Antonio, the drama would reincarnate the popular Sturm und Drang topic under a classicist guise of "universally human" relevance. Ziolkowski's new frame resets *Tasso* in the classical triad together with *Iphigenie* and *Die natürliche Tochter*, taking interpretation back to structuralist basics in a manner imitative of "comparative anatomy." Yet Ziolkowski finds that of the three classical dramas, *Tasso* fits his skeleton least, because this work is "more complex" than the other two.

Still more openly frustrated by the inconclusive history of *Tasso* criticism, Stuart Atkins in a *Festschrift* for Henry Nordmeyer (also published in *Carleton Germanic Papers* 1973) yet shows how much can be gained through a focus on partial aspects and from the work of previous critics, as he reviews them at length. Atkins's focus is on formal categories, especially those relating to genre and the reworking of traditions, and it is by this route that he finally ventures out on a new perspective of his own: *Tasso* should be viewed as a "heroic pastoral," a genre that presents not a special case of The Poet, but life's tribulations for Everyman.

Even as the experts despaired over it, scholarly readers continued to take delight in the drama. This *Tasso* paradox is exemplified and explicitly stated by John Edgar Prudhoe, who wrestles helplessly with the text in his *Theatre of Goethe and Schiller* (1973). The hero's "Hamlet-like complexity," he finds, is one of the reasons why, despite the botched ending, the drama "fascinates us more at each new acquaintance" (181–3). Another delighted reader was Alan Menhennet, for whom *Tasso* is the supreme symbol of the "classical synthesis" of *Order and Freedom* (title of his 1973 book) that the epoch of Goethe and Schiller attained. In this Goethean work, Menhennet sees the objectivity of form create a perfect balance for the hero's inwardness and subjectivity.

Critics who limited themselves to particular aspects of the drama instead of attempting an interpretation of the whole, generally came up happier and with genuine results to show for their effort. Lieselotte Blumenthal's idea (1959) that "Arkadien" should be understood as a game of poetic-mythic fiction that the characters self-consciously play, still needs to be explored. Johannes Mantey's laborious dissertation on *Sprachstil in Goethes "Tasso"* (published the same year in the German Democratic Republic) offers a useful if incomplete inventory of thematic words and their questionable meanings. The exploration of key concepts in *Tasso*, such as freedom, happiness, property, merit and so forth, from his position inside East Germany add to Mantey's study a strange sort of relevance for the historian of GDR culture.

Two superb essays, by Edmund Papst and T. M. Holmes, managed to throw light into previously ignored corners. The fourth act with its excess of monologues and the question about Tasso's insanity had always been a particular problem. Admirers of the drama routinely avoided discussing it. Papst's essay in *PEGS* of 1964 makes act 4 the subject of a theoretically founded "genealogy of delusion." In another innovative approach, Holmes's article in the *Modern Language Review* of 1970 combines psycho-analytical theory with a Marxian perspective on history. Holmes was the first Western critic to focus on historical context and ideological conflict in *Tasso*. Inspired by the historical turn of Hölderlin criticism initiated by Pierre Bertaux, he traces the return of the repressed in Tasso's conflicted attitude of "Homage and Revolt" (title of his essay) towards the Duke.

Finally, to no one's surprise, Tasso's final speech continued to fascinate, with the result as inconclusive as ever. Leonard Forster's lucid reading in the *Festschrift* for Roy Pascal (1969) should have laid to rest the tribulations aroused by Peacock and Gray on the (un)readability of Tasso's last lines. On the other hand, J. R. Williams's reflections on "Reflections" in that final speech (*PEGS* 1977) might stand as an exemplar of the dilemma, deplored by Magill and Atkins, that *Tasso* presents to criticism. With too many forebears, too much pre-trodden ground, the epigone Williams, defensive and insistent, resorts indiscriminately to a whole spectrum of Goethe texts for help with the meaning of a single image. Fortunately, help was on the way. In the same year, two studies out of Germany would initiate a new era of viewing *Tasso* inside out, their sociohistorical approach offering, in Hans Rudolf Vaget's phrase "einen Tasso von außen [a Tasso from outside]."

Unlike *Iphigenie*, *Tasso* did not arouse the passions of the academy in the Great Classics War of the 1970s. Ever the esoteric play, the drama of artistic self-reflection, it lacked the status of exemplary school classic that had propelled *Iphigenie* to the forefront of the German classics controversy. It is doubtful if *Tasso* would ever have come out of the narcissistic closet but for Peter Stein's provocative production on the Bremen stage in 1969. No theatrical event has had a comparable impact on academic criticism. Again unlike *Iphigenie*, where the decisive turn in criticism issued from within the scholarly institution — a *Germanistentag* no less — the impulse for the *Tasso* renaissance came from outside the grove of academe. And the scholarly establishment indeed perceived and repulsed the Bremen staging as an invasion. Not until 1977, the annus mirabilis in *Tasso* criticism, did the reaction to Stein's production show up in mainstream scholarship, to be followed by a second wave of *Tasso* enthusiasm three years later. *Tasso* criticism had come back to Germany with a vengeance.

On one side, Bremen was forcing traditionalists to reexamine their bases and to come up with new ideas in defense of accepted Tasso doctrine. On the other side, Bremen had opened a window for the new school of *Literatursoziologie* to recognize in *Tasso* a demonstration model for the thesis that social conditions, especially those of power and class, were first causes in literary history. Most decisive for the Tasso impact, however, was the fact that here a persistent theme of German history surfaced: the question of intellectuals and politics, so familiar in the topos *Geist und Macht* [spirit and power] or, in the leftist version now revived: "Intellektuellenmisere [misery of the intellectuals]" (Grimm 1977). *Tasso*, no longer limited to the travails of The Poet, with whom scholars could sympathize but not identify, had thus once more, as at the turn of the last century, moved into the dimension of identification.

The new wave of 1977 had promised a renaissance of sociohistorical and political perspectives, but already with the second wave in 1980 the tide was turning. As Hans Rudolf Vaget asked somewhat belatedly for "a Tasso from outside" (1980), the mainstream was again changing direction away from the political back to the personal, from literature as a social institution to the poet's psyche. In a strangely incestuous move of mutual support, the two most influential Tasso readings of the next decade proclaimed the drama a "psychogram" of poetic melancholy (Hinderer and Borchmeyer 1980).

The tug-of-war between "Tasso from outside" and "Tasso from inside" continued until the late eighties, with the sociohistorical camp increasingly outgunned. The overall result was again a stalemate, or rather, a stall-out. The harvest from the 1982 anniversary year makes this evident. In symposia and journal essays we see scholars taking sides, repeating themselves and others, and occasionally giving explicit vent to their frustrations over the inconclusiveness in Tasso criticism.

And so, while new perspectives emerged during the eighties, the difference from *Iphigenie* criticism remained marked. As regards quantity, output on *Tasso* was a mere trickle. Concerning quality, where the Taurian drama engaged a multiplicity of ideological interests and historical contexts — from feminism and othering to international law — the play of Ferrara returned to its traditional place of exclusion: the preserve of the intellect and more particularly of aesthetics. *Tasso* was examined predominantly as part of highbrow intellectual and aesthetic history, as a stop on the long road of Western cultural tradition. The new focus on literary theory in American criticism touched this drama only marginally. The mainstream found the way back to its old bed: puzzling over the ending, dissolving the obstreperous text into Goethe's oeuvre, or, in introductions to the two Goethe editions at the end of the decade, perpetuating the view of *Tasso* as the drama of The Artist's endangered psyche: "Künstlerpathologie."

The Tasso year 1977 proved the skepticism of Atkins and Magill wrong with a truly amazing demonstration of force and variety in no less than seven reconsiderations of the drama, issuing from four distinct camps in British and especially German scholarship. Essays in *PEGS* and *German Life and Letters* continued the British (Wilkinsonian) line of close reading and, in the case of William F. Yuill, showed that a precise and subtle investigation of the rhetorical features could only begin to mine the productive potential of this sophisticated Goethean text.

From the opposite corner, Ilse Graham's new approach via a much improved version of psychoanalysis, in her book *Goethe, Portrait of the Artist*, repositioned Tasso, drama and hero, in the context of Goethe's own creative development. While Graham did not offer a new interpretation, referring the reader instead to her reading of 1973, her scrutiny of a wealth of biographical texts (Goethe's diaries, letters, source material for *Italienische Reise*) radically changed the figure and signification of Tasso.

But the really new criticism was happening in Germany, unquestionably in reaction to the Bremen staging. It needs to be kept in mind that the Bremen production involved more than just the performance, even including the sensational reviews, the tours, and prizes. The exceptional impact was due to a new product on the book market: the *Regiebuch*, of which the Bremen *Tasso* was the third instance. The *Regiebuch* generally aims to "present" the performance to the reader by means of photographs, the stage version of the text, and documentary texts supporting the ideology behind the production. In the case of the Bremen *Tasso*, the dramaturgical license taken with Goethe's text was one of the main reasons for literary scholars to get involved and incensed. Furthermore, the iconoclastic views — presenting Tasso as a pathetic court clown, for instance — expressed in the accompanying texts by actors, directors, and theater critics, were enough to drive the Goethe tradition itself to madness.

It is thus not surprising that even with a long delay of eight years, the first responses came not from inside Goethe scholarship, but from the antiestablishment wing of the German intellectual scene. Bremen had made Tasso topical enough to be recruited as an agent for contemporary literary discourse. Reinhold Grimm (not a Goethe scholar) in his essay on "Dichterhelden [poet-heroes]" published in a prominent organ of the new literary left (*Basis. Jahrbuch für deutsche Gegenwartsliteratur*), claims Goethe's drama as the first literary work to have addressed the sad history of German intellectuals' lack of interest in politics. "Intellektuellenmisere," a term coined by the nineteenth century Marxist critic, Franz Mehring, had become one of the buzzwords of the rebellious generation of 1968. Goethe's *Tasso* now was seen as a pioneering text of self-criticism, an aide in the campaign against the academic and literary establishment.

The self-critical perspective drives the argument, too, in one of two seminal studies on German Classicism to be published that year: Christa Bürger's *Ursprung der bürgerlichen Institution Kunst im höfischen Weimar* (1977). In Bürger's book, *Tasso* serves as a well-known text, a classic, to support the main thrust of her sociohistorical inquiry into the relation between art and the state in eighteenth century Germany. Bürger's view on *Tasso* achieved prominence when Karl Otto Conrady published it concurrently in his revisionist volume on the Age of Goethe: *Deutsche Literatur zur Zeit der Klassik* (1977).

From then on, the Tasso controversy had found a new polarity. It was Rasch and Ryan versus Bürger and Bremen, "Tasso from inside" versus "Tasso from outside." Independent of the pros and cons over her explicit ideological stance, Bürger brought to the Tasso debate of the next decade a number of fresh ideas, concepts, and terms. Moreover, where the *Tasso* of Bremen had aimed to actualize — pillorying the present-day situation of artists and actors — Bürger changed direction to historicize. She moved the court of Ferrara out of its Renaissance distance and irrelevance into the Age of Goethe, presenting *Tasso* as a reading of the Adornian dialectic of the Enlightenment.

The most fertile of her initiatives proved to be the focus on patronage. In her Marxist materialist view of history, *Tasso* presents a structural change of that crucial institution for artistic production, reflecting similar changes in Goethe's own era. Bürger follows current Marxist doctrine, which saw in the eighteenth century a period of transition from an earlier, good concept of literature inspired by the bourgeois Enlightenment, toward a later concept of art informed by the bad values of court society and bourgeois capitalism. Goethe's *Tasso* would demonstrate the historical contradictions that characterize periods of transition. For Bürger, the drama creates an illusion of court and poet united by bourgeois family bonds and the Enlightenment ideology of *Humanität*, in order to draw attention to the hidden reality of absolutism, whose political interests use and functionalize the poet. In Bürger's reading, Tasso's path in the drama designs a historically new, bad role for art: autonomy. From the position of the new German Left, which demanded political commitment from writers and artists, autonomy meant art's alienation from and irrelevance to the world of power and real life. Bürger's Tasso is an anachronism and at the same time he anticipates the role of the artist as outsider in the nineteenth century. Goethe's text reflects critically on the "crisis of self-worth of the bourgeois writer," which in Bürger's view precipitated the birth of modern authorial consciousness. Despite its brevity and sketchiness, Bürger's essay contains a wealth of original insights that deserve to be further explored, such as instances of value reversal in Tasso's embrace of the Princess and in the epiphanies of truth in Tasso's hallucinations.

The other essential new *Tasso* reading of 1977, by Dieter Borchmeyer in his *Höfische Gesellschaft und Französische Revolution bei Goethe* [Courtly Society and French Revolution in Goethe], shares Bürger's sociohistorical perspective but not her politics, and, in contrast with Bürger's inspired glimpses from the outside, presents the thorough inquiry of a Goethe scholar and philologist. While Bürger was concerned with the social history of power and action, Borchmeyer's focus is on the sociology of attitude and behavior, on the ethics and aesthetics of different social classes. Where Bürger's sociology hails from the radical German left, Borchmeyer's authorities on sociohistory are the moderates associated with the Frankfurt School — Elias, Lepenies, Koselleck, Habermas — and, in a long overdue discovery, the British line represented by Walter Bruford.

Besides *Wilhelm Meister*, *Torquato Tasso* serves Borchmeyer as paradigmatic example to illustrate a crisis in the aristocratic value system ("höfisch-repräsentativ") of the late eighteenth century and its relationship to an emergent "bourgeois aesthetic." Rejecting Lawrence Ryan's philosophical ("spekulativ") approach (1965), Borchmeyer aims to undergird Rasch's portrait of the poet (1954) with a sociohistorical base, as illustrated in decorum, rhetorical and poetic practices, behavioral conventions. First to appreciate and explore Neumann's encyclopedic project of 1965, Borchmeyer adopts a relational structure for his own reading, but with the focus firmly on Tasso, and with the surprising result that Goethe's hero is deemed asocial, defined by "Gesellschaftslosigkeit." Victim of anachronistic, Don Quixotean fantasies, Borchmeyer's Tasso inhabits a "world of mere appearances." This poet is radically unpolitical, like his suggested model in Goethe's own time, Klopstock, merely "scheinrevolutionär [pseudorevolutionary]," and prone to "subjektivistisches Rütteln an eingebildeten Ketten [subjectivistic shaking of his imagined chains]" (70ff., 89f.).

As Borchmeyer moves ever closer to Staiger's position of *Dichterschelte* [poet bashing], blaming "modern aesthetic consciousness embodied in Tasso" for the alienation of art from society, he discovers parallels between Goethe's drama and Molière's *Misanthrope*, thus joining Staiger in his reading of *Tasso* as a character drama. By the end of his analysis, Borchmeyer's focus has shifted drastically away from his sociohistorical starting line to a perspective of individual psychology. Like Molière's hero Alceste, Goethe's hero is a "melancholic," who reflects the interest of the Age of Goethe in temperamentology. It is this angle on melancholy which would increasingly determine Borchmeyer's successive readings of *Tasso* in 1980, 1984, 1985, and 1988.

Reacting strongly against the classics bashers, in his widely read introduction to *Weimarer Klassik* (1980) Borchmeyer pursues an ideological agenda of his own, in which he aims to reempower the classics by establishing a connection between the writings of Goethe and Schiller, and political reform efforts in the German states. Borchmeyer is having a hard time recruiting *Tasso* for this argument since he has to read against the grain of the critical tradition. His interpretation wavers between his earlier sociohistorical categories ("collision of aesthetic value systems") and a new focus on the alienated poet. His view of the protagonist now is profoundly ambivalent. Following the sociohistorical stance of the 1977 book, Tasso still is in the wrong — anachronistic, subjectivist, illusionist. However, as Borchmeyer moves ever closer to the position of Wolfdietrich Rasch (1954), Tasso is also in the right, because his rootedness in mythic origins

("Vertrautheit mit mythischen Urzuständen") is the "deepest reason" of
the alienation between poet and society.

Borchmeyer's readings in the anniversary year 1982 (published in 1984
and 1985) complete the shift towards the private and individual perspective. The theme of *Tasso* now is an issue of existential psychology: "Das
Unglück Dichter zu sein [The Misfortune of Being a Poet]" (title of the
1985 publication). The other reading takes a leaf from Rasch's symbolic
laurel wreath ("Der unfruchtbare Lorbeer [The Barren Laurel]" is the title
of Borchmeyer's 1984 publication) and makes Tasso once again a brother
of Werther and Wagner.

Borchmeyer (who was writing a book on Wagner at the time) sees in
Goethe's drama an instance of Enlightenment criticism of "furor poeti-
cus," in the spirit of Schiller's castigation of the Sturm und Drang holdo-
ver, Gottfried August Bürger. On these terms *Tasso* is an indictment of
cultivated melancholy, that mark of modern poetic consciousness: "die
moderne artistische Leidensmetaphysik als pathologisches Produkt einer
um sich selbst kreisenden Subjektivität [the modern artistic metaphysics of
suffering as the pathological product of a subjectivity circling about itself]"
(1985, 84). By the end of the decade, in Borchmeyer's commentary in the
Deutscher Klassiker Verlag edition of Goethe's works (1988), the equation between artist and pathology in *Tasso* is complete: "The first artist
drama in world literature is a downright compendium of artist pathology
(1422)."

Borchmeyer was not alone in turning *Tasso* back outside in as early as
1980. Walter Hinderer, whom Borchmeyer quotes approvingly, did likewise in the first volume of the new Reclam series on the classical dramatic
canon: *Goethes Dramen. Neue Interpretationen*, published in the same
year. Hans Rudolf Vaget's plea to keep the sociohistorical perspective
open, "Um einen Tasso von außen bittend" (in *Deutsche Vierteljahresschrift für Literaturwissenschaft und Geistesgeschichte* 1980), was indeed
timely, but scholars over the next decade overwhelmingly chose to ignore
it.

Vaget's study stands today as a model of sociohistorical contextualization for literary criticism, argued consistently in the best philological tradition, and still waiting for adepts. In his effort to supply the missing factual
base for Bürger's programmatic divorce of art from power, Vaget widens
the focus of patronage from the figure of the ruler to encompass the
courtly ruling class of artistic dilettantes. The decisive factor in Vaget's argument is not "Mäzenat [patronage]" but "Musenhof [court of the
muses]." Tasso's failure would express Goethe's protest against the dilet-
tante aesthetic of Weimar court society, a protest that Vaget sees formal-
ized later in Goethe-Schiller's joint educational effort, the "Weimarer
Klassik-Programm."

Tasso study in the eighties took an intriguing new turn, toward the intellectual, not the sociopolitical aspects of history. One might think that Neumann's approach of 1965, predating the upheavals of 1968 and highly commended by both Borchmeyer and Hinderer, was finally coming into its own, as scholars began to tap into the rich thesaurus of aesthetic and cultural history that the text of *Tasso* represents. Another source for this new interest can be seen in the need to reconsider the status of German Classicism in the wake of the contentious seventies. In addition, with the internationalization of Goethe studies in general, and following Harold Bloom's innovative approach to literary influence in America, the relation of *Tasso* to intellectual and aesthetic history offered new paths of inquiry.

First in this new field, Gabriele Girschner's dissertation of 1981 displayed an unwieldy mass of material from aesthetic tradition in the background of *Tasso*. More recently, Rudolf Brandmeyer's focus on the heroic motif (1987) explored the aesthetic debate in the Age of Goethe, with Schiller and Schlegel reenacting the *querelle des anciens et modernes* [controversy between classicists and modernists] of the French sixteenth century. Across the Atlantic, *Tasso* served to deconstruct Kant with the aid of Hegel, Nietzsche, and Derrida (Ronell 1985), whereas in a British view *Tasso* exemplifies the opposite: a late Enlightenment effort at Kantian emancipation (Reed 1989). *Tasso*, we see, continued to generate contraries.

So, too, when American critics reflecting the advance of feminism there replaced the German focus on the hero with a new look at the Princess. After Ronell, who made the two Leonores vehicles of philosophical debate, the Princess affirms the traditional function of Goethe's female figures as symbols of an ideal (Ammerlahn 1990), or she deconstructs Goethean women as carriers of patriarchy (Wagner 1990). The ending, too, still tantalizes. New keys were sought in gestic language (Hart 1986), in hermeticism (Schanze 1989), and in the most microscopic examination to date of the final speech (Kruse 1990).

If we look at the big Goethe projects framing the eighties — the new *Hamburger Ausgabe* (1981), the *Münchener Ausgabe* (1990), and Nicholas Boyle's biography (1991 for the first volume) — it seems clear that "Tasso from inside" has completed his comeback. Stuart Atkins (*Hamburger Ausgabe* 1981) retreats from the sociohistorical fray to the classicist positions of Staiger, von Wiese, and Peacock. For Atkins, *Tasso* is a character drama with the intention to reveal an unbalanced and subjectivist personality. Saving the essential poet from the modern afflictions of subjectivism and madness introduced by the Romantics, Atkins pronounces Tasso's "pathology" curable. Atkins's emphasis, however, is on the formal features of *Tasso*'s language. As he explores style, rhetoric, and meter he finds in their harmonizing effect the norm by which to judge Tasso's extremist character wanting. In a moderato variation on Staiger's

"Dichterschelte," Atkins thus sacrifices Tasso the nonpoet in order to save *Tasso* the drama.

Hartmut Reinhardt in the *Münchener Ausgabe* rejects the sociohistorical perspective explicitly. Stepping back more than a century to quote at length a performance review by Theodor Fontane, Reinhardt empathizes with that eminent writer's "Ratlosigkeit [perplexity]" vis-a-vis the "shrinkage" of Tasso interpretation in the sociological climate of the late nineteenth century. Reinhardt's own "Ratlosigkeit" is evident as he relies on other critics for interpretation, dropping names and quoting voluminously. He finds his own voice, however, in the interest of dehistoricizing and depoliticizing *Tasso*. With extraordinary emphasis he asserts that Goethe's drama is absolutely clueless on the contemporary unfolding of the French Revolution: "Ein Wetterleuchten des Wandels wird in dieser Richtung (1789!) nicht auch nur von fern sichtbar [no sheet-lightning announcing change in this direction (1789!) is visible even in the remotest distance]" (923). We note the return of Brandes and Robertson here, two critics apparently unknown to Reinhardt although they are much closer in time than Fontane.

The most remarkable aspect of Reinhardt's account is the return of another forgotten figure in the history of Tasso criticism, Richard Wagner, propelled by the pervasive Borchmeyer influence here. For Reinhardt, Wagner stands as the decisive critic to propound what *Tasso* is all about: the drama of the artist. And, as Reinhardt completes Wagner's interpretation, Tasso is the artist apart from society, separated from the world of normal people by necessity as well as choice — or possibly in a sour-grapes move. Reinhardt's sub-title states it as "Die Künstler-Problematik: Autonomie und Pathologie [the problematic of the artist: autonomy and pathology]."

Nicholas Boyle, finally, assigns *Tasso* a key position in Goethe's inner biography (1991). "Spiel zum Abschied [farewell play]" indeed (title of an article by Helmut Merkl in *Euphorion* 1988), the drama for Boyle marks the half-time point in Goethe's development. A ritual of leave-taking, as Goethe mails off the manuscript on the day before his fortieth birthday, *Tasso* represents the conclusion of the first phase in Goethe's productive career: "the poetry of desire." From this perspective of closure Boyle's focus is on Tasso the poet, who turns desire into loss; the protagonist in a drama that represents the genesis of dementia according to "the perverse logic of madness" (610). More important, *Tasso* serves to define the "poetry of desire," Boyle's central perspective on Goethe in the first volume (and the volume subtitle) of his biography.

Boyle defines poetry of desire, Tasso's and Goethe's, as a transcendental kind of poetry; it is the attempt to realize in language — in symbol or "sacrament" (617) — what Faust strives to achieve in life: perfection, presence, duration. The key passage for Boyle to this poetological problem is the silkworm metaphor, where poetry is shown to self-destruct. The final imagery, on this view, merely marks the end of transcendental poetry as understood by Boyle: presenting the turn of poetry of desire into poetry of loss — and madness (625). Boyle's probing analysis, combining the tradition of close reading with exhaustive contextualization within individual and cultural history, gives unexpected comfort to the historian of Tasso criticism. His reading of this perplexing text proves that all is not lost, that there are, on the contrary, a host of windows yet to be opened, perspectives to be attempted, avenues to be explored, for a most promising beginning of Tasso interpretation of the nineties.

3: *Die natürliche Tochter*

UNTIL 1918

IF THE NINETEENTH century, until the advent of the *Künstlerdrama* [artist drama] model, did not know what to make of *Tasso*, the embarrassment presented by *Die natürliche Tochter* was worse. Faced with the question of what to do about this last of Goethe's supposedly classical dramas, scholars in fact decided to do precisely nothing. Through the first decade of the twentieth century there was not a single interpretive study devoted to the work. Biographers Lewes and Bielschowsky belittled or skipped it; editors of Goethe's works avoided discussing it by offering instead source material and a selection from standard opinions: Schiller, Fichte, Herder, Körner. If we look at what there is, and there is still a lot, we find a picture of scholarship in disarray. This is the most speckled, variegated, difficult stretch in the history of Goethe drama criticism.

What makes it so difficult to read as history is the pattern of seesawing between extremes. Successive readings oscillate, with varying amplitudes, on the major points of contention: low or high aesthetic value; public or private theme; historico-political or universally human (*allgemeinmenschlich*) import. There is no development, let alone consensus, on any of these points during the entire period. The only development to be observed, in fact, is a process of shrinkage. We see the critical horizon narrowing, the number of points addressed or insights reached decreasing. On the other hand, we find an increase in rhetorical insistence, especially on the negative, and an increasing pattern of repetitions and clichés. What this period of criticism offers is a history of obscurantism, a counterpoint to the expected path of enlightenment, as Goethe scholarship emerged and developed in the second half of the nineteenth century. Why? What was the problem that made this of all Goethe dramas such a stumbling block for criticism?

It was a variety of problems that provoked this erratic history, concerning disciplinary, aesthetic, and ideological issues. In the absence of an established opinion on the drama, the critical discipline found itself destabilized. Worst of all, and frequently mentioned, was the wide disagreement among the Weimar greats themselves, Goethe's friends and contemporary luminaries. With the usual authorities canceling each other out, there existed no authoritative opinion, no doctrine. Rather than contradict Schiller's and Fichte's high praise by siding with Herder or Körner, or assert, as Lewes could afford from his outsider's stance, that praise from Schiller and Fichte spoke against the drama, scholars withheld their own judgment, at most cautiously mixing praise and blame, preferably quoting selectively from the Weimar authorities.

If there was anything critics in general could agree on, it was the aesthetic side: this drama was not one of Goethe's artistic successes. Expressions of opinion fluctuated widely, however. The damning phrase of one reviewer contemporary with Goethe: "marmorglatt und marmorkalt [smooth and cold as marble]," was stereotypically repeated or just as stereotypically, its repetition deplored. Many conceded a particular aesthetic flaw — most frequently: flat characters or "uneigentliche Sprache [improper, not literal language]" — while explaining away other supposed shortcomings. Apologists and accusers alike sought to place blame for this drama's shape that was so different from its closest predecessors in form, *Tasso* and *Iphigenie*.

Among preferred places of blame: Goethe's interest in drama theory reinforced by Schiller's influence; Goethe's absorption in nature studies with their generalizing tendency; the unsuitable source material that made ennobling, that is, idealizing and abstracting treatment necessary; or, invidiously suggested by Kotzebue at the beginning of the century and revived by the emergent youth cult at its end, old age. Quite clearly, the age of realism had no taste for the drama's tendency toward allegory and abstraction, for this new style that announced postclassicist Goethe, the author of *Faust Part II*.

Another problem was the well-known fact that the drama was originally planned as the first part of a longer work: return of the *Tasso* dilemma of the inconclusive ending, but the dilemma sharpened by the knowledge that a specific ending was envisioned. To appreciate the scholars' quandary one should imagine that Goethe had never published the second part of *Faust* and left unanswered the question whether his hero would be damned or saved. Tantalizingly, however, Goethe's sketches for the planned sequel to *Die natürliche Tochter* had been published; and it was precisely their vagueness that enticed scholars to speculate widely and wildly on the putative course of dramatic events. (Could Goethe have planned this?)

The heroine would suffer a sacrificial death, saving her country, King, and (princely) family, or she would be destroyed by the anarchic masses together with country, King, and family. Alternatively she would experience a conversion from absolute royalism to side with her bourgeois husband, whereupon she would either be killed by one of the radical parties or lead the way to conciliation all around and a utopian state, which again might take the form of a constitutional monarchy or a bourgeois republic. Obviously, scholars read their wishful thinking into Eugenie's story, as they interpreted Goethe's thoughts on the course of revolutions and history according to their own fears and desires about contemporary events.

Writing on *Die natürliche Tochter* demonstrates that for nineteenth century Germany the issue of revolution was a matter of current events, not historical past. It is this fact that makes the criticism of that era so fascinating. German critics reacted to revolutionary history as it was played out again and again by their restless neighbor, France, always with the possibility of leaping across the border, as it had happened in the aftermath of 1789 and again in 1848. Historians have extensively documented the overwhelmingly conservative position of German Goethe scholarship of the time. What is interesting here are the ways this conservatism translated into diverse reactions of avoidance, displacement, substitution, or compensation as literary scholars dealt with the work which Goethe, according to his familiar statement, had created to express his ideas on that burning historico-political issue of the French Revolution.

With rare exceptions, our critics reveal less a conservative politics than a fear of politics, the apolitical conservatism of the evolving *Bildungsbürgertum* [educated bourgeoisie], which found itself in harmony with another much quoted and misquoted Goethe phrase: "politisch Lied, ein garstig Lied [political song, a nasty song]." Which of course also meant that the critics lacked political understanding and interest: they preferred to see *Die natürliche Tochter* as the tragedy of an individual, "Charaktertragödie," or, with the Duke as center, the tragedy of a family. The patriarchal mentality of the age could appreciate this drama on the sorrows of a father, the mature Goethe's pendant to his youthful Werther novel.

On the basis of the generic names of the dramatis personae, critics also took the drama out of its historico-political context to declare that it was a play on revolution "an sich," not on the particular event of the French Revolution. A variant of this approach accompanied the advent of scientific naturalism: Goethe wrote a "natural history of revolution," where politics was irrelevant since humans, in the naturalist doctrine, lacked free will. And of course we find the reduction favored by classicists, who made particulars such as politics and history disappear in the universal (*das Allgemein-Menschliche*).

Where political content was allowed, opinions alternated between extremes: the drama was pro- or antirevolution. For these critics, Goethe's own position on revolution and politics was at issue as well, but discussions were, in the main, brief and superficial, conclusions remained cautious and noncommittal. Marked reticence, too, reigned where the drama's critique of the ancien régime was concerned, with the exception of two points. One was the weak King, but who was also declared so kind and "liebreich [loving]" that, as one prorevolutionary critic put it, any thought of revolution would appear crazy and criminal.

The other point frequently discussed was the "lettre de cachet," the royal document that signs Eugenie over to the Hofmeisterin. Much philological acuity was expended in debating whether the King's signature on the decree was authentic or forged. Most striking is the treatment of the two officials, Gouverneur and Äbtissin. When they are mentioned at all, their knee-jerk reaction is simply passed over in silence or belittled as "almost comical." It took the outsider, Brandes, at the end of the Wilhelminian era to note the relevance of this "blind obedience" of functionaries, which reminded him of the Dreyfus case.

The more openly political readings share another feature of nineteenth century conservatism: nationalism or more precisely, Francophobia, revealed more or less openly. This aspect emerged increasingly in the years after the Franco-Prussian war of 1870–71, sometimes in rather infantile ways (Strehlke 1879), sometimes revealing the need to justify the war and its revolutionary consequences for France (Geiger 1883, Scherer 1883). Schröer's extraordinary challenge in the *Nationallitteratur* edition (1882–97) highlights the pervasiveness of this sort of political actualization: "Es ist vielleicht gewagt, es heutzutage auszusprechen, daß es einen höheren Standort giebt als den nationalen [It is perhaps a risk to state nowadays that there is a higher point of view than the national one]" (254). It was Gundolf, none less, who in 1916, toward the close of our first period raised the anti-French animus to authentic xenophobia (perhaps explicable in the middle of the next Franco-German war), which may well be one reason why he refused to deal seriously with this most specifically French of Goethe's works.

Hardly more comfortable than the political implications were the issues of civil and private morals raised by the drama. Critics expressed acute discomfort with the central topic of illegitimacy, often shying away from the "awkward title" (Engel 1909) and substituting "Eugenie." To apologize for Goethe's choice of topic and to make the "widrige [repulsive]" matter more palatable by humanizing it, they would point out biographical connections: Goethe's serious illness made him worry about his own illegitimate son; and, a rather unknown tidbit, a daughter (illegitimate, too, of course) was born and died during the drama's genesis. Eugenie's illegitimacy was the main reason why critics considered the subject matter unsuitable for Goethe's august thematic intentions and why they would argue against the play's political import.

The ending of the drama with the "Scheinehe [pseudomarriage]" demanded by Eugenie transgressed almost more against the patriarchal conventions of the time. Compared even with reactions to the scandalous ending of *Stella* advocating a *mariage à trois*, we find an amazing degree of avoidance, denial, and outright protest. An intriguing study of detail might explore the ways in which the infringement on conjugal rights, the dominant posture of the woman, and the questioning of the civil institution of marriage were felt to be, as one critic said, "verletzend [hurtful]." It is curious, too, that for all his righteousness and generosity the Gerichtsrat found no admirers; this bourgeois was no identification figure for his bourgeois critics, who damned him with lame praise. If the drama offered an identification figure at all, it was that of the grieving father — but only in his private role which, moreover, compelled a highly selective reading of the problematic third act.

This brings us to the last awkwardness facing our critics: the moral ambiguity of the characters and, by implication, the moral ambivalence of this Goethean drama, exhibited so blatantly in act 3. Critics show a rare unanimity here: they preferred to ignore the moral twilight zone, sometimes with a devious acknowledgment of "psychological improbabilities." Character analysis, the favorite approach to dramatic literature during this period, was studiously avoided. When characters were discussed in any detail, the focus was on Eugenie, Duke, and King. The unsavory characters — Hofmeisterin, Sekretär, Weltgeistlicher — got a bare minimum of text or a subtle cosmetic treatment that embellished the former two, but made the latter into an unambiguous blackguard. Practically without exception, objections to the drama's moral ambivalence, or worse yet to Goethe's moral skepticism, remained unacknowledged, or at most surfaced in finding fault with a style that allowed "Edle und Schurken [the noble and the villains]" to speak exactly the same language.

Since there was essentially no development, but much repetition in criticism over the period, we will focus on major exponents of the positions outlined above. To begin with our Königsberg philosopher, Karl Rosencranz, means to realize what the next half century might have produced if the paths he opened had been explored. Immediately following Rosencranz's book on Goethe (1847) it was undoubtedly the revolutionary events of 1848 and the repressive aftermath that foreclosed political perspectives on the drama. Discovering, as Rosencranz did, in *Die natürliche Tochter* a fundamental discourse on communism * and declaring private property the drama's central issue — Rosencranz even quotes Proudhon's provocative slogan: "property is theft" (361) — is hard to imagine after 1848, the year of revolutions in Germany and of the *Communist Manifesto*. Likewise, rejection of the drama for being antidemocratic and antirevolutionary by the liberal constitutionalist Georg Gottfried Gervinus (1842), was possible only before the 1848 watershed.

* See the enigmatic reference to the invention of airplanes as necessary precondition for Communism as political reality (362).

Property relations, however, are not the sole focus of Rosencranz's extensive analysis. As with *Iphigenie* and *Tasso,* he devotes two chapters to *Die natürliche Tochter,* the last time for a century (until Staiger) that the drama was accorded such significance in a Goethe monograph. Rosencranz's other themes pertain to the political and public sphere as well, although he tries to arrange a detour into the private sector on the marriage question, as we shall see. His second focus is the issue of class. Class structure for Rosencranz is encoded as illegitimacy in the title, drives the plot, generates conflicts and reversals, and creates Eugenie's fateful character as parvenu and transgressor.

It is in his third main theme, the motif of marriage, that an ideological blind spot manifests itself in a number of interesting deviations. Although his discussion concerns the legal aspect of marriage and its crucial plot function — in a bourgeois marriage Eugenie would lose her name and her claim to aristocratic legitimacy — Rosencranz yet assigns marriage to the universally human sphere, "*das allgemein menschliche,*" declaring matrimony a law of human nature exempt from ideological critique (364). He stresses the significance of a woman's loss of name in marriage, but in an odd argument he illustrates his point with the privileged situation of aristocratic women, who could retain their names, not with bourgeois marriage law as it applied to the case at hand. As he slides back and forth between what he knows is civil law and what he wishes to see as human nature — all the way back to the apple and Eve — he offers a striking sample of selective perception and engages in an amazing bit of mythification.

Quoting the first and last lines of the Gerichtsrat's scary and lengthy definition of a husband's despotic power over his wife, Rosencranz completely ignores the substance of that definition and merely makes the point that the husband's right supersedes even that of the King. Here civil society, originary human nature ("Urverhältnis der Menschheit"), and sentimental mythmaking join in Rosencranz's argument to safeguard the ideology of marriage:

> [Die Ehe] ist das Urverhältnis der Menschheit . . . Sie ist das Prinzip aller gesellschaftlichen Ordnung. Sie umzirkt das Weib mit heiligem Zauberkreise und bereitet das Haus zum Asyl der Sitte. [Marriage is the originary relation of mankind . . . Marriage is the principle of all social order. Marriage encircles woman with a holy magic circle and makes the home a refuge of morals]" (366).

Such mushy language is quite out of character for this sober Hegelian. It would seem that this Goethean drama inspired even rationalists to dream. Like many of his later colleagues, Rosencranz projects his own wishes on Goethe's planned sequel. He forecasts glorification of the bourgeois lifestyle in idyllic country privacy, and, for the body politic, the eventual emergence of a new, unified nation after the social and political catharsis of revolutionary upheaval is past.

The future projections of Heinrich Düntzer, in his *Erläuterungen* to the classics series, were far more extensive and specific. He devotes a full fifteen pages, more than 10 percent of his text, to narrating the sequel as if there really existed two additional dramas. It is to this sequel, too, that he assigns any political meanings Goethe might have intended, which leaves him free to read the extant drama in emphatically private, depoliticized ways. For Düntzer, the planned trilogy's aim was a constitutional monarchy, which would combine strong government with individual freedom. He thus made Goethe the contemporary in spirit of German patriots in 1859 (publication year of Düntzer's first edition), who clung to just such hopes after their failure in 1848.

In the second edition, published three years after the establishment of the Wilhelminian Empire, Düntzer could see these hopes fulfilled in the new, strong German monarchy: "den echten neuerdings so glänzend bewährten deutschen Sinn [hat Goethe] so innig gehegt wie irgend ein anderer unserer Dichter [Goethe, as fervently as any other of our poets, harbored the genuine German mind which has proved itself so splendidly in recent times]" (88). The Francophobia that engulfed Germany in the seventies would explain the way in which Düntzer revised Goethe on the subject matter of his drama. Goethe did not object, he assures us, to the French *Revolution* but to its "Bewältigung [coping with, overcoming]." Furthermore, Goethe's objection was not to the *French* Revolution, but to any "gewaltsamer Umsturz [violent overturning of government]." In fact, Düntzer's conclusion with its emphatic gesture of denial concerning Goethe's intentions in this drama could serve as a motto for his interpretive effort to avoid anything that might be understood in political or historical terms: "[Goethe wollte] ja gerade nur jede geschichtliche Anlehnung vermeiden . . . nur nicht die Beziehung auf ein bestimmtes Land [Goethe strove precisely to avoid at all costs any historical association . . . no connection whatever with a particular country]" (143).

If Düntzer avoided history and politics on the public side by a universalizing move ("da das Ganze eben allgemein menschlich gehalten sein sollte [since the whole was after all supposed to be in a universally human mode]" 143), he did the same on the private side by a naturalizing strategy. All dramatic action derives from the nature of the tragic heroine, "Heldenjungfrau" Eugenie, the drama therefore belongs to the genre of "Charaktertragödie." This strategy allows Düntzer to weight his standard segment of character analysis heavily in favor of the central figure, an innocent female victim of envy and intrigue, and to slight the others, who present far more of a problem because of their morally mixed natures and because they are the agents in the political drama, which Düntzer is trying to avoid. His most glaring avoidance here concerns the two knee-jerk officials, Gouverneur and Äbtissin. All he tells us about them in his characteristic future perfect subjunctive mood, deferring certitude to the unwritten parts of the trilogy, is that their characters would have been developed in the sequel (139).

As for the three morally ambiguous conspirators, Düntzer manages to present the Hofmeisterin as an all-good mother figure, even at the cost of putting Eugenie in the wrong, because she "ihren treuen Willen so sehr verkennen kann [can so thoroughly misunderstand her loyal intentions]." In an amazing distortion of textual fact, he adjusts the liaison between Hofmeisterin and Sekretär to the benefit of the woman. On the scale of nineteenth century bourgeois thought, any woman's value rises through appropriate role behavior: to love and be loved. ("Für ihren Wert spricht auch die Liebe." 140) He does his best to save the Sekretär, giving him a good heart, compassion, and a conscience finally overcome by dangerous political addiction.

Düntzer's archvillain is the intellectual in pursuit of higher worldly status, the figure of the Weltgeistlicher. In order to paint him all in black, Düntzer ignores entirely the strange dialogue with the Herzog in act 3. The only way in which the moral ambiguity of the drama emerges in Düntzer's account is in disguise. Düntzer displaces the problem onto language and onto the unloved French; Goethe was forced to write like this in order to depict irreligious and therefore debased French Enlightenment culture: "[weil] er den vornehmen Ton einer überbildeten, glaubenslosen Zeit nachbilden mußte [because he had to imitate the genteel tone of an overeducated, faithless epoch]" (75).

Düntzer was the only critic in the nineteenth century to get that close to individual characters with their questionable morality. Others preferred to refer vaguely to "psychological improbabilities," or they joined the trend to universalize in terms of human nature or fateful reality. Goedeke in the Cotta edition of Goethe's works (1866) and Hettner in his literary history (1870), for instance, were united in their appeal to universals, yet nevertheless arrived at opposite extremes. Goedeke offers a biographical subtext by informing on Goethe's own sorrows of a father. His humanizing approach leads him to perceive in the drama, finally, "a picture of beautiful humanity freed from contingencies," comparable to the *Iphigenie* model.

Hettner by contrast, who also glances back to *Iphigenie,* condemns the later drama for its dehumanizing treatment of individuals. He objects that the characters here are mere conceptual constructs, puppets in a "natural history of revolution." Grimm, too, in his Goethe lectures (1877) took up the idea of natural history, but he tries to develop a positive association by linking the drama with the scientific perspective of *Die Wahlverwandtschaften,* emphasizing the temporal proximity of the two works. Yet he displays acute discomfort at Goethe's "retrospective fatalism" concerning history, which distilled complex individuals into chemically pure varieties of political will. "It is frightening to see these aesthetically prepared figures appearing and acting . . . in a cold necessity, as if one set in motion a pendulum in a vacuum" (Volume 2, 182).

Readings after the Franco-Prussian War of 1870–71 took a turn toward political perspectives in an effort to actualize Goethe's drama in a more or less nationalist spirit. A crass example among our critics comes from Strehlke, editor of the Hempel edition (1868–79). His anti-French prejudice conditions his rejection of this drama, which in his view unquestionably presents "impressions of contemporary events." His own impressions of contemporary events reflect most strongly on Goethe's French source, the memoirs of a purported princess of the Bourbon dynasty. The narrator of this autobiography exhibits, he finds, "the French national character unable to bear with dignity deserved or undeserved misfortune, as today's events confirm" (10).

Other readings reveal a more troubled position, as Goethe's drama served to wrestle with the disastrous events of the latest revolution in France following the French defeat in 1871 at the hand of the Prussian army, and including the brutality and bloodshed of the Paris Commune. In both Geiger's and Scherer's discourses (1883) on the causes of the first French Revolution represented in Goethe's drama, there is an undertone of justifying or at least exculpating the German role in precipitating the more recent upheaval.

Scherer's account, surprisingly extensive for the format of his literary history, is largely devoted to political history and presents a scathing and detailed critique of government failure and its dire consequences. (Could the dismal situation of the Hapsburg Empire — Scherer was Viennese — have inspired him here?) His speculations on the unwritten parts of the "trilogy" read like a summary narrative of recent French history up to the provisional postwar government of General Mac-Mahon, when "in dem Widerstreite der Stände nach vielem Blutvergießen die militärische Gewalt das Feld behauptet [in the conflict of classes after much bloodshed, military force holds the field]" (561).

Geiger's main emphasis in his introduction to the Grote edition of Goethe's works (1883) is on the problems presented by Eugenie's unconventional marriage proposal. Yet he, too, sees the most momentous issue addressed by the drama in the revolution. His historicist perspective gives the great event its due significance, with a disclaimer of customary anti-French stereotypes. Goethe intended to show "das Ringen einer großen Nation nach Neuordnung ihrer Verhältnisse und in Folge dessen die Umwälzung der ganzen Welt [the struggle of a great nation for reform of its situation and in consequence the revolution of the entire world]." Historical consciousness further leads him to conclude the discussion of the drama's political aspect with an actualizing gesture. He draws a line from the original event in 1789 to the latest French revolution of 1871, whose "schauerliche [horrific]" events are still a vivid memory. History demands "that the misdeeds of the fathers must be atoned by horrific suffering of the sons" (Volume 5, vii). The sins of the fathers, in this argument, exculpate outside agents — the Prussian armies — as mere executors of historical necessity.

But the historian's wise equanimity quite deserts Geiger when he turns to his other focus, the conditional marriage proposal. Overwhelmed by naive patriarchal indignation, he considers it at great length as the sole moral issue of the drama; the moral ambiguities of the three conspirators do not interest him in the least. A student of pre-Freudian sexual morality would recognize characteristic symptoms in Geiger's protest against the "impossible" condition of male abstinence, against the woman setting and the man accepting this condition, and against a virgin's possessing such knowledge about conjugal mores (xiii). His outburst against the "hurtful" moral transgression in the marriage issue is the turning point for Geiger's value judgment.

From now on, his reading denounces the drama, not in his own words but in selective quotation and interpretation of critical authorities. To this end he even replaces the standard authorities, Schiller and Fichte, who had high praise for the drama, by the wives of Schiller and Herder, whose views accorded with Geiger's own objections. In the later preface to the Hesse edition of 1901, Geiger allowed the drama exactly one sentence, enough to reveal the reason for such neglect: "die [natürliche Tochter] als Drama zu verherrlichen gewiß keinem besonnen Urteilenden einfallen wird [to glorify the {Natural Daughter} as drama will certainly not occur to anyone possessing good judgment]" (58).

Schröer's introduction in the *Nationalliteratur* edition (1882–97) betrays all too clearly the need to save the drama from detractors such as Geiger. Wildly defensive and speculating widely on the sequel, he ranges all over the landscape in order to discover new points for his rescue mission, yet it is interesting to note that most of his argument bears on the drama's political aspects. More obviously than any previous critic Schröer used the drama to pursue his own political agenda. Reclaiming Goethe from anti-French nationalists, he dared pronounce that there was a higher standpoint than nationalism.

Beyond that, and surely shocking to the monarchist persuasion shared by most of his profession, Schröer claimed Goethe for the republican cause. He, too, found his particular dream of a future state forecast in Goethe's sequel, but there is an interesting new aspect to his construction of the unfinished drama. Eugenie will have to be converted from her royalist belief. She will have to realize that monarchy is no longer historically adequate. After the disappearance of patriarchal social relations with the advent of modern industrial society, absolute monarchy in Schröer's view — attributed to Goethe, of course — is an anachronism.

In propounding his view about the putative development of the drama, Schröer delivers an extensive critique of the hierarchical monarchic state, where the essentially conservative civil and military services would inevitably impede the establishment of a "Rechtsstaat [government of laws]." One might object that the uncanny relevance to the Wilhelminian state found in Schröer's critique is merely the effect of historical retrospect. Yet there can be no doubt about Schröer's critical politics in this instance. His open protest against the nationalist perspective unambiguously signals his position. We find another version of Schröer's critical politics encoded in the use he makes of Faust's final vision of a desirable future state: "auf freiem Grund mit freiem Volke stehn [stand on free soil with a free people]." Reading these words politically, Schröer declares that Goethe intended republican liberty to define the future "Staatseinrichtung [state organization]" of his unfinished trilogy (265).

With the start of the next century, three decades after the events of 1870–71, criticism of *Die natürliche Tochter* experienced a brief period of normalcy. Meyer's and Witkowski's monographs (1895 and 1899) and Köster in the *Jubiläums-Ausgabe* (1902) discuss questions of form, content, background, themes, and ideas academically: without personal or political emotions, with attention to stylistic, rhetorical, and thematic detail, and finally even with some new insights.

Still, one should not look for insights in Witkowski. He takes to new extremes the familiar diagnosis of abstraction and idealization, with the novelty, however, of unqualified endorsement. Witkowski's aestheticizing approach was in tune with turn-of-the-century perspectives on literary criticism in general. His aesthetic perspective helps to remove the drama from politics and history. In stark opposition to naturalist doctrine, in Witkowski's view truth is to be sought in ideas, not in real events and situations. Historical and political reality therefore, "die tatsächlichen Vorgänge," would be "Verhüllung [cover-up]," hiding the truth to be represented, namely, "revolution *per se* . . . the great catastrophe of monarchy" (emphasis mine).

Along with historical reality, Witkowski dismisses "alles Stoffartige [everything pertaining to subject matter]" (he uses Schiller's term approvingly): substance is irrelevant, the drama can be discussed strictly in terms of form. In Witkowski's reconstruction of literary history, Goethe was inspired by the collaboration with Schiller on their classicist aesthetic program to practice "Gedankenkunst [art of thought]." For *Die natürliche Tochter* this meant creating not characters but characteristics: royal weakness, court corruption, bourgeois high-mindedness. In this way Witkowski gets around the bothersome question of moral ambiguity; morality, like politics, is *stoffartig* [material] and therefore to be ignored.

Witkowski's reading supplies an elitist explanation for the drama's history of rejection. He states explicitly what Körner's much-quoted analysis of the unenthusiastic audience reaction in Goethe's own time had intimated: this was a work reserved for the happy few endowed with enough "strength of imagination given to only few in all epochs," enough imagination to appreciate the pure beauty of *Gedankenkunst* [art of ideas]: "pure beauty . . . the noblest form, images, . . . profound pronouncements on the great questions of mankind." Antidemocratic exclusion as a bonding device of the newly forming academic class speaks in his dismissal of "die übrigen aber [the rest of the people however]," who will turn their backs on this sublime work because of their lower needs for "stronger sensual impulses" (199f.).

Both Meyer (1895) and Köster (1902), following another contemporary trend, separate form and *Stoff* [material] to consider *Die natürliche Tochter* a drama of ideas after the Shavian and Ibsenian models. In marked contrast to Witkowski, both judge the formal qualities severely, with Köster attempting the first detailed critique of language. He explains Goethe's rhetoric of abstraction in terms of the antinaturalist intentions of classicism, yet faults the poet for the sententious, didactic, repetitious, and self-commenting speech of his characters. Above all, Köster complains in a *Tasso* pun heavy with irony, the poet lets them talk too much about their suffering: "gab ihnen allen der Dichter zu sagen, wie sie leiden."

Most interesting for our investigation is the manner in which Köster uses form to get around the drama's moral ambivalence, that silenced and repressed dilemma of *Natürliche Tochter* criticism. He displaces the question of morality into the field of language, which he has already subjected to severe blame. The worst problem with the drama's language, he states, and "profoundly hurtful for many" is the deliberate way in which the villains of the piece express their "calm and lack of contrition," whereby "the impression of depravity is heightened to the point of terror [ins Entsetzliche]" (xxxif.). Clearly Köster is deeply troubled by the presence of evil in this work and avoids dealing with it by confusing form with substance.

On the side of substance, Köster is the first productively to compare this drama to *Iphigenie*, with the surprising result that the later work is placed on a markedly higher ethical plane. Where Iphigenie was a divine instrument with a mission limited to her family, and with success already inscribed in the divine plan, Eugenie is a free agent charged with a higher mission that will pit her against her family. Unlike her predecessor Iphigenie, that re-creation of antique myth, the modern heroine Eugenie, contemporary of Goethe's own time, will not succeed in asserting individuality against the moving forces of history. And here we see another feature of early twentieth century German ideology emerge: an antidemocratic death mystique, the cult of the heroic individual who can demonstrate his (in this case, her) superior worth only by death.

In dem brutaleren Massenandrang der Gegenwart aber erliegt die einzelne schwache Kämpferin. Sie kann wie alle tragischen reinen Siegergestalten ihren ewigen Triumph nur durch einen zeitlichen Tod besiegeln [In the more brutal attack from the masses of the present age the single weak fighter succumbs. Like all tragic and pure victorious figures she can seal her eternal triumph only through a temporal death]" (xxvi).

Here, in considering the role of the individual, Köster's unwillingness to deal with history on real terms drives him to escape into heroic myth.

Concerning the historic event that produced this drama, the same unwillingness takes the form of derealization. Köster in fact emphasizes the enormous impact the French Revolution had on Goethe, but it is curious to see in his discussion of that impact how he projects his own fear of revolution into spooky experiences for Goethe, transforming reality into mere phenomena and perceptions: "schaurig beunruhigend und verwirrend . . . Gespenst . . . unheimlich-ungewöhnliche Erscheinung [horrifyingly disquieting and confusing . . . ghost . . . uncanny-unusual phenomenon]." Writing this drama would have been Goethe's effort to exorcise the fearsome phenomenon, to erase it not only subjectively from his own consciousness, but objectively from the world: "das Phänomen . . . aus der Welt schaffen" (xxvif.).

Where Köster derealized by first evoking and then exorcising the uncanny in history, Meyer (1895) privatizes the historico-political element by translating it into Nietzschean terms of will to power, generational warfare, and worship of the life force. His reading places him in the context of the youth revolt, of the father-offspring opposition which left such a pronounced mark in German literary history of the early twentieth century. The revolution, according to Meyer, signified for Goethe the struggle between desire and non-desire ("Begehr und Entsagung"), and the focus of his drama is the father-daughter relation. The father, to satisfy his desire for power, wrongfully raises his daughter so as to instill in her that same desire, creates her as instrument to serve his own desire, and eventually destroys her. The ending, for Meyer, is unmitigated tragedy. Eugenie, by renouncing legitimacy and the life it might hold for her in accordance with her father's goal, has her existence broken, her essence destroyed. It is easy to see which side Meyer is on. He emphasizes the youth factor ("the aging poet desires youthful figures") when he notes that Goethe made his characters much younger than they were in his source, the French memoir, and that he recycled motifs and language from his own youthful poetic works.

While Meyer takes a strong stand against the drama's stereotypical detractors, he still considers it a diminished work: diminished in originality, in youthful vigor, in creative force. For this biographer the drama marks the turning point in Goethe's creative life from the upward direction of youth to the downward path of aging: "der sinkenden Hälfte [the sinking half]." *Die natürliche Tochter* signals for Meyer a downward turn in history, too: from the era of Weimar's greatness to — well, its epigonic afterlife. As product and symptom of a period of transition, this drama, in Meyer's view, could hardly be a great work (310–18).

The seesaw pattern in evaluating *Die natürliche Tochter* remained in force during the waning years of the Wilhelminian era. After the measured scholarly appreciation of the three critics, Witkowski, Meyer, and Köster, around the turn of the century, Eduard Engel's treatment in his Goethe monograph a decade later (1909) can only be called hysterical. He tells us so himself when he reports that under the imbalance of the antagonistic forces in this drama, "one literally suffers physically." His interpretation illustrates a distinctive characteristic of this first period of *Natürliche Tochter* criticism: on the whole, the critics offered more insights about themselves than about the drama.

The first question to arise about Engel is why he devoted so much text (four pages) to a "verunglücktes [failed] Drama," which he obviously disliked intensely. One could suggest that Engel intended a rebuttal of the elitist stance taken in Witkowski's monograph ten years earlier. Engel protests in the name of the educated middle class, more democratically minded at least in theory, who found themselves ignored in Goethe's drama and by critics like Witkowski, in favor of a questionable intellectual aristocracy. And while Witkowski blithely dismissed substance in order to praise the drama's sublime style, Engel targets his most scathing criticism precisely at Goethe's effort to overcome "'alles Stoffartige' [all material substance]." Most unkind of all, he quotes a good number of lines from the drama to make his point that the effort produced a "uneigentlich [non-literal]" language that went all the way to "Sprachwidrigkeit [repulsive language]" and "Schwulst [bombast]."

Style, however, is merely a subsidiary issue for Engel; his main quarrel is with the drama's disregard for the "Volk." In contrast with officialdom (Gouverneur and Äbtissin) the people are kept offstage, although in Engel's view it is the people who are the decisive instance of appeal in Eugenie's search for help. More serious yet, and here Engel's rhetoric gets truly impassioned, is Goethe's unsuitable choice of subject matter. Engel's contention that the questionable rights of some princess were inappropriate to represent the great struggle for human rights of an entire oppressed people, recalls the *Vormärz* accusations of Goethe as a *Fürstenknecht* [princes' slave]. Significantly, Engel here quotes Börne's negative judgment on this drama as "Weltgeschichte als Hofgeschichte [world history as court {hi}story]." It is the mistaken equation of these incommensurate concepts that dooms Goethe's play, and Engel's affective language leaves no doubt as to his own political feelings. On one side of the unequal equation he places "an unknown mistreated half-princess . . . some Princess Conti or other . . . and her after all very doubtful rights." He weights the other side of the scale with "centuries-old repression and pillaging of an entire great people . . . the reconquest of human rights . . . and a striving upwards of a class from the yoke of slavery to civil freedom."

It may seem surprising that besides his political passion there is any room for moral indignation, yet Engel is the first to object specifically, even if still displaced into a critique of language, to the dialogue between Weltgeistlicher and Herzog in the third act. (His moral outrage includes the Sekretär here.) "Wenn diese Schurken in feierlich stilisierten Reden den trostlos jammernden Vater ansalbadern . . . so wird unser Ekel unerträglich und alle Stilisierungskünste des Dichters erzeugen nur den Eindruck innerer Stillosigkeit [When these villains in ceremonially stylized speeches babble at the father in his inconsolable lament . . . our revulsion becomes intolerable and all of the poet's artful stylizations produce nothing but the impression of inner lack of style]" (399–403).

Despite Engel's idiosyncratic attack, the fortunes of *Die natürliche Tochter* seemed to take a turn for the better; normalization seemed to continue as academic critics were trying to naturalize, finally, Goethe's *Natural Daughter* in the pedagogical province. In a first step, two essays in major periodicals (Paul Hoffmann in *Euphorion* and Eugen Kilian in the *Goethe Jahrbuch* 1911) tested the waters by way of the theater, which in the new age of symbolist poetry was showing some interest in the drama that had not been publicly performed since Goethe's lifetime.

The following year saw two book publications: a brief study on language aspects (Fries 1912) and a substantial book by establishment philologist Gustav Kettner (1912), who aimed to update Düntzer for the new century, as he states in the preface, in order to lay the foundation for scholarly work on the long-neglected drama. A tradition of academic *Natürliche Tochter* criticism was in the making, until Gundolf's damning treatment in his Goethe book of 1916 aborted the launch attempt.

Gustav Kettner wants to place the drama as a third member into the *Iphigenie-Tasso* chain, under categories established by critics such as Scherer and Steinweg: *Seelendrama, Leidensdrama, tragédie classique* [soul drama, drama of suffering, French classicist tragedy]. In the aspect of form Kettner demonstrates the drama's "high classicism"; concerning substance, his central theme of "Entsagung [renunciation]" also continues the *Iphigenie-Tasso* model, but with a nod in the direction of the Nietzsche-Schopenhauer Zeitgeist. The three main characters, Eugenie, Herzog, Gerichtsrat, with emphasis on Eugenie, have to make their way from desire to non-desire and thereby find a harmonious, ethical existence.

Other aspects of Kettner's updating effort bear on the historico-political moment. In accordance with his classicist perspective, Kettner still banishes historical referentiality: the play is not about the French Revolution, it presents history as parable, but as a parable which invites application to the present world. He devotes much text to a discussion of the "Zeithintergrund [background of the times]" presented in the drama, and, more striking still, except for the heroine he subsumes all the characters under the heading "Zeithintergrund." In his analysis, the characters are constitutive facets or representations of a typified political context.

He becomes the first applicator of his parable of history, as he reads his own time through Goethe's text, even if in the customary timid and veiled manner of scholarly decorum. The present shines through Kettner's reading of the past text in notable instances. The Mönch's cultural pessimism applies to all times of decadence ("at *all* times, especially in periods of a highly developed civilization " 115). The aristocratic usurpation of power is the result of a monarch's weakness ("Monarchy thus has become de facto rule of the nobility. And how the aristocracy exploit this position!" 94). State functionaries demonstrate silent obedience ("in schweigendem Gehorsam vollziehen die Beamten der Verwaltung und der Justiz die Befehle des Königs" 89).

On this last point Kettner is especially explicit. For the first time in our critical history, the Gerichtsrat comes in for extensive analysis, primarily in his political function. As Kettner explicates how this figure represents "a politically indifferent citizenry [bourgeoisie]" not merely as type "but literally as the ideal of the *citizen* [*bourgeois*]," we see the critic in the throes of ambivalent identification. The Gerichtsrat's ideal-bourgeois predicament of impotence in the face of arbitrary power finds Kettner's empathy, but at the same time Kettner's apologetic rhetoric reveals that he is aware of the ethical duplicity of such acquiescence. "He foregoes measuring with the yardstick of bourgeois morals [the struggles of the powerful which defy every law]. He recognizes a raison d'état which can command to commit injustice. The 'entsetzliche Gewalt' [horrible violence] outrages him, even if he is clearly aware of the pointlessness of any resistance" (106f.).

Despite the political subtext, the focus of Kettner's analysis is on the private aspects. Character and family factors are the driving power, the motivating impetus of this "first part" of Goethe's dramatic project. In fact, Kettner artfully points out flaws and lacunae in dramatic motivation and then gets around them by hypothesizing that Goethe superimposed the political implications on the action only in a later phase, "erst nachträglich" (85). The political, then, was merely an afterthought, irrelevant to the meaning of this play.

Symptomatic of Kettner's resistance to the political significance is his discussion of the royal document that decrees Eugenie's subjugation, whose authenticity had been much debated in the critical tradition. Kettner opts for authenticity but then engages in a long discourse of denial (82–88), an intricate ratiocination in defense of the kind King (83f.), who could not possibly have done such a thing knowingly or willingly: a royalist's rationalization based on much speculation: "vielleicht . . . mag . . . [perhaps . . . may . . .]" (85f.).

The exclusion of the political also motivates Kettner's explanation of why Goethe did not complete his project. The sequel, he argues, would have had to be political. Goethe, however, having chosen a classicist vessel for his thoughts on the revolution, came to realize that classicist form and political content were incompatible: "Increasingly [Goethe] had to become aware of the inner contradiction between the classicist form and the political content" (59).

If Kettner purged politics from *Die Natürliche Tochter* so that he might shelter the work in the niche of Goethean classicism, it was precisely on these grounds that Gundolf, four years later (1916), expelled the drama from the Goethe canon: this was a political text and therefore unclassicist and un-Goethean. Gundolf reacts to previous criticism all the way back to Herder: repeating, augmenting, revising, refuting, or expanding although without mentioning any names. His unacknowledged rebuttal of Witkowski, for instance, sets a nice counterpoint to Engel's refutation, seven years earlier, in the spirit of democracy. Gundolf identifies the elitist bias in Witkowski's praise ("contradiction to the judgment of the majority and gourmet taste") and transposes the earlier critic's positive terms into a negative key. Witkowski's praise for Goethe's "Gedankenkunst [art of ideas]" in this drama returns in Gundolf's reading as "dekoratives Geistgewebe . . . motivierter Denk — traum [decorative spirit-texture . . . motivated thought-dream]." Herder's laudatory metaphor for *Die natürliche Tochter* as a "Silberbleistift [silver pencil]" drawing reappears in Gundolf's negative phrase: "blaß und leer wie Stahlstiche jener Zeit [pale and empty like the steel engravings of that time]."

Ostensibly Gundolf's critique concerns aesthetic matters in order to explain the drama's failure through "misunderstood theory" — again repeating earlier analyses — and by contrasting the botched imitation with its original, *Iphigenie*. But what is so striking in Gundolf's text is that he never considers the drama itself, that he does not mention a single character or plot feature. He tells us what this work is not, on one and one-half pages: not-*Iphigenie*, not-*Tasso*; but he does not tell us what it is — except in this summary: "[Goethe's] theoretical drama [is] . . . an artificial product."

An omission of this sort signaled to Goethe scholars that the work was not worth their attention; it intended the exclusion of *Die natürliche Tochter* from the canon or, to use Gundolf's terminology in this chapter, the elimination of a foreign body, of alien matter from the body of Goethean works. While Gundolf does not use the word *Fremdkörper* [foreign body] itself, metaphors of foreign bodies frame his argument on Goethe's drama on the French Revolution.

Whereas he dedicates a separate chapter to all other major works, he subsumes *Die natürliche Tochter* under a chapter entitled "Die Revolution." The text of this chapter bears the familiar marks of ideological consciousness that we observed in the preceding history of criticism — reduction of history and politics to human nature, of social and collective events to individual agency — with one crucial difference. Previous criticism, on the whole, had exhibited aversion to political and revolutionary aspects because of a more or less naive lack of interest and understanding. Gundolf's aversion is deliberate and principled. His argument against politics and the Revolution rests on three premises, which recall other Zeitgeist documents such as Thomas Mann's *Betrachtungen eines Unpolitischen.* The first premise holds that politics ("Staats- und Parteitreiben") is not germane ("ungemäß") to a person of genius such as Goethe or anyone who would take him as a model: "no genius can be a party person or even a patriot in the sense of the state functionary or citizen."

On Gundolf's second premise, the democratic goals of the revolution, "the great abstract principles liberty, equality, fraternity," are "side issues" compared to the essential goal of human existence: realizing the humane ideal, cultivating beautiful humanity in the individual person. Gundolf's language remains in the abstract here, but the opposition of low-valued political life to high-valued inner life is evident in his terms: "rund und frei ausgebildetes . . . schönes und harmonisches Menschentum [developed and shaped round and free . . . beautiful and harmonious humanity]."

According to Gundolf's third premise, the French Revolution was alien to Goethe's genius because it was French. It was a foreign body that the Goethean-German organism could not integrate. Gundolf carefully constructs Goethe as a national poet, as he addresses the period in Goethe's life after his return from Italy, which was also the time of the French Revolution. The chapter on revolution and *Die natürliche Tochter* follows an ultrashort chapter on "Theater," which narrates Goethe's efforts to create a national theater in contrast to his earlier work for a court theater. As Gundolf tells it, post-Italian Goethe's "'theatralische Sendung' [theatrical mission]" became a *nationale Sendung,* precisely in the *völkisch* terms current at the time. "What is new in Goethe's theater efforts now . . . is the will to educate a people [Volk], or rather a 'Volkheit,' for the stage," and later, together with Schiller "to create as an after-effect [nachträglich] a national drama, i.e. unity of stage and people" (466f.).

As Gundolf next outlines Goethe's poetic attempts to deal with the revolution he distinguishes three steps, the first two treating the event "in German": as the revolution affected or was reflected by the German people "auf deutschem Boden [on German soil]." A veritable flood of the lexeme *deutsch* infuses the text here, culminating in one of the most quoted lines from *Hermann und Dorothea,* the work which criticism had overwhelmingly embraced as *the* Goethean representation of the

French Revolution (in Gundolf's phrase: "als einer Menschheits- und Deutschheits-erschütterung [as a convulsion of mankind and German-kind]"):

> "'Nicht dem Deutschen geziemt es, die fürchterliche Bewegung Fortzuleiten und auch zu wanken hierhin und dorthin.' [It does not behoove the German to transmit the dreadful movement and also to waver this way and that.]"

Here the body metaphors enter the picture, metaphors that locate the German and the Goethean encounter with the French Revolution in the field of disease or (xeno)phobia:

> Gerade dies betonte Goethe, daß . . . Übertragung der Symptome auf andere Körper ein Aberwitz sei: er hatte zu sehr den Sinn für das einmalig gewordene Eigengewächs, um deutschen Körper mit französischen Arzneien heilen zu wollen. Darum betonte . . . seine Darstellung gern das *Gefährliche* einer fremden großen Einwirkung [Goethe emphasized precisely this that . . . transmission of symptoms to other bodies was an absurdity: he had too much sense for the uniquely developed home growth and thus could not want to cure German body with French medicine. For this reason his representation tended to emphasize the *dangerous aspect* of a great alien impact]" (Gundolf's emphasis).

In his third step of dealing with the historic event, the writing of *Die natürliche Tochter*, Goethe attempted to represent the French phenomenon itself, "den *Gehalt* und Grund der Revolution [the *essence* and causes of the revolution]." Note Gundolf's one-sided emphasis on the term for the essence of the phenomenon, while de-emphasizing the causes of the revolution, which on Gundolf's view would not have been accessible to Goethe. In his misguided attempt to understand the alien phenomenon, Goethe went against his own better knowledge about incompatible organisms. *Die natürliche Tochter* thus had to become an alien, symptom of Goethe's self-alienation, and that is why Gundolf must reject it. His aesthetic criticism of the drama, then, is an effort at rationalization: finding grounds for his xenophobic rejection of Goethe's foreign work in terms of the rational discourse of his discipline. Gundolf's concluding sentence confirms the diagnosis of alienation: "So bleibt das Werk uns ehrwürdig als ein Versuch des großen Mannes das große *fremde* Ereignis auf seine Weise groß zu sehen [thus the work remains venerable for us as the attempt of the great man to see the great alien event great in his way]" (emphasis mine) (466–75).

On the heels of Gundolf's demolition of *Die natürliche Tochter* followed, seesawing again, a patriotic reclamation under the title: *Unser großes vaterländisches Frauendrama. Studien zu Goethes "Natürlicher Tochter"* [Our Great Patriotic Woman's Drama. Studies on Goethe's

"*Natürliche Tochter*"] (M. Möller 1917). Unfortunately the work does not exist in any American library — ironic testimony to the political destiny of this embattled drama. It is easy to understand why in 1917, the year America entered the war against Germany, a book with this title would have been unwelcome here.

FROM 1918 TO 1945

There is not much of a story to tell about the period from the end of the First to the end of the Second World War. Gundolf had expelled *Die natürliche Tochter* so effectively that it took until the late thirties for scholars to challenge the ruling opinion and try to rescue this Goethean work: his "Liebling Eugenie [favorite, Eugenie]" as they would explain apologetically. The historian might see a connection between the exiled drama and the mythic motif of "das edle Blut im Exil [noble blood in exile]" it inspired in the first of its rescuers, comparatist (and poet) Max Kommerell, in 1936. The literary scholar is tempted to draw a further connection between the conclusion of Goethe's text with its play on burial and resurrection, and the historical fate of the drama: the belated rescue attempts of the late thirties were buried in the ensuing war but played a decisive role in the drama's astounding postwar resurrection.

An earlier attempt, by Melitta Gerhard in the new journal *Deutsche Vierteljahresschrift für Literaturwissenschaft und Geistesgeschichte* (1923), to save *Die natürliche Tochter* on Gundolf's own terms was of no avail. Gerhard argues on the basis of biography against Gundolf, that Goethe's experience of the revolution had the intensity and impact of a psychic trauma. In her view the much maligned form of the drama is an objective correlate of experiential substance: the text's control, distance, and degree of abstraction signal the effort to repress, to hide the traumatic emotional truth.

Introductions to the two major editions of the period did nothing to change the situation. Theater practitioner Ernst Hardt in the Ullstein edition of the same year enthuses vaguely about the play but is far more concerned with Goethe's politics, which he offers as a compromise solution to the contemporary left-right antagonism: Goethe was a conservative similar to British aristocracy, "supportive of the state through inner formation and culture" (31).

Three years later in the *Festausgabe* Robert Petsch had little to say for the drama. His repetitive pattern of comparing *Die natürliche Tochter* with other Goethean works in a mode of mitigated negation ("not so much . . . but instead") sounds like the thirteenth fairy in *Sleeping Beauty* trying to undo the curse of her predecessor. Petsch's conventional reading of the theme as decayed monarchism ("vermorschter Absolutismus"), and his focus on idealistic Eugenie, pure fool doomed to a tragic end ("Volltragödie"), give the drama a distinctly out-of-date flavor, little prone to excite contemporary interest. Still more anachronistic is his treatment of the Gerichtsrat, who interests him not in the slightest. For Petsch this character represents nineteenth century federalism opposing the centralist forces of history, not the middle class bourgeois, whose ascendancy in political power we have found reflected in the earlier criticism.

Under Petsch's pen *Die natürliche Tochter* became a historical drama, a work merely of historical significance for monarchist conservatives. From this perspective it makes sense that the only "critic" he mentions by name should be Otto Ludwig, the mid-nineteenth century author of historical dramas. Petsch's historical orientation shows, too, in his devoting the bulk of his text to paraphernalia of biography, source material, and an egregiously long and detailed narrative of the putative future course of the drama that Goethe did not write.

A defensive stance emerges as he deals with aesthetic aspects, finally turning to outright critique. He assures us that Goethe was not swayed by Schiller's theories; that the abstract characters were not a result of geriatric debility; that the representation of world history in a trivial intrigue was not an error but artistic intention; that the stylization of language served to express not a particular "life form" but "world interpretation." Yet it is precisely on language, the crucial aspect of literary form for Petsch, that his judgment finally turns against *Die natürliche Tochter* as he restates Engel's devastating condemnation of the silver-tongued villains, if in more decorous terms. He warns that Goethe's rhetoric skirts moral disaster when the sublime is only a dash away from the — objectionable ("auf der Messerschneide zwischen dem Erhabenen und — dem Bedenklichen"). In Petsch's opinion this drama should definitely not be staged. Its improper language, which seems to glorify the "secular, all too secular goals" of the wicked, might give the wrong ideas to the public at large, of whom Petsch holds a very undemocratic opinion: "the brutal vulgarity of the average man" has ever been a handicap for the better angels of mankind in history. Petsch's attempt to secure a "place of honor" for this text at least among the small circle of experts who can appreciate the poet's intentions, ends by severely limiting the honor. Goethe's drama is finally a failure, a grand experiment to come to grips with historical catastrophe that remained incomplete: "großartiges Fragment" (397f.).

With friends like this, who needs enemies. Petsch's introduction did nothing to prevent, in the second volume of Korff's *Geist der Goethezeit* published four years later (1930), the outright ejection of the drama from the realm of ideas. In a vivid illustration of what one of the drama's later rescuers, Rudolf Alexander Schröder, called the "Vorgänger und

Nachtreter [forerunner and afterstepper]" syndrome (1938), Korff copied Gundolf in a more openly *Blut und Boden* [blood and soil] vein. The work, he finds, sorely lacks "Goethean poet's blood." Declaring it, with Petsch, a fragment ("Torso"), he can then, now following Gundolf, ignore it in favor of *Hermann und Dorothea* for giving us the authentically Goethean ideas on revolution.

The German situation in turn did so little to stimulate English criticism, that Robertson in his monograph (1927) could afford to repeat negative clichés about a work he may never have read. (His plot narrative is erroneous.) Fairley in his anti-Robertson study of 1932 sees no need to correct Robertson on this point. For a *Goethe as Revealed in His Poetry* the un-Goethean *Natürliche Tochter* would be irrelevant; Fairley does not even mention the work.

There is, however, an aspect to this apparent nonstory that makes it worth telling after all. The Goethe year 1932 rekindled interest in his "political" play; after a twenty-year interval there was even a stage performance.* It is difficult today to imagine the intense ideological atmosphere in which Goethe, this "greatest of Germans," was commemorated, claimed, and reclaimed by the various parties in their final battle for power on the eve of the Third Reich. Abandoned by Goethe scholarship, its complex problems unexplored and uncontested, *Die natürliche Tochter* was just waiting to be picked up by ideologues to serve their apologetic or propagandistic purposes. It took three such unabashedly ideological publications (1933–35) to provoke the three belated efforts at interpretation by literary scholars Max Kommerell, Rudolf Alexander Schröder, and Kurt May (1936–39), which would provide the foundation for *Natürliche Tochter* criticism after 1945.

One of the ideologues can be dealt with very briefly. *Studienrat* [Gymnasium teacher] Wilhelm Willige, in a pedagogical journal (1934), used Goethe's text for a naive exhortation of youth in the spirit of heroic faith and self-sacrifice for folk and fatherland. To be taken more seriously is Willige's repeat performance, under an ideologically honed title ("Gemeinschaftsgesinnung [community mindedness]"), a year later in the official journal for German teachers in secondary schools, *Zeitschrift für Deutschkunde*. His essay leaves nothing to be desired for a model German teacher from hell in one of Wolfgang Borchert's postwar stories, as he presents an interpretation of *Die natürliche Tochter* that carries all the right messages. Without reference to the critical status of the drama, without documentation or annotation, the essay clearly is out of bounds of the scholarly discourse. Its publication nevertheless demonstrates what can happen if a critical vacuum is allowed to develop around a major work of a major poet.

---

* In Dresden 1932; see Willige 1934.

Of wider significance is the other instance of ideological appropriation, an essay by Adolf Grabowsky published in the *Zeitschrift für Politik* (1933), which he coedited. Grabowsky is familiar with the Gundolf-induced critical paralysis and levels some heavy charges at Goethe scholarship generally. He presents interesting new views of literary aspects designed to redeem *Die natürliche Tochter* from limbo: the drama is the beginning of Goethean romanticism, not the weak tail end of his classicism; the father-daughter relation is modeled on Goethe's relation to Christiane Vulpius and carries complex erotic and gender-conflict meanings; Eugenie's fringe situation between two classes is fraught with the ambivalent experience of Goethe's own, and even more Christiane's social "Zwitterexistenz [hybrid existence]."

But Grabowsky's main focus is political. For him, the key to understanding the difficult work and the reason why Goethe did not write the sequel, is Goethe's attitude to politics. Here again, the absorption of Weimar era intellectuals in the controversy over "politics yes — politics no" supplies the background. Predictably, as editor of a journal for politics, Grabowsky argues for intellectuals to engage actively in politics and uses Goethe's drama as evidence to support his argument. According to Grabowsky, in the heroine's crucial decision to dedicate her life to a political future Goethe rehearsed for himself the "Wandlung [transformation]" from a private to a political existence — but then he did not go through with it. He did not write the sequel where Eugenie would have had to engage in political action, not merely anticipate it.

Concerning the goals of political action in his own time, Grabowsky leaves his readers in no doubt. Again claiming Goethe's biography ("he was a conservative revolutionary" 107) and the drama for supporting evidence, he agitates for "conservative revolution." He discovers the ideology of conservative revolution in *Die natürliche Tochter*. The drama's spirit is nationalist and *völkisch* but not democratic; the plot reveals the need for social and governmental "Umsturz [revolution]," and embraces a despotic Führer mystique ("der heftige Wunsch nach wirklichen Führern . . . begnadete Führer . . . aber nicht aus dem Recht der Masse, sondern aus eigenem Recht [the vehement desire for real leaders . . . supremely gifted leaders . . . not by the right of the masses, but by their own right]" 103).

In 1951 a substantially revised version of this essay became the first postwar study of *Die natürliche Tochter*. Published in the *Goethe Jahrbuch* under the slightly revised title, "Goethes *Natürliche Tochter* als Bekenntnis," — the original had been entitled: "Goethes *Natürliche Tochter* als politisches Bekenntnis" — it has since been carried in Goethe literature as a study of the drama as expression of an existential crisis. Needless to say, in the 1951 version the political focus was gone, Goethe's political orientation had been changed to a lukewarm liberalism, Grabowsky's to a sort of apolitical existentialism that pronounced itself pro-life and therefore pro-change. In the confused history of twentieth century Germany, Goethe's political drama had become an exhibit for intellectuals' nimble adaptation to changing political circumstances, and for the astonishing feats of historical forgetfulness.*

The reappropriation of the alienated drama by literary criticism in the late thirties had a propitious start in two respects. Two critics who took up the cause, Kommerell and Schröder, brought fresh perspectives from their own work as creative writers, and in Kommerell's case from the new methods developed by comparative literature. Furthermore, it so happened that the three essays which comprise the prewar *Natürliche Tochter* renaissance took their explorations each into a different basic dimension of a literary work: the structuring motif or fable (Kommerell); the ideational substance (Schröder); and the forms of representation (May). In this way the drama was revealed as a fully fashioned aesthetic object worthy of scholarly attention, which demonstrably repaid critical labor. It was the same multidimensionality that made this slim body of publications serve as model for the broad postwar surge of critical interest in *Die natürliche Tochter*.

Despite the prominent display in postwar *Natürliche Tochter* criticism, especially in Josef Kunz's commentary in the *Hamburger Ausgabe* (1952), Max Kommerell's focus is not on the drama itself. In his brief but beautifully crafted essay in the *Neue Rundschau* (1936), *Die natürliche Tochter* is one of many works Kommerell uses to trace the motif of "das edle Blut im Exil [the noble blood in exile]" through Goethe's oeuvre. Yet he makes this text his centerpiece. On two pages in the middle of the essay, under the subheading, "Iphigenie, Elpenor, Natürliche Tochter," Kommerell gives it the longest, most detailed and sustained analysis of the works he considers. Taking his start from (Gundolfian) *Wesensschau* [view of the essence] — "Goethes Wesen ist auf Dauer gerichtet [Goethe's essence is oriented toward permanence]" — Kommerell follows the motif of the exiled prince or princess beyond Goethe through folk and other traditional literature all the way back to the myths of antiquity. His archeology demonstrates the comparatist's method of reading the archetype through its multiple representations. It was this approach, and the existential meanings Kommerell discovered on the way, that was eagerly grasped by postwar criticism. In the context of its own time and of the situation of German Goethe scholarship, Kommerell's reading was an attempt to cope with the troubling course of current history. Kommerell proposed a mythic vision, where history appears as bad in-between times ("Zwischenzeit"), with nature as the guarantor of eventual restoration of

---

* Hermann's "Auswahlbibliographie" in *Goethes Dramen* (Hinderer 1980, 342) lists a compound error. The first publication is given without "politisches" in the title; the 1951 publication is called a "Wiederabdruck."

good times ("Wiederherstellung"). Or, in the language of ideology critique, Kommerell performed a reduction of history to mythology with evidence supplied by high literature and folk art.

He categorically opposes bad "Geschichte [history]" to good "Gedichte [poetry]": "Das Alte Wahre [ist] der Stoff allen Gedichtes [Originary Truth is the subject matter of all poetic literature]." Concerning Goethe and *Die natürliche Tochter* specifically, Kommerell's myth of eternal recurrence subsumes the political history. The drama is "the universal, the recurrent [narrated] as a political event," Kommerell asserts in his introduction; and again in the conclusion: "[political history] becomes myth in the drama."

But as the critic traces his archetype in Goethe's works, we see his own historical situation shining through. The motif of nobility in exile is portrayed as the deep structure in family, social hierarchy, and identity. When the social elite ("Oberschicht") experiences an identity crisis because it is no longer pure; when the best are tarnished or driven out; when the truly great can be heroic no longer in action, merely in victimization, death, or exile; when followers and servants ("Kanzler und Priester" as in Hitler's title *Reichskanzler*) usurp sovereign powers; when poets can only find their identities as exiles: then is the era of illegitimacy, a time of usurped power. Myth decrees, however, that this interregnum ("Zwischenzeit") be followed by "return of time," when true identities will be revealed and true order restored, as modeled archetypally in Odysseus's "recognition and homecoming" and at least anticipated in Goethe's *Die natürliche Tochter*.

The poet and consummate artist Rudolf Alexander Schröder would seem an unlikely critic to take an interest in Goethe's embattled drama. His essay in the *Goethe-Kalender* of 1938 is clearly motivated by the political situation and by Schröder's own opposition to the Nazi regime. Schröder was a member of the *Bekennende Kirche* (the anti-Nazi part of the German Protestant Church), and his contemporaries, or at least the readers of the *Goethe-Kalender*, would receive his essay with that perspective in mind. Today's readers will find his text an intriguing study in *Tarnsprache*, the language of camouflage. In a far more subtle and literary way than the earlier ideologues, Willige and Grabowsky — whose existence he does not acknowledge — Schröder actualizes *Die natürliche Tochter* as Goethe's teaching voice warning against the dangers of revolutionary times still continuing today. We can hear through his reading a pervasive insecurity and a mounting fear in the face of the future, beginning with the collective "Erschütterung [strong emotional impact] " experienced at the unique Munich performance of the drama on the eve of the First World War ("ein paar Jahre vor dem Krieg" in Schröder's 1938 chronology). It is the recollection of this catharsis through the dire forebodings of the play that now, on the eve of another war, serves as the starting point for Schröder's analysis of Goethe's text.

Going all the way back to the insightful "philosopher" Rosencranz, blasting later critics as "Vorgänger und Nachtreter [forerunners and aftersteppers]," he insists on the political meaning of the drama. Schröder himself, however, offers an explanation for the history of misunderstanding that he deplores. In his emphasis the drama is essentially symbolic, not typical, idealizing, and abstracting as traditional criticism maintained. Schröder takes pains to point out that the meaning of symbols cannot be neatly limited. Thus Goethe's symbolic "meaning" includes the present and the future — the revolution of Goethe's time and "our time" — extending the personal into the political, the spiritual into the historical.

Schröder's reading of Goethe's symbols reveals a mythic conception of history, which allows him to connect the drama with classical antiquity and with his own, Christian mythology. In his use of the symbol to expand the textual meaning, including both plot and characters, from the private and personal into the public and political, the focus is on power. The figure and fate of the Herzog, in Schröder's reading, recall on the personal level the ironic tragedy of Oedipus, who suffered the deserved consequences of hubris or "Gottverlassenheit [divine abandonment]." The collapse of the father in the third act, however, is a prelude to the collapse of the ancien régime — with unmistakable allusions to the current regime in power in Germany.

Schröder's most emphatic rhetoric throws into focus the figure of the King as an ambiguous symbol of power, which in Schröder's Christian view is by definition ambivalent. Royal "impotence" claiming to be "omnipotence" produces idolatry in the first two acts. The last two acts reveal the "zweideutiges Götzenbild [ambivalent idol]" of secular omnipotence ("Erdenallmacht") as satanic and destructive. Eugenie, finally, *die natürliche Tochter*, is natural woman, whose egregious Fall is the harbinger of her future existence in living death ("Scheintod"), and whose musings on guilt spring from the issue of "originary sin." In his discussion of the ending, Schröder moves the figure of Eugenie back into the field of political meaning in unusually explicit terms. Her renunciation in the personal sphere will transform into historical power. As she disappears into anonymity Schröder looks ahead to the day of revolution, when the anonymous masses will fashion precisely from their anonymity "the most terrible instrument of power of all times."

Schröder perceives Goethe's solution to the enigma of history as ambiguous: "One can call [the solution] . . . a reconciliation and at the same time a catastrophe," as ambiguous as the drama as a whole. His own conclusion, that *Die natürliche Tochter* was Goethe's testament of "unausschöpfliche Belehrung in unausdeutbare Zukunft weisend [inexhaustible instruction pointing into an uninterpretable future]," is not just a clever bit of rhetoric, it expresses the mood of uncertainty in the face of current historical developments. But beyond the reaction to political reality,

Schröder's reading uncovers indeterminacy in the literary text, a phenomenon that he locates in his innovative concept of the symbol. It speaks for the quality of Goethe's text that despite Schröder's Christian-exegetical prejudice, he did perceive the inexhaustible meaning potential of this drama.

In marked contrast with Schröder's regime-critical stance, Kurt May, in the last study of the thirties (1939), is in thrall to the new ideology. Yet, unlike Grabowsky and Willige, he does not attempt to appropriate Goethe's text; on the contrary, he offers an argument for the rejection of the drama on ideological grounds at the same time as he makes an explicit methodological case for its aesthetic appreciation. We witness here the origin of what came to be called *werkimmanente Interpretation* [intratextual interpretation]. After Robert Petsch's essay in 1937 on *Iphigenie* in the same forum, the *Goethe Jahrbuch*, May in 1939, dedicating his own study to Petsch, pioneers Petsch's text-based approach in explicit contradistinction to the Gundolf-Korff line based on life and thought, which had up to then dominated Goethe scholarship.

If May does not mention Gundolf or Korff, nor any other critic except Petsch and Kettner, this points to another root of the new method of *Interpretation*: the insularity of German academic criticism of the period. In a case of critical neglect, such as *Die natürliche Tochter*, the insularity came to approach the discursive space of a tabula rasa. Critical discourse now excluded, in addition to the unmentionable ideologues Grabowsky and Willige, exiles and Jews. One could not write about Gerhard and Gundolf, who were the only two voices who had said anything substantial on the drama since post-Neanderthal Kettner. May in fact uses major points made by Gerhard and Grabowsky, but without attribution in either case (148f.,157).

May's effort to separate and thereby save interpretation from ideology results on the one hand in more attention to textuality: "Gestaltung [formation]" is a major focus of his essay. On the other hand, May's own situation in the midst of ideological conflict transforms his study into a search for distance and objectivity, for balance and compromise, and finally turns into ambiguity. In frequent methodological asides, he insists on distancing. Goethe's text must be approached as past, as part of its own historical context different from every present, as evidence therefore of a "fremd [foreign, alien]" mentality that could no longer be considered normative. May practices historicization as emancipation from Goethe, the now irrelevant mentor.

However, his very belief in the objectivity of distance is modeled on Goethe's own alleged distancing, in the writing of his drama, from the oppressive presence of the French Revolution. In a variant of the pattern of identification, May projects onto Goethe his own belief in the objectiv-

ity of form, in the restorative, even healing (*bewältigend*) power of representation — the belief which is the foundation of his interpretive method.

In the text itself, May finds everywhere the effects of distancing in a
lesser degree of reality, which, however, is disturbingly ambiguous: the
"Wirklichkeitsgrad einer seltsam zweideutigen Halbgeschichtlichkeit [de-
gree of reality of a strangely ambiguous half-historicity]." He locates this
half-historicity in the mysterious dramatic events and in the nonevents,
when decisive agents and actions are suppressed; in the anonymous characters who symbolize themselves and their ilk; and in the schematized scenic
settings that anticipate symbolist and expressionist drama, where statu-
esque figures interact in a neatly scripted choreography. Distancing produced a more clearly definable objectivity in Goethe's language, to which
May devotes the longest and most detailed part of his examination. He
shows how the entire range of linguistic elements — diction, meter and
rhythm, grammar, syntax, sententious style — strive to transform tempo-
rality into permanence, to transcend history in the "Überzeitlich-Über-
geschichtliche [supra-temporal, supra-historical nature]" of "permanent
Being" (160, 158).

May sees the same principle of reality reduction at work at the level of
substance, where the social and political forces of history are transformed
into tensions and interactions that lead not to solution but to balance,
compromise, and ambiguity. And it is here that May's own ideological
conflict surfaces in the position he assigns to Goethe and in his own response to Goethe's position. On one side he places, in Nietzschean terms,
the ineffectual monarch whose "disturbingly weakened consciousness of
dominance and broken instincts of power" have forfeited his claim to rule
and, with empathetic admiration, the doomed idealist Eugenie. On the
other side he sees "the God-ordained right in its own order . . . human
culture altogether . . . the moral and religious order of mankind" threatened by selfish individuals. Equally selfish is the populace, driven by
wholly negative democratic interests: "the liberation of all individuals to
achieve equality, which means for each the satisfaction of their own arbitrary desires."

The middle position between the warring sides is assigned to the
Gerichtsrat, representing the Goethean compromise of *Bürgerlichkeit* [civil
society of peculiar, nineteenth century German type]. Here May's rhetoric
proclaims unreserved approval, yet his Biedermeier subtext calls up the solidity, limitation, and stagnation associated with that era: "an inner realm
of permanence and security . . . sheltered in unshaken and unshakable
originary forms of human existence" (151f.). And then, in a surprising
turn, May rejects the Goethean compromise in terms that reveal his own
ideological ambivalence.

May's contemporary readers, he tells them, will feel in Goethe's compromise, in the "defensive posture of *bürgerlich* man of the early Bieder-

meier era," a tension with the "'political' in the present meaning of the term." This tension, May argues, can only be resolved by perceiving Goethe's position as belonging to a long gone past history. For May there is an "infinite distance" between Goethe's values and those of his present time, one and a half centuries later. May does not embrace the new values wholeheartedly but with ambivalence, in a willy-nilly compromise. If he justifies the new, political values of the Third Reich by the dangers threatening the state ("dangers which threaten us in the realm of the 'violent', movement of history, in our situation among world powers"), he yet recognizes an element of compulsion in that new order: "so gebietend wie gerechtfertigt [as commanding as it is justified]."

May's ambivalence shows above all in his final gesture of nostalgic regret toward the solution of secure *Bürgerlichkeit* offered in the drama. "In the end there is — an awakening as if from a dream of vanished prehistory [Vorzeit]." The beautiful prehistoric dream of peace was engulfed in history; it has been taken away from May's own time by historical events, as he assures his readers in emphatic repetition: "Uns ist nicht mehr gegeben noch möglich noch erfahrungsmäßig erlaubt . . . in jenem inneren Bereich der Dauer . . . geborgen zu leben [To us it is no longer given nor possible nor permitted by experience to live sheltered in that inner realm of permanence]." Nostalgic regret, however, is balanced in May's concluding paragraph by enthusiastic acclaim for "an emphatically 'political' literature, in the new sense of the term," which would adequately replace Goethe's no longer adequate work. While political literature of this sort already exists but presumably lacks aesthetic quality, May fervently hopes for a renaissance of drama: "A future German drama, which we longingly await, will be political and poetic" (162f.).

Finally and just as decisively as Gundolf and Korff had effected the disappearance of *Die natürliche Tochter*, if with delayed impact due to the war hiatus, Emil Staiger in 1939 from his offstage Swiss vantage point set the stage for the drama's postwar resurgence.* His unassuming study of three poets, *Die Zeit als Einbildungskraft des Dichters* [Time as the imagination of the poet], modestly subtitled *Untersuchungen zu Gedichten von Brentano, Goethe und Keller*, was to become a basic book in postwar scholarship's rebirth in the name of *Werkimmanenz*.

At the time of first publication, Staiger's book engaged in a veritable strategy of stealth to smuggle the exiled drama back into the Goethe canon. *Die natürliche Tochter* does not appear in chapter titles or in the table of contents; there are no chapter abstracts where the drama would be mentioned, nor is there an index. Staiger has hidden his contraband well.

---

* The middle chapter of his book, which concerns us here, is based on a course given at the University of Zürich in summer 1938. First published in 1939, the second edition in 1953, with new copyright, was the real take-off point for this important study.

Yet *Die natürliche Tochter* is the centerpiece in his enthronement of Goethean Classicism as new humanism, based on neo-Kantian transcendentalism and Humboldtian "Innerlichkeit [inwardness]." As he undertakes to dismantle the traditional methods of German literary studies, from Scherer-type philology to Gundolfian *Erlebnisdichtung* [poetry of experience] and Korffian *Geistesgeschichte* [intellectual history] he selects for one of his linchpins the Goethean work that Gundolf and Korff had so signally discarded.

The central chapter of his triptych of poets deals with Goethe and purports to interpret the poem "Dauer im Wechsel," yet Staiger takes most of his evidence from our drama's third act, "which shall occupy us many more times" (113). Given the status non gratus of the work and particularly of act 3, this programmatic gesture had iconoclastic overtones. More revolutionary still was Staiger's demonstration of how his decontextualized method of interpretation would allow problematic issues of real life and history to be ignored. Without even a hint of the moral dilemmas that had so vexed previous critics, Staiger liberally quotes the Weltgeistlicher as pure spokesman of Spirit, who would embody the Staiger-Goethean philosophy of permanence in change.

Staiger's rehabilitation of *Die natürliche Tochter* was complete. If the purpose of his argument prevented his presenting a sustained interpretation of the work as a whole, he nevertheless addressed and transvalued, often with amazingly adulatory rhetoric, precisely those aspects that had caused qualms and controversies in the past. His purification of the Weltgeistlicher is only the most egregious example. He gets rid of the stumbling block of the French Revolution by declaring political and historical reality incompatible with Goethe's classical view of time as essentially stationary, in the sense of the Greek *kairos* [moment of fulfilled time].

From this perspective a revolution is incomprehensible and thus an impossible subject for poetic treatment. Revolution is to be ignored as "das Nichtige . . . das Sinnlos-Ungestalte [the nothingness . . . the meaningless monstrosity]." The blame then for Goethe's failure to cope poetically with the revolution in this drama, a failure represented by the problematic figures of Sekretär, Hofmeisterin, and Weltgeistlicher, should be placed on history itself. The three figures need not be considered as characters; it is really History that shows up, through their words, as the *figura non grata* in the poetic work.

Eugenie, by contrast, is raised in Staiger's revaluation to signify the highest achievement of Goethe's art: in her figure experience and idea unite in symbolic representation. Staiger postulates that such symbolic art inspires in the reader a similar synthesis of experience and idea, enabling through readerly "Nachvollziehn [imitative performance]" an ideal experience: "den Augenblick, in dem das Ewige aufglänzt [the moment in which the eternal radiates]" (157). Staiger solves another problem of long standing in *Natürliche Tochter* criticism. He saves the anonymous figures from abstraction and from the negative connotations of the type, or worse yet stereotype, into the positive category of ideal-type. Staiger derives his concept of the ideal-type from Goethe's *Urpflanze* [archetypal plant] and then transforms it into classicist Goethe's understanding of the symbol. The symbol in this understanding is an artifice ("Kunstmittel") used to announce signification.

Staiger's prime example of this symbolic function is the drama's "significant" opening: Eugenie's fall from the horse promising her eventual "Auferstehung [resurrection]" (137f.). For the symbol as embodiment of ideal experience in a rhetoric of the sublime, Staiger chooses the dressing scene, when Eugenie puts on the clothes and jewels from the forbidden treasure. Reproducing Goethe's rhetoric of the sublime here, Staiger does his best to convey exalted meaning to the banal scene. (I apologize in advance for the touch of absurdity in the following quotation and for the awkward translation of Staiger's impossible text.) The event proffers the

> unbegreiflich schöner Anblick, wie der Mensch das scheinbar ganz Zufällige, Spielerische des Tags mit Bedeutsamkeit durchwirkt und so das wohl nur Goethe in solchem Zauber eigentümliche Schillern zwischen 'Jetzt und Da' und 'Jederzeit,' das eben den klassischen Augenblick ausmacht, zustandekommt [incomprehensibly beautiful sight of man weaving signification through what appears to be entirely incidental and playful in everyday life and in this way generates a fluctuation between 'Now and Here' and 'Every-time', which is probably in this degree of magic uniquely Goethean, and which precisely constitutes the classical moment] (139).

Staiger's revisionist reading divests this scene of its heroic meaning, where past criticism had seen the *Heldenjungfrau* assuming her sacrificial role on the altar of monarchy. He invests her instead with the higher status of New Woman in the hoped-for renaissance of the Goethean spirit. Among postwar critics, Staiger disciples all, Eugenie in her new role would experience a veritable apotheosis.

Likewise in the area of language, where the drama's detractors had found plentiful ammunition, Staiger sees spirit doing its work of *Aufhebung* [sublimation] on reality and on the hearer or reader. The sententiousness on this view is evidence of "spiritual union," the verse, especially in the stichomythic passages, of a symmetry a priori, performing in the interplay of meter and rhythm a balance of magic and control that irresistibly yet freely draws the hearer into its spell. The conspicuous paraphrases finally, those awkward "Umwendungen" for which Petsch tried so hard to apologize, arouse Staiger's highest enthusiasm. "In the incomparably beautiful phrases" such as "der Stirne schöner Raum [the forehead's beautiful space]" he sees Herder's *Silberstift* effect: language making reality transparent for spirit (142 f.).

For postwar critics, especially after republication of Staiger's book in 1953, this interpretation of *Die natürliche Tochter* was an epiphany. The slate was wiped clean again of earlier criticism with its manifold objections. The erstwhile ill-reputed drama was spectacularly rehabilitated. Moreover, Staiger's method had shown how to cull pure thoughts from impure texts. As postwar Goethe scholarship searched for new beginnings after its ideological disaster, here were new discoveries to be made, fresh fields to be plowed in the terra incognita of this neglected Goethean drama.

SINCE 1945

The key to the astounding success story of *Die natürliche Tochter* after 1945 can be seen in the fact that criticism had to start from scratch. This had its disadvantages, as our exploration will show; but they were far outweighed by the advantages. Any scholar can imagine what it must have meant to find a fresh text in the overworked Goethe canon. Moreover the situation of German academics, more or less compromised by their immediate past performance in the Hitler era, made the opportunity of a new beginning particularly welcome. It meant not having to look at the past but being able instead to stride forward unencumbered; in fact it meant a *Stunde Null*, Zero Hour: the historical situation claimed and proclaimed by the writers of the new postwar German literature.

With the exception of Kettner's philological dinosaur of 1912 and Schröder's *Goethe-Kalender* essay of 1938, there was no usable work on *Die natürliche Tochter*. Melitta Gerhard's lone article of 1923 had effectively disappeared from view until its republication in 1966. Kurt May's article in the *Goethe Jahrbuch* (1939) should have been part of the embarrassment over the scholarly past. If the essay was nevertheless cited in bibliographies of early postwar critics, it only goes to show the dearth of work on the piece. Korff's standard work on *Goethezeit* (1930), dismissing the drama with one sentence, had created a vacuum that simply called out to be filled. And while there was no body of criticism dealing with the work itself, the drama was not entirely absent from academic writing; it was hibernating, as it were, in diaspora. We have seen the significant presence of *Die natürliche Tochter* in Emil Staiger's 1939 study, *Die Zeit als Einbildungskraft des Dichters*. With the advance of *werkimmanent* interpretation and Staiger's rise to a leadership position in the new method, his book had become a basic text of postwar literary studies.

Another basic book helped spread the gospel of Eugenie among Goethe professionals, even if somewhat more slowly due to its considerable bulk, but in the final analysis far more effectively. It was Wilhelm Emrich's *Symbolik von "Faust II": Sinn und Vorformen* [Symbolism of "Faust II": significance and preformations], first published in 1943, at a time when no one in Germany had attention to spare for heavy academic tomes on esoteric literature such as the second part of *Faust*. Emrich counted *Die natürliche Tochter* among the significant *Vorformen* of *Faust II* symbolism; in fact, he paid the drama so much attention that the first critical study of *Die natürliche Tochter* in English could declare that as far as symbolism was concerned, Emrich had said it all (Boeschenstein 1956). The profession at large obviously did not think so, and after Emrich's second edition in 1957, with a third following in 1964, mining Emrich was the favorite method of *Natürliche Tochter* criticism until the paradigm change in German scholarship of the late seventies.

Other reasons for the drama to be brought out of the closet had to do with literary developments in general. As we have seen, the fact that Goethe never wrote the sequel had counted as a major point against the extant text, which might at best be considered, apologetically stated, "ein großartiges Fragment [a grand fragment]" (Petsch 1926). But now, at a time when Kafka's unfinished novels were being discovered as masterworks, the status of fragment was no longer necessarily a liability. To the critical avant-garde it could instead be an attraction. It is surely no accident that Emrich, who had meanwhile taken up Kafka in a big way, should become the most passionate champion of Goethe's long neglected drama.

By the same token, as the focus in Goethe scholarship shifted from classicist perfection to the postclassicist works and particularly *Faust II* with their multiplicity of unconventional forms, a different light fell on the weird form of *Die natürliche Tochter*. Formerly decried as belated, failed or overdrawn classicism, the drama was now said to constitute an art form sui generis, provisionally termed "incomparable" (von Wiese 1948; Staiger 1952 [Volume 2, 1956]). It was this formal aspect that would later pit traditionalists against modernists, as both camps staked their claims to Goethe's last completed drama in outwardly classical form.

Concerning content, finally, this most contemporary of Goethe's major dramatic works and the only one with explicitly political and social themes, offered significant contributions in the various campaigns to reconsider and reshape the image of Goethe. The first campaign on the bicentenary occasion was too early for our drama, which in 1949 was still in hibernation; we have seen how *Iphigenie* and the avoidance of tragedy held sway. But in the next round, in the classics war of the seventies, *Die natürliche Tochter* became a major player, an antidote to *Iphigenie*. In the same measure that *Iphigenie*, the exemplary (school) classic, came under attack as affirmative literature in thrall to false consciousness, "Eugenie," the not-yet-canonical un-classic, was promoted as testimony for Goethe's sociopolitical consciousness. It was at this point that the first real discussion of the drama took place; the lack of focus and perspective in criticism of the time shows the problems of integrating a new work into the canon.

By the last wave of Goethe revision, in the anniversary year 1982, *Die natürliche Tochter* was well and truly launched as a major ingredient of the new Goethe image. Witness the volume, *Bausteine zu einem neuen Goethe*, issuing from a 1984 conference (published in 1987), where two of the ten essays deal with our drama. Finally, too, from 1982, German scholars began to publish journal articles on the drama. Up to then all special studies had appeared in English publications, with two significant exceptions of American and British authors writing in German journals (Burckhardt in the *Germanisch-Romanische Monatsschrift* 1960, Peacock in *Deutsche Vierteljahresschrift* 1962), exceptions that indeed make our point.

What the postwar history of *Die natürliche Tochter* illustrates in fascinating detail is the road of admission to the canon, or: the making of a classic. It was a rocky road. Sole among the first group of postwar critics, Benno von Wiese in *Die deutsche Tragödie von Lessing bis Hebbel* (1948) proclaimed the discovery of a major new tragedy. Free to read the unknown work ("the least perceived until today" 110) any way he wanted, he ranged widely over a host of perspectives, exhibiting the riches the text held for further exploration. After von Wiese had put the drama on the map, it fell to Josef Kunz in the first postwar Goethe edition (*Hamburger Ausgabe* 1952) to set the discursive frame for the new classic.

Once the foundation had been laid, criticism began, but only in British and American journals. Discussion in Germany remained at the dissertation level for a while yet, with vigorous support from senior scholars to be sure (Staiger for Bänninger 1957, Bergsträsser for Stammen 1966). As Staiger and von Wiese kept pushing for the new classic, the chapters on *Die natürliche Tochter* in their respective volumes (*Goethe* 1952 [Volume 2, 1956]; *Das deutsche Drama* [essay by Hans-Egon Hass], 1958) finally achieved the canonization of the drama.

Following Staiger's lead in the fifties, mining Emrich for symbolism reigned supreme in German approaches until the sociohistorical wave hit in 1977. English criticism, meanwhile, had pursued a number of different approaches subjecting the classic-in-the-making to the usual range of disciplinary tests, while following the German attempts to create another masterwork with open skepticism, and falling silent during the decade of the late seventies and eighties when the Germans finally came to terms with their new classic. On the German side, sociohistorical critics debated the political content, arguing for or against a German *Sonderweg* [third way] around the French Revolution in Goethe's play.

It was against this school that Emrich set out on a crusade starting as far back as 1964, on the one hand reclaiming for historicity his work on

Goethe's symbolism from the formalist symbolizers, on the other hand actualizing *Die natürliche Tochter* in the service of a cultural critique of apocalyptic dimensions. The two editions of the eighties (Stuart Atkins in the new *Hamburger Ausgabe* 1981; Victor Lange in the *Münchener Ausgabe* 1986) mirror the schism in criticism, if along different lines. Atkins marginalizes the drama as a lesser classic, a mere appendage to the more important earlier and later works, whereas Lange declares it central for a new, experimental Goethean poetics.

By the late eighties, these various controversies had widened the discursive horizon enough so that literary criticism might begin in earnest. It was no longer a question of whether to admit the text to the canon, but of defining the place it should occupy. And so we begin to see dispassionate considerations of historical, political, philosophical contexts; of relations with Goethean thought and writings, particularly in nonliterary dimensions such as art and science; of evolving concepts of genre and literary theory. At the end of the decade, Bernhard Böschenstein's book edition of Goethe's text (1990), together with its autobiographical French source (in German translation) and Böschenstein's three essays that had reframed the discussion beginning in 1985, made it official: *Die natürliche Tochter* had achieved the status of the classic; she had won a room of her own.

When in the anniversary year 1949 Ortega y Gasset, in a famous formulation, was seeking "a Goethe for the shipwrecked," Benno von Wiese had already found him in his history of *German Tragedy* (1948), and most particularly in *Die natürliche Tochter*. There is no mistaking von Wiese's passionate interest in Eugenie's history, embedded in a rhetoric of fear and the sublime, in marked contrast to his ambivalence on *Iphigenie* and his cool rehabilitation of *Tasso*. The root of the changed attitude is the critic's identification with this Goethean heroine, victim of catastrophic history, whose fate and figure von Wiese ennobles by reinterpreting victim as sacrifice and historic catastrophe as tragedy. This drama, he declares, is Goethe's text on "the essential nature of history itself as ineluctably tragic."

Von Wiese's view of history harbors a deep paradox. On the one hand history appears mythicized as tragedy, as an anonymous and demonic power annihilating individual will, utilizing and eventually destroying indiscriminately the good and the wicked. On the other hand, von Wiese belittles history as a lie, a web of deceptions and illusions, a mere "pseudotragedy," which the third act of Goethe's drama serves to illustrate. In either case it would be pointless to analyze history. The only attitude possible is one of fatalism, and von Wiese goes way back into critical history to unearth an authority for this view of *Die natürliche Tochter*. He not only quotes with appreciation Herman Grimm's diagnosis of 1877: "fatalism turned backward," but universalizes Grimm's judgment to bear on all of history. In von Wiese's view, "one might just as well call [history] 'fatalism turned forward'" (120). Consequently the real historical context in the background of Goethe's play as well as the political players with their questionable morals are absent from von Wiese's reading. They function as mere instruments of the "schauerlichen [horrific]" power of total disorganization that is history.

Sole object of interest is the victim, Eugenie, with the strongest focus on act 5, of which von Wiese offers the first close reading ever. For in Eugenie, the victim can be shown to turn into sacrifice. Both meanings coincide in the German word *Opfer,* but von Wiese makes his intended meaning clear by emphasizing in Eugenie's role the function of "representative renunciation and sacrifice, which alone yet guarantees healing to the country threatened by catastrophe" (119). Eugenie is the model of right behavior in difficult times; in her decision not to follow the Mönch's advice to emigrate, von Wiese constructs a legitimation for the so-called inner exile of German intellectuals during the Hitler era.

It is on this point, the question of emigration, that von Wiese's identification with Goethe's heroine hinges. His inordinately prolix discussion of this topic rests on the subtext of recent history, including personal history. A few samples must suffice to make the point. When the Mönch declares Eugenie's loss suffered in her "banishment" to be a benefit, he means "not at all a personal saving of oneself but instead the salvation from the imminent catastrophe of history, which his prophetic vision reveals to be precisely the fate of those who *must* remain behind in the homeland [in der Heimat zurückbleiben *müssen*] (emphasis mine)." "Müssen" as the modality of staying home is a particularly revealing interpretation of Eugenie's options. After quoting at length the Mönch's vision of total destruction of the city, von Wiese reiterates his revaluation of emigration versus staying at home, which he attributes, of course, to Goethe's figure in this drama: "emigration means blessing, grace, a gift from fate; the fatherland, the world at home, however, faces a catastrophe which we have already characterized as the total disorganization of history" (118f.).

Von Wiese closes with the sacralization of Eugenie's victimhood or sacrifice. Initiated by the Mönch into a "Christianity turned inward" (117), Eugenie can promise the miracle of purification. She has become a Christ-like figure giving hope and faith to her sullied fatherland, which von Wiese immediately expands from an individual country to encompass all mankind. "Her unique nature is destined from now on to be the pure sacrifice [Opfer] for a mankind having become impure through history. Only in this way, in Goethe's opinion, can the healing [Heilung] for the endangered country continue to be hoped for and believed" (120). Finally, Eugenie's original task of "saving the fatherland" is displaced by a new function: "Heilung [healing, cure]." She is to cure the ill of impurity that history has visited on her country. At this point an antonymic rhetoric centered on the terms *pure* and *impure* invades von Wiese's text. Clearly, von Wiese's context here is not the French Revolution, nor Goethe's Germany of 1800, but his own contemporary time and place.

After von Wiese had discovered in Goethe's long neglected drama a major statement on history as tragedy, it fell to Josef Kunz in the *Hamburger Ausgabe* (1952) to undergird the newly prominent work with a foundation in literary history and critical discourse. Where von Wiese implicitly mythicized history, Kunz explicitly installs a new myth in Goethe's drama: the myth of the lost center, "Verlust der Mitte," as expressed in a key formula of existentialist thought of the time. Kunz's mythological reading comes well credentialed philosophically, not only via existentialism, and ends up in a metaphysics of politics and of history. For Kunz the political sphere is the battleground of good essentialism versus bad nominalism or Hegelian particularism. The nominalist figures in *Die natürliche Tochter* are the representatives of the aristocratic *fronde*, who challenge the organic entelechy of the state. The state is seen in terms championed by Max Weber: charismatic government embodied in the figure of the King.

The battle of philosophies is embedded in a triadic view of history, which Kunz, while acknowledging his debt to Kommerell's *Zwischenzeit* [in-between time] motif, links to its gnostic roots. In Kunz's gnostic scheme, Eugenie's role is that of redeemer who has to wait out in hiding the *zwischenzeitlich* phase of historical crisis. Hiding and waiting ("Verborgenheit") is for Kunz the central theme of the drama. Time, timeliness, untimely acts, the law of the hour — these are crucial guideposts in his reading. The drama's time is not historic time but mythic time: Kunz repeatedly insists on "the mythic schema of the drama." And Eugenie's story is not a personal history, nor even yet symbolic of political history, but "mythic fate."

Indeed Kunz proposes a full-blown mythology, as he substitutes mythologic for dramaturgical categories such as the psychology of the figures or the pragmatic motivation of events. Learning from Staiger (1939), Kunz advises that such dramaturgical considerations should be ignored, just like the "Peinliche [embarrassing, painful matter]" in the dialogue of Herzog and Weltgeistlicher in the third act. Emrich's symbols, too, the silent symbolism of things and events as well as the verbal symbolism of metaphors, are pressed into service to convey a self-contained myth where "Hintergründigkeit" and "Hinweischarakter" [backgroundedness and associative nature] rule. (Emrich would later protest such misappropriation.)

Perhaps the most influential feature of Kunz's interpretation were his notes on individual passages of the text. Here he supplied a veritable inventory of significant motifs, words, and themes that would long inspire and challenge critics. Highlighting archetypes such as rebirth, vital energy, hubris, and *kairos*, or the archaic magic of things, the ritual power of gestures, and the aura of words such as *Glück*, *Verstand*, and *Sorge* [luck-happiness, reason, care], Kunz demonstrated the depth and breadth of this text and thus its qualification for the rank of classic.

At the pole opposite to Kunz's mythological metaphysics stands a book-length study by Verena Bänninger (1957), published under the auspices of Emil Staiger one year after Staiger's own new interpretation of *Die natürliche Tochter* in the second volume of his *Goethe* monograph. Bänninger, a disciple of the Staiger-Kayser school, offers a particularly clear instance of the power struggle in postwar German literary studies between southern (Swiss) formalism and northern (Frankfurt to Hamburg) existentialism. At this moment in *Natürliche Tochter* criticism, in the experimental phase of classic-making, claims with totalitarian range were put forth in a field free from a critical tradition that would impose limitations on new perspectives. Bänninger's meager list of literature on *Die natürliche Tochter*, more than half of which is strictly positivist philology of the old school, makes the point: there was as yet no "body of criticism" on this drama.

Speaking of beginnings: Schiller, whose formula of "alles Stoffliche aufgezehrt [all matter absorbed]" stood at the origin of *Natürliche Tochter* criticism, would be pleased. In Bänninger's interpretation, form absorbs content absolutely, with one significant exception: the problem of the father. For Bänninger, the King's misguided paternalism is the root of the dramatic conflict; in the peripeteia of act 3 the Duke's bad fathering is raised to the level of the demonic and grotesque. Other than that, Bänninger translates all action into terms of form. The drama's overall theme is conflict and change of the roles humans play, each role instantiating a basic sphere of life. The dramatic process consists in appearance and disappearance, in self-reflexive theater whose function it is to make something momentarily visible.

Bänninger's concept of form is derived from a theatrical model. Based on Goethe's active interest in French classical theater in connection with his theater work in Weimar at the time of *Die natürliche Tochter*, Bänninger finds in this drama an aesthetic of absolute theater. Figures, gestures, scenes, and words present; they make abstractions concrete and concepts visible; they do not represent. Here the medium is itself the message, this is "Augentheater, 'spectaculum'" (47, 114), a ritual of showing, not an attempt to signify hidden meanings and inner processes. This distinction allows Bänninger to emphasize the distance of *Die natürliche Tochter* from the classicism of *Iphigenie* and *Tasso*, where outer acts, words, gestures signified inner events. Here as in Racine's dramatic works, she maintains, outer remains outer: "man does not express himself, he (re)presents himself" (125).

Bänninger's immediately useful contribution to *Natürliche Tochter* criticism lay in the close examination she performed on a wide range of textual elements: figures, spaces, structures, events, gestures, and especially language. On the other hand, her new approach from the perspective of representation, theatricality, and French classicism as good as disappeared from the critical scene for many years. The new German classic was not to be founded on a French model; its symbolism was not to be deprived of philosophical depth and cultural sophistication; the cathartic tragedy of history was not to be reduced to a mere spectacle.

The spirit of Zurich favored the success of *Die natürliche Tochter* in many ways. Bänninger's demonstration that here was a "sprachliches Kunstwerk [work of art in language]" according to the most demanding specifications of the Staiger-Kayser method,* came three years after the Artemis (Zurich) *Gedenkausgabe* volume (1954) that contained the drama. Kurt May's introduction, a new and improved version of his 1939 essay, agglomerates ideas of Staiger (1939), Emrich, and von Wiese, while expanding on his own formal considerations. Most remarkable of all, the Zurich *Schauspielhaus* staged its first performance of the drama that same year, 1954: a noteworthy experience according to an admiring essay by Fritz Ernst in the *Neue Zürcher Zeitung*. By including this essay two years later in a volume entitled *Meisterdramen* [master dramas], Ernst confirmed the excellent quality of *Die natürliche Tochter*. At long last, Goethe's strange drama had made it to master status even on the stage.

It was all the more surprising then to hear Emil Staiger himself sounding an ambivalent note in the second volume of his *Goethe* monograph (1952; Volume 2 in 1956), as he set out to assign the new classic its place in Goethe's oeuvre, life, and thought. The road to prove the "incomparable" excellencies of this text even to himself, it seems to the critic, is fraught with dangerous pitfalls. The wrong approach, he fears, will founder on "apparent mistakes, apparent inconsistencies . . . Only the greatest caution will enable us to distill into firm conviction our intuition of a perfection which is incomparable" (372).

Most obvious in Staiger's reading is the effort to make the forthcoming classic interesting to his contemporaries. His aim is not to add yet one more text to the great works of the past but to enlist the new recruit in a campaign against the Zeitgeist. Staiger was the first postwar critic to propose *Die natürliche Tochter* as a critique of modernity, which included but went far beyond the antipolitical impulse of nineteenth century critics. For Staiger, the political in this drama is a metaphor for "Geist der Zeit," which threatens humanity with dissolution through "Begehren [desire]" and "ungestalte Gewalt [unshapable, monstrous violence]." Staiger's emphasis on *ungestalt*, on the political as that which resists artistic shaping, points to his overall method of evading moral problems — ethical, political, historical, social — by transferring them into the aesthetic dimension.

---

* Wolfgang Kayser's book of 1948, *Das sprachliche Kunstwerk*, published by Francke in Zürich, had become a basic book on method.

The "political" spirit of the modern era, according to Staiger, has wiped out individuality: thus the anonymity of the drama's characters. Politics has overpowered and made irrelevant individual ethics and responsibility.

The focus of his interpretation is act 5 with the entrance of the Mönch, a messenger from another world. Staiger embraces the Mönch's animus against the Zeitgeist to a point of near identification. In his reading, this figure represents an earlier world for Goethe and for history: the Iphigenian world of antiquity contrasting its "zarte Menschlichkeit [tender humanity]" with the "Nacht der Neuzeit [night of modernity]." From that other world Staiger imports into Eugenie's encounter with the Mönch the Iphigenian concept of a spiritually unalienated humanity ("I and Thou and man and God are interwoven indissolubly" 399). He grieves that such a concept of humanity is out of date in the modern age, in the world of power and bureaucracy symbolized in the "paper," the royal document concerning Eugenie.

In the most actualizing passage of his interpretation, Staiger, calling on Goethe for support, mounts an impassioned polemic against writing as the dead letter killing the living word. At the same time he is fully conscious of the paradoxical stance he — and Goethe — are taking. "The apparently harmless sentence which, pronounced by the man who has written close to one hundred thousand pages, sounds almost like a joke: that writing was an abuse of language, acquires a monstrous meaning." Staiger illustrates the monstrous meaning of Goethe's sentence by the image of the *Schreibtischtäter* [desk perpetrator], a topos much in vogue at the time reflecting on the crimes of the Nazi era. "Alone in a room, in front of a white paper, a ruler who feels threatened orders without hesitation the terrible act whose consequences he does not see with his own eyes." Staiger takes two pages for his fable of modern bureaucracy, of "files" at war against humanity, and concludes with a proper moral: "With such documents, however, which speak no man's language, the modern world is ruled; doomed is any attempt to assert the preciousness and dignity of God's creature against it" (395f.).

The only right conclusion for Eugenie's story, in Staiger's view, is for her to withdraw from the modern world corrupted by paper power and legalistic ethics, represented in the embarrassing marriage proposal. The only healthy sphere of life left in the modern era is nature, a concept that Staiger springs on us unprepared, after he has just as surprisingly skipped any discussion of the ending. Taking Goethe as his model here, who also skips disagreeable thoughts in his dramatic writing ("Goethe cannot persuade himself to let the decision develop in Eugenie"; he drops the curtain and continues later, according to Staiger), Staiger avails himself of the right to skip over the legal and psychological perplexities of the ending and proposes instead his simple solution: "Eugenie vanishes from the world, returns . . . to the simple development of nature" (400).

Less obvious than his antimodern ideology are Staiger's qualms concerning the aesthetic qualities of the work. In the interest of promoting the classic he keeps his doubts well below the surface, so well hidden in fact that English criticism over the next decade attacked him as one of the prime panegyrists of *Die natürliche Tochter*. Staiger's problem is that he cannot, in an interpretation of the drama as a whole, follow his own advice of 1939, so gratefully accepted by Josef Kunz: simply to ignore psychology, motivation, dramaturgy (what Kunz called "the pragmatic nexus") and just listen to the words as pronouncements of Goethe's philosophy.

Staiger tries to deal with the problem in the first half of the chapter by clearing out of the way critical objections, including his own, so that he might then start over from a clean slate with the interpretation proper. He openly admits certain flaws in the work. The doublespeak of the villains shows the limits of Goethe's genius; the inappropriate prolixity of some characters is evidence of the aging author's preaching (380); the inconclusive ending is a failure of dramatic art (400). He will correct Goethe's misleading language ("we feel compelled to state" that Eugenie's guilt speculation is mistaken, 393), and detect an imbalance between reflection and reality in the verse, which he takes as evidence of a crisis in Goethe's command of meter at the time of the drama's composition. He even states in passing that Goethe chose the wrong genre; the sequel would have made it still more evident "that the story is basically not dramatic but novelistic" (401f.).

The greatest difficulties, predictably, arise from act 3. Here Staiger finds himself forced to return to his awkward position of 1939: forget this is a drama, think of it as just poetry! This in turn leads him to glorify incongruity as mastery ("truly royal strategy!") and to indulge in Goethe idolatry, where excessive rhetoric aims to lull his reader into allowing the beautiful music of Goethe's poetry to overwhelm the possible meanings. "Every event . . . touches upon the slumbering strings of the harp of Goethe's soul and makes the powerful instrument vibrate with its plenitude of sounds. What do we care about the proximate cause when such a music resounds?" The music of his own words has finally succeeded in overcoming Staiger's objections, too, and he can begin his reading of the third act: "Now we, too, no longer take offense at the controversial third act" (381f.).

The effort it has cost him, however, appears over the two pages of his reading of act 3 in a rhetoric of exhortation against doubts ("But don't let us insist! Let's follow the voice of our heart! . . . The scene does not suffer through this point. To the contrary!"), and in the projection of his own "Anstrengung [effort]" onto the text and its author. "The third act is abstract . . . because the last things . . . must be defended with a tremendous effort. The language of the unique work testifies to the same effort" (383f.).

Staiger had presented *Die natürliche Tochter* as a complex work and, first in the postwar period, achieved an integrated interpretation that encompassed the multiple aspects of Goethe's play. But in straining to enthrone the new classic in a safe place in the Goethe canon he overstressed the praise and covered up the complexities of the drama. Reading his chapter leaves one uncomfortable; the Goethean text seems stranger than ever, truly "incomparable," but in a different sense than that intended by Staiger. In no small part can Staiger's chapter be seen as the agent provocateur of critical protests over the next two decades, especially among English critics, who during that time undertook the effort to get a "clean" reading of the new arrival on the Goethe scene.

No such qualms and ambivalences bothered German critics. Here it was a question of sanctioning and celebrating the drama's canonical status, mining and synthesizing the work of Staiger, Kunz, and Emrich. What emerged particularly clearly was their emphasis on aesthetic and formalist aspects and on personal as against political meanings. Staiger's translation of the political into the aesthetic dimension had opened this path. Revolution was a figure for disorder, "Ungestaltes"; politics was a function of form, as in Theo Stammen's voluminous study (published 1966 with an updated introduction, but essentially a 1961 dissertation), *Goethe und die Französische Revolution: Eine Interpretation der "Natürlichen Tochter."* Here Goethe is presented as a "political morphologist," who deals with social and political crises in history by constructing a figurative dream of ideas. (Witkowski's approach of 1899 comes to mind.)

The essay by Hans-Egon Hass in von Wiese's normative anthology, *Das deutsche Drama* (1958), served to confirm the classic status of *Die natürliche Tochter*. By its mere inclusion in this volume the drama joined the ranks of major texts that are supposed to constitute the category and history of German Drama. Far from qualms or doubts of the Staiger kind, Hass elegantly synthesizes Emrich, Kunz, the new May, and Staiger, on the basis of a Gundolf turned inside out. The result is *Die natürliche Tochter* as a network of symbols woven around selected foci which emphasize the personal. The theme of this ironic tragedy is the discrepancy between "Schein" and "Wesen [appearance and essence]."

The high points in Hass's reading of the drama are the scene of Eugenie defining herself by putting on the forbidden clothes and jewelry, and act 3 as the philosophical counterpart of that scene in the register of the Herzog. Both protagonists, Eugenie and the Herzog, are victims of the appearance-essence delusion and both overcome their victimization through private acts of renunciation ("Entsagung").

An article by Wolfgang Staroste in the *Schiller Jahrbuch* of 1963 engages in surface-mining of the German symbolist critics; its most significant feature is the fact that Staroste completely ignored English criticism, which had produced a substantial body of texts. Paul Böckmann's essay in the *Festschrift* for Bruno Marckwardt of 1961, on the other hand, takes symbolist readings to the extreme in order to construct *Die natürliche Tochter*, on the authority of Goethe entering his age of wisdom, as a safe house for the spirit. Here spirit lives in the autonomous symbol, removed from public view and political activity. From his existentialist perspective, Böckmann asserts the superiority of the spirit living "im Verborgenen [hidden away]," its autonomy, freedom, and essential truth.

Böckmann's interpretation replays a traditional theme of German Goethe scholarship: the foundation of the academic ivory tower on identification with Goethe's (allegedly) unpolitical life and thought (see especially 16f., 22f.). His reading hinges on the motif of secrecy, on a paradoxical play of binary terms, contrasting "das verborgene und das offenbare Geheimnis [the hidden and the revealed secret]." Böckmann insists that, despite the autonomy of symbols within the textual "network of associations," the reader yet must supplement symbolic meanings from his or her own imagination. Indeed the text appeals to the reader to furnish the necessary supplement ("wir sehen uns aufgefordert . . . von uns supplierend vollzogen werden müssen" 18). With his investigation of symbolism, Böckmann's reading of *Die natürliche Tochter* anticipated such later key concepts of literary theory as Wolfgang Iser's "appeal structure" or the Derridian supplement.

English criticism accepted the new German classic only reluctantly and never without reservations. Barker Fairley's unremittingly negative judgment in his 1947 *Study of Goethe* remained a powerful obstacle to the drama's recognition as a major Goethean work. If we recall von Wiese's exaltation of the same text around the same time, the extreme divergence between English and German views in the postwar era shows up in stark relief. In the view of Fairley and subsequent English critics, above all Ronald Peacock, the specifically Goethean type of poetry excluded political subjects. This most political of Goethe's works therefore had to be a failure, testimony of the poet's defeat: "evidence . . . of the maladjustment of Goethe's genius to the European crisis" (Fairley 160).

Fairley's prohibition did not prevent, however, some experimental probings into this "ghost of a play" (159) that could generate such a schism within the critical profession. So while the fifties saw Peacock's adamant rejection, there is also the first salvage attempt on the terms of English Goethe discourse in a pair of *PEGS* essays, encouraged no doubt by the editorship of Goethe promoter Elizabeth M. Wilkinson.

The first essay, by Hermann Boeschenstein (1956) uncovers a plethora of motifs, myths, and messages in this transitional text, as Boeschenstein sees *Die natürliche Tochter*, marking a paradigm change in Goethe's oeuvre. Under the impact of Napoleonic history Goethe's focus would have shifted from female passivity, as in his heroic saints Iphigenie, Prinzessin, Gretchen, and Makarie, to male activism aiming, of course, toward

Faust II. The most interesting figure for Boeschenstein, and the most intriguing feature of his reading, is the Weltgeistliche seen as an adumbration of Faustian activism. This most controversial character in *Natürliche Tochter* criticism is the " *Urbild* " of the new "man of energy" in tune with his historical moment at the beginning of the nineteenth century, whose pragmatic ruthlessness lays down "the principle of rule by terror." In a move of actualization reminiscent of the *Iphigenie* criticism of the time, but so far missing from writing on this drama, Boeschenstein considers the essential truth of this dramatic character validated by recent history: "the master-liars and perverters of public opinion of a more recent vintage have nothing over him" (39f.).

Sylvia P. Jenkins's essay in *PEGS* three years later insists on the drama's success *as drama,* not merely as a network of motifs, ideas, and symbols. Her original contribution, however, lies in the area of motif, which takes her like Boeschenstein into Christian mythology. Where Boeschenstein suggested a neo-Miltonic myth of "paradise regained" for the nucleus of Eugenie's mission, Jenkins discovers in Eugenie's fate the biblical Joseph story as a prefiguration of Christ buried and resurrected to become the savior of his people.

There is perhaps no better example of the schismatic potential of *Die natürliche Tochter* than the case of Ronald Peacock, where schism may be said to have taken the form of critical schizophrenia. As early as 1946 Peacock had disqualified the drama from competing in "Goethe's Version of Poetic Drama" (title of a *PEGS* essay), the subgenre which was, after Wilkinson and Willoughby's work on *Egmont* and *Tasso,* all the rage in British criticism. Four years later, Peacock signally excluded *Die natürliche Tochter* from his reading of *Goethe's Major Plays* (1959), which put him at sharp disagreement with the recent canonization of the work by Staiger, Bänninger, and Hass. He felt compelled to justify this exclusion through a demonstration of the drama's "Incompleteness and Discrepancy" in the same year (*Festschrift* for James Boyd 1959), in an essay that spectacularly foregrounds the reasons for schismatic criticism's history.

Yet a mere three years later, in an essay published in the *Deutsche Vierteljahresschrift* (1962), Peacock seemed to have come to terms with the troublesome drama. He had discovered a principle of interpretation which allowed him finally to accept and appreciate *Die natürliche Tochter* as a major statement of Germany's greatest poet. It is difficult to account for this about-face. Apparently, Peacock had not read Burckhardt, who had been first to reveal the challenging depth of this text from a perspective that yet was highly critical and thus in accordance with British interpretive principles. One hates to think that Peacock's epiphany was owed to Grabowsky's expurgated article of 1951, but the evidence suggests exactly that. Grabowsky is the only critic Peacock not merely mentions by name, but extensively absorbs and, fortunately, transcends in his own interpretation.

In his 1959 essay on "Incompleteness and Discrepancy in *Die natürliche Tochter*" Peacock mounts a frontal attack on postwar German idolizers. Not only does he recall the objections of earlier critics, reminding the classic-makers that there is no such thing as a tabula rasa after a century and a half of critical history. He also draws up an account of new reasons why this text, for all its beauties of individual passages, must not be ranked a "masterwork" in the definition of the era, that is, a complex but integrated and well-rounded whole. Unkindest of all, he is the first to exhibit in detail just those lines, especially in act 3, that criticism so far had merely referred to, and then silenced, as "embarrassing." Peacock is doing what Staiger did in reverse. Where Staiger had tried to shape and mold his reading carefully so as to reveal the "incomparable perfection" of the text, Peacock wades in, with blunt language, to strip bare the incomprehensible imperfections: "discrepancy is the hallmark of the work" (126).

He comes down particularly hard on Eugenie, apotheosized not just by the German idolizers but installed in the transcendent realm of the Savior by *PEGS* essayists Boeschenstein and Jenkins as well. When Eugenie rejects the advice of the Mönch and decides to use the Gerichtsrat instead, as Peacock tells it, at the very moment when the *PEGS* authors had initiated her sacralization, she appears "both harder and coarser, a little repellent, if the truth were told" (126). Telling the truth about why this text has been a critical embarrassment is precisely Peacock's project. Calling a spade a spade, he exposes the "squalid relationship" of the "sordid characters" Hofmeisterin and Sekretär, and debunks the supposedly august *Schmuckszene* [dressing scene] as girlish, domestic, and intimate, with its final line of alleged tragic irony ("Das Schicksal, das dich trifft, unwiderruflich [the fate that awaits you, irrevocably]") sounding not sublime but "extremely crude" (127f.) to his ears.

After this blast of vituperation it is perhaps not altogether surprising to find Peacock trying to make amends in his next essay (1962). Published in German, in a German journal (*Deutsche Vierteljahresschrift*), the article is explicitly intended as a conciliatory gesture towards the German mainstream of *Natürliche Tochter* appreciation: Peacock starts out by referring to the criticism of his earlier article. He now solves the problem of discrepancy by dividing the text into two dramas: one political, the other personal, in order then to discuss only the second, as the title announces: "Goethes *Die natürliche Tochter* als Erlebnisdichtung." In Peacock's view the political drama creates all the problems, the personal drama supplies the answers so that we can after all escape from bewildering strangeness into sense and consistency: "a subjective drama of emotion . . . which gives a meaning and focus to many passages which otherwise appear strange and incomprehensible."

Peacock's reading of Goethe's "subjective drama of emotion" opens a new door. His understanding of subjectivity goes beyond the definition in traditional criticism: as ideology, worldview, and opinion. Subjectivity for him includes the body and the (Freudian) psyche. The subjective experience in this drama is Goethe's traumatic experience of death, faced in his severe health crisis around 1800. Peacock traces in the text the imprint of physicality, of urgent desire (for life), of neurosis, compulsiveness, and obsession. The drama as a whole transacts the struggle between life and death.

For Peacock, the urgency of this ultimate human issue coupled with the intensity of desire and emotion, particularly in the ecstatic love between father and daughter, accounts for the hyperbolic style and explains the many strange aspects that have given critics so much trouble. When, in conclusion, Peacock warns against trying to unify this multilayered text, we see how he has solved the problem of *Die natürliche Tochter:* by interpreting incompleteness as depth which calls for probing exploration, and discrepancy as complexity which challenges critical labor.

Had Peacock been aware of Sigurd Burckhardt's essay two years earlier (1960), he could have seen how the depth and complexity of this drama created not just problems for critics, but offered opportunities for wide-ranging and thought-provoking conjecture and interpretation. It is significant that Burckhardt achieved his advance in perspective and results from the vantage point of another text, not on the basis of *Die natürliche Tochter* itself. This classic was still in the making; in order to find its place in the canon it needed to be approached from the established works. Staiger and Kunz, after Emrich, had placed it at the threshold to postclassical, "late Goethe." Burckhardt took the opposite stance and reattached the drama to its traditional predecessors *Iphigenie* and *Tasso* as part of Goethe's "blank-verse trilogy." His pretext for looking backwards is thus formal, but the move is prompted by considerations of substance and methodology.

As Burckhardt evaluates the contest of methods in the case of *Die natürliche Tochter* he places the "new method" of interpretation practiced by Staiger and Bänninger ahead of the old philological reading on the basis of the work as a torso. His own method, a third approach designed to overcome the shortcomings of the other two, integrates form and substance in the mediating body of language. Burckhardt's premise is that for Goethe "form is . . . meaning," and for *Die natürliche Tochter* "form is . . . in the work as a whole, metaphor." Read through the body of its linguistic form (which includes dramaturgy and dramatic structure), the drama about Eugenie is Goethe's "counter-Iphigenie."

If Burckhardt's essay is proof of the productive potential of a compare-and-contrast approach, it also illustrates the drawbacks of this procedure, that is, the temptation to set one text up as the norm, the standard against which the other text is read and evaluated. Possibly impelled by the contemporary fight over *Iphigenie* and humanity, Burckhardt sets *Iphigenie* as the absolute norm, not just within Goethe's oeuvre but in literature altogether, insofar as literature conforms to Burckhardt's definition of an essential enterprise of the human spirit. His essay on *Die natürliche Tochter* is almost as much an essay about *Iphigenie*. If Goethe had written nothing but *Iphigenie,* he assures us, we would "have him as a whole; we need nothing more in order to understand him, his true nature and his creative will." As he had argued in his essay of 1956 on *Iphigenie,* in this drama *logos* reveals itself; interpreting this text is "natural theology," and worshipping this work is "natural religion." No wonder then that compared to such perfection *Die natürliche Tochter* is doomed.

On the other hand, Burckhardt's critical reading of the latter drama spells doom for its venerated counter-image, *Iphigenie,* as well, for history knows no absolutes. If, following Burckhardt, in the problematic later work Goethe indeed recanted his earlier drama of realized human idealism, then this would imply a historical deconstruction of the erroneous assumptions about human perfectibility as embodied in *Iphigenie.* Goethe would have responded to the course of historical experience, personal as well as cultural-political, by adjusting his views of mankind to the point where he judged his earlier creation to be "damnably humane." And indeed Burckhardt reads *Die natürliche Tochter* historically. In the context of Goethe's personal history the work is evidence of an identity crisis. At the same time Burckhardt considers the drama as testimony to the split between the professional poet Goethe and the Zeitgeist that rejected his works. In Burckhardt's frame of cultural history *Die natürliche Tochter* stands as radical critique of Enlightenment ideology.

True to his interpretive principle of language as existential metaphor, the focus of Burckhardt's critique is on the word as carrier of ideas, and on the precise functioning of the word in this carrier role. In the double name Eugenie-*Natürliche Tochter,* the word splits the self of the only figure that is named. The drama thus signals the eighteenth century's ambivalence toward a debased concept of nature, where *natural* meant arbitrary and illegitimate. It is an ambivalence that Burckhardt finds reproduced in the drama's overall presentation of a "rococo nature" in "baroque language." Unity of word and message in *Iphigenie* contrasts with the chasm between signifier and signified in this drama, which indulges in puns and language games to the point of farce.

Worst of all for Burckhardt, the split between signifier and signified generates a vast array of language abuses. Pieces of paper masquerade as actions: Eugenie's sonnet, the royal document, the marriage that will exist merely on paper. More serious is Eugenie's sin against the word, that is, her broken promise not to open the treasure. Language is abused in the debased meaning of the *secret,* a meaning that has fallen from its biblical origin to the level of gossip; in the word instrumentalized as political means of exchange; in the pervasive presence of the lie. The fate of such a world, as envisioned by the Mönch, is chaos: the inevitable consequence of "the law of linguistic entropy" (88).

For Burckhardt, too, the third act is central, but again, in contradistinction to its centrality in *Iphigenie,* for a "monstrous" reason: precisely *because* it is so hard to understand. For the message of this "monstrous" middle act is that the word cannot be understood. In the post-Iphigenian age truth does not exist. Facts here produce hypotheses, not true knowledge. In a nutshell, this act contains for Burckhardt the relation between Goethe's two dramas, which he states characteristically in religious terms: revelation in *Iphigenie* versus mystification in *Die natürliche Tochter.*

Two decades later, German critics fighting the classics war were doing the reverse of what Burckhardt had done: playing off the good, because critical and political, *Natürliche Tochter* against the discredited, because affirmative and personal, *Iphigenie.* The interest of American and British scholarship meanwhile, never very strong to begin with, had withered away. Two articles in *PEGS* (1971 and 1974) were the only journal publications; their main import is their reflection of the controversial history of criticism.

F. J. Lamport (1974) states the unrelieved trouble the play constitutes for an ethically based and language-oriented criticism: he finds the drama essentially uninterpretable; in other words, not a fit subject for literary criticism. The work itself, in Lamport's mind, casts an unfavorable light on the revered author, Goethe, whose language here "muffles, deadens, smooths out, glosses over the echoes and pre-echoes of not-so-distant catastrophe" (60f.).

In the threshold year 1977, which saw the second rebirth of *Die Natürliche Tochter* in Germany in preparation of the classics war, English criticism concluded with a chapter in Ilse Graham's *Goethe, Portrait of the Artist.* There would be silence from the American and British side for over a decade, with the noteworthy fact, however, of American scholars writing in German publications, a phenomenon anticipated in Burckhardt's and Peacock's essays of 1960 and 1962. The conjecture must at least be ventured that Burckhardt's critique had been understood rather too well by English criticism. If interpreting *Die natürliche Tochter* meant endangering that ideal Goethean work, *Iphigenie,* then it was preferable to jettison the problematic text in order to keep *Iphigenie* safe.

In Ilse Graham's psychobiographic project to draw the portrait of the creative artist, *Die natürliche Tochter* occupies a crucial place. Following Peacock's latest essay, Graham sees the roots of the work in Goethe's life and death crisis; the drama's essence and subject is the testing out of the shakily recovered poet's creative energy. The world of the drama, for Graham, is not political or historical reality but a totally inner "universe of discourse," linked with a fragile "economy of creativity." Focus of that universe is Eugenie, ambivalent symbol of production which, as process, configures infinite creativity and striving on the one hand and, on the other, as product, signifies the finality and rigidity of form. Graham calls attention to the predominant motif of the artifact in the textual imagery — the exact opposite of the critical emphasis on organic imagery heretofore.

The problematic third act is central to her argument. In an explicit challenge to Staiger's dismissal of dramaturgy and psychology here, she offers an integrated reading of this act. The father-daughter relation is a relation of "generation" and "Bildung [formation]," which in turn means both "Hervorgebrachtwerdendes und Hervorgebrachtes [something in the process of being produced and the finished product]." The dialogue of Herzog and Weltgeistlicher translates the theme of production and product into the sphere of artistic creation. The birth of *Gestalt* at the close of the dialogue is a defense against loss and can be understood as a dramatic transaction of the Goethe poem thematized by Staiger (1939): "Dauer im Wechsel [permanence in change]." Graham's connection of the father-daughter relation with *Euphrosyne,* Goethe's elegy on the young actress Christiane Becker, deserves to be further explored.

But her main emphasis is on the ambiguity and ambivalence, including the ambisexual nature of the ambiguously and significantly named heroine. In this view, *Eugenie* embodies the fundamental insecurity of the creative artist Goethe in a traumatic moment of his life. The heroine's complex character also prefigures, in Graham's reading of literary history, Kleist's ambiguous women. Penthesilea and Käthchen are demonic sleepwalkers who, as figures in their dramas, remain mysteries that resisted the poet's effort to shape them into a communicable artistic form. The key motif of the mystery in Goethe's drama intimates, for Graham, that artistic creation can succeed only momentarily and incompletely in revealing any genuine mystery. Eventually, the mystery will have to return to its original state of unrevealed uncreatedness: like her sonnet Eugenie has to go back into the closet (esp. 280f.).

Not quite as spectacular a vintage as for *Tasso,* where seven interpretations appeared, the year 1977 yet saw the official entry of *Die natürliche Tochter* in the German classics war. In addition to Graham's, three more readings of the fledgling classic were advanced to mark new positions in the revaluation of Goethe and Weimar Classicism. The three readings, by Ehrhard Bahr, Dieter Borchmeyer, and Wilhelm Emrich, set the frame for the *Natürliche Tochter* debate of the next decade: it was to be a contest between historicization and actualization. With the general turn of German literary scholars toward intellectual history, the historicizers won in the end. But the most fascinating aspect of that decade is on the side of actualization: it is, in short, the Emrich story, which because of its continued impact on the ongoing debate will be told first.

An in-depth narrative of this story would have to be a history not just of postwar German studies, but would have to go back all the way to the early thirties, when scholars found themselves polarized between politicization and withdrawal into inner exile. Emrich told part of that history himself in a 1967 address on Radio Bremen (Emrich 1968), at a moment when a similar polarity, if under different denominations, was being replayed in the late sixties. At issue then as now was the role of literary scholars, guardians of the spirit as they saw themselves in the German academic tradition, in the wars of ideologies. And then as now, in Emrich's personal account and in academic history, one of the poles was represented by Theodor W. Adorno, young Emrich's mentor at Frankfurt University and now, more than thirty years later, inspiring the rising generation of scholars in a way best described in Goethe's poem of the Sorcerer's Apprentice (17–30).

An abbreviated version of our story might begin with Emrich's first book after the 1957 republication of his now famous *Symbolik von "Faust II"*: a collection of essays programmatically entitled *Protest und Verheißung* [Protest and Promise] (1960). At a moment when Staiger-and Kayser-type *Werkimmanenz* and Heideggerian transcendental existentialism were in full bloom, Emrich explicitly turned against the mainstream in German literary criticism. Opposing "ontology or metaphysics of truth" as well as "a timeless aesthetic or autonomy of form and a so-called 'pure' ahistorical *Werkimmanenz*" (7), he insisted on the historicity of literature in order to claim a role for literature as cultural critique targeted at the modern age of science and technology.

A champion of literature as the creed of modern man replacing Christianity, Emrich asserts a superior status for literary truth against the truths offered by the mathematical sciences. Literature and her priests, the literary scholars, have the right and the duty to deconstruct, to reveal the fallacies of "modern barbarism," and to raise historical consciousness as the path to eventual salvation in a new promised land: "to awaken consciousness through insight into the truth which is mediated by poetry and which reveals the structure of our reality in order to translate it into a new order" (10).

While in 1960 modern literature and particularly Kafka served as standard bearer in Emrich's crusade of "Protest and Promise," four years later Emrich appointed *Die Natürliche Tochter* to this honor in his campaign against the ideologized literature of the New German Left. In one of his regular contributions to a weekly paper, he juxtaposed the Goethean drama, then unknown even to the educated elite, with a current theater hit glorified by general critical acclaim: Peter Weiss's *Marat/Sade*. Surely Goethe's drama had never found itself in stranger company than in Emrich's eye-catching title, "Marquis de Sade und die natürliche Tochter."

More extraordinary yet, this text which had traditionally been downgraded for its aesthetic flaws — indication of an unfortunate lapse in Goethe's poetic faculties — was chosen to demonstrate the principle of absolute aesthetic quality. Comparing the two dramas by Weiss and Goethe, Emrich demonstrates his belief, against contemporary criticism's abstinence from evaluation, in a hierarchy of aesthetic values: "different artistic ranks within and despite all historical relativizations" (54). For Emrich there are better and worse literary works, and compared to the Goethe text of small renown, the famous *Marat/Sade* is definitely worse.

It should be noted as a point of historical irony or justice that Emrich's elevation of *Die natürliche Tochter* occurred in the same year that the downfall of her close relative, *Iphigenie*, began with Martin Walser's attack at the 1964 *Germanistentag*. Both Eugenie's promoter and Iphigenie's detractor took the same perspective of historical consciousness, political responsibility, and critical aesthetic. Yet where *Iphigenie* was found irremediably wanting in every respect, Emrich declared her neglected stepsister Eugenie an embodiment of the most advanced state of modern critical mentality, in a dramatic text fully aware of the problem of power relations in an historical context. "You won't find it any more 'modern' even in the modern writers . . . . [Goethe's drama] sustains the dialectic and reveals the unity of the apparently inexorable antinomies of our human society" (55).

Emrich's challenge in the journalistic forum would surely have passed unnoticed in academic criticism. However, his essay in the *Festschrift* for Victor Lange in the crucial year 1977 pitted his view of the drama as an anticipatory vision of modern times, "Zur Ursprungsgeschichte der modernen Welt," against two sociohistorical readings of the same year, which aimed to integrate the drama into a revisionist history of German Classicism: Ehrhard Bahr's essay in Conrady's volume *Deutsche Literatur zur Zeit der Klassik*, and Dieter Borchmeyer's chapter in his *Höfische Gesellschaft und Französische Revolution*.

Emrich's reading adapts *Die natürliche Tochter* to a neoconservative critique of modern mass culture. More particularly and pointedly, Emrich's critique targets his own branch of that culture: German intellectuals and the universities. He takes on the two major trends of the seventies: the politicized Left that he sees borne to triumph on the wings of "Massenjubel [mass applause]," and the silent majority's withdrawal into the ivory tower of "Verinnerlichung [inwardness]" and idolatry of historicism.

He opposes the pure symbolism of the disciples of Staiger, Kayser, and Kunz disciples, as he reclaims *Die natürliche Tochter* from the miners of his *Symbolik von "Faust II."* In retrospect, he insists on the historicity of his own reading of *Faust II*, and now he explicitly proposes to read its "Vorform [preformation]," *Die natürliche Tochter*, as an historical allegory of genius exiled from modern culture. It should be remembered that at that time allegory was anathema to literary criticism. Despised — using Goethe's own bon mot — as the bad counterpart of the symbol, allegory was the literal-minded, clumsy image-making practiced by unsophisticated earlier eras.

Anathema, too, in the sociopolitical orientation of German criticism, was Emrich's focus on the excellent individual. There can be no question but that precisely this anti-individualist Zeitgeist was the subtext of Emrich's glorification of individualism in the figure of Eugenie. Drawing support for the theme of the ostracized individual from other Goethean works, Emrich propounds his heresy in a provocative terminology borrowed from the current gospel of *mündige Bürgerlichkeit* [autonomous citizenship]. His pro-individualist subtext shows through most clearly when he takes recourse to Goethe's own famously irrational terms of *Persönlichkeit* [personality] and *das Dämonische* [the daemonic], without attempting in the least to suggest a definition. In Emrich's reading, the world of the drama that denies legitimacy to genius Eugenie is the "desert" of nineteenth and twentieth century culture, with the traditional villains of the piece, Weltgeistlicher, Sekretär, and Hofmeisterin as representatives.

Emrich saves his most withering words for the Weltgeistliche. The designation, *Weltgeistlicher*, that Goethe chose for this figure, is the key to his nature. Appointed to mediate between *Geist* and *Welt*, spirit and world, he betrays and corrupts both. He is an allegory of the decadence of Spirit that Emrich's sarcastic rhetoric attributes to contemporary intellectuals: "'Geist', der sich nur noch masochistisch in Angstorgien und gesellschaftskritischen Weltschmerztiraden wälzt ['Spirit' reduced to indulging masochistically in orgies of anxiety, criticism of society, and *Weltschmerz* tirades]" (177). The words of this worldly spiritual leader in act 3 herald the institutionalized decadence exhibited in the last two acts by government, the church, and the law. The Herzog "in fact represents the type of the 'man of spirit' here," who wrestles with the "monstrous temptations" of the modern intellectual by ideology and demagoguery, and by escapism into the worship of dead artworks of the past.

The pessimism of the 1977 essay is refined and surpassed in Emrich's last reading of our drama in an essay first published in 1982. Here the dialectic of the Enlightenment developed by Emrich's teacher, Adorno, finds a radical application, as Emrich uses the work of the greatest poet of the German Enlightenment to recant the principles of poetic work as well as of his own work as a literary critic. The irony of the occasion was not lost on him. He presented his essay first in Marbach, repository of classical German literature, at an anniversary celebration of Goethe's death.

While his interpretation of *Die natürliche Tochter* is far less extensive — the drama is only one of five discussed, and Emrich refers the reader to his 1977 essay for the longer version — there are two substantial developments since the earlier article. The first concerns the place Emrich assigns the drama in Goethe's oeuvre. In fact, he designs a new structure of signification in Goethe, the oeuvre and the cultural icon. In this new structure, *Die natürliche Tochter* is neither a prefiguration of late Goethe, as his *Symbolik von "Faust II"* saw it, nor part of the classical triad together with *Iphigenie* and *Tasso*, as emphasized in standard readings of the recent past (Kunz, Staiger, Hass, Burckhardt, Ziolkowski, Marahrens). Instead, Emrich draws a line from *Die natürliche Tochter* back into Goethe's work to its very beginnings. From *Götz* to *Egmont, Iphigenie, Tasso*, and finally to this drama composed at the turn of the nineteenth century, he reads the allegory of genius exiled by modern history and culture. Unacknowledged, probably unwittingly as in the 1977 essay, in which Adorno's influence appeared, the influence of another of Emrich's teachers at Frankfurt in the thirties emerges here: Max Kommerell. We remember Kommerell's seminal motif of "nobility in exile," which he, too, traced through a multitude of Goethe texts.[*] For Emrich now, *Die natürliche Tochter* is the most trenchant statement of what he considers the fundamental problem of German history: the alienation of power from spirit, the tragedy of *Geist und Macht*, "the two hostile brothers who command the scene to this day" (157).

Far more radical than this rather obvious actualization of meaning is the other development since the 1977 reading. A profound language pessimism calls in question the critic's very self-identity. In Emrich's deconstruction of Goethe's drama, language self-de(con)structs, too. The 1977 reading had found two languages in contest: corrupt and perverted political language (Weltgeistlicher, Sekretär) stood against the authentic language of poetry that could speak essential truths (Mönch). But Emrich had planted the self-destructive seed even then, when he highlighted Eugenie's accusation of linguistic rape against the Hofmeisterin. Now there is no more "good" as distinct from "bad" language. All language has been penetrated by the evils of modernity, which Emrich still blames on politicization, including also and spectacularly Goethe's language.

Despair breathes through aggressivity as Emrich launches his polemic against his public, the *Bildungsbürgertum* [educated elite], and against the foundation of his life's work: literature.

> Only if one understands this does one get an intuition of the bottom-less, dizzying abyss that lies hidden in Goethe's classical language, which sounds so muted and harmonious . . . . The appearance of the formally perfect language does not imply a perfect, whole world, as the clueless *Bildungsbürgertum* believed, but on the contrary harbors conflicts and terror in itself (159).

[*] Emrich's remarks on Kommerell in the 1967 radio address throw light on his own belligerence now (Emrich 1968).

Language as shaped by society penetrates and dominates the language of spirit as well . . . . a fact which all the desperate emancipation attempts of modern poets cannot change. This is the true reason of the hopeless, steadily progressing withering-away of poetry in the twentieth century (161).

Here literary criticism undermines itself as Emrich indicts all language as corrupt. Usurped by an alien power, by the anti-Spirit ("Geist und Widergeist" was another Emrich book title), language is alienated from spirit, can no longer represent spirit, and is therefore no longer accessible to spirit: inaccessible for spirit's creative work in poetry as well as for spirit's analytical work in criticism. Consequently, and with rhetorical overstress on consequentiality, Emrich's 1982 reading of *Die natürliche Tochter* ends with a death wish: "Folgerichtig sehnt sich daher Eugenie hinab zu den Toten [Consequently Eugenie therefore longs to join the dead below]." Eugenie's death wish is, of course, not the end of the drama; nor is it the oft-quoted apocalyptic vision of the Mönch, though Emrich makes it look that way.

In conclusion he returns once more to Kommerell (again unrecognized) for a cyclic view of history. Emrich's emphasis, however, is not on the hope for a return of better times, but on the necessary destruction that must precede rejuvenation, an emphasis he buttresses with a late Goethe quotation: "I foresee the time when God will no longer find joy in mankind and when He will once more have to smash everything for a rejuvenated creation" (162). There is no more devastating example of the subversive power of this problematic Goethean drama than Emrich's reading. The fact that it was republished in 1987 in a volume entitled *Bausteine zu einem neuen Goethe* (Chiarini 1987) seems to declare that this is the view of New Goethe, a Goethe for our times.

The historicizers on the opposite side of Emrich's actualization campaign during the late seventies and eighties make far less exciting reading. Still, their approach had just as much to do with contemporary German developments as Emrich's, even if not as immediately and openly. They did not aim to withdraw Goethe and themselves from the ideological and political battles of the day into the distance of past history. On the contrary, with the issue of German revolutionary traditions or the lack thereof at the top of the intellectual agenda, the new classic became a test case to decide whether Goethe could be expelled from or repossessed for political-historical consciousness. The question was whether Goethe was part of the problem of German intellectual and political history — the so-called *deutsche Misere* in the parlance of the time — or part of the solution. And predictably, opinions diverged.

Of the two historicizers of 1977, Ehrhard Bahr claims Goethe for good history. Bahr makes much of the plans for the sequel and of relations between Goethe's text and specific historical figures and events, in order to show that the drama is indeed about revolutionary history. According to Bahr, Goethe read his revolutionary history correctly. First, because the ruling aristocracy in his drama fails the test for legitimacy and therefore the right to govern, when they refuse to legitimize Eugenie; second, because in the figure of the Gerichtsrat, Goethe designated the bourgeoisie as the revolutionary class and the ruling class of the future.

For the second of the 1977 historicizers, however, Goethe had it all wrong. It was precisely for not having recognized the revolutionary role of the bourgeoisie that Dieter Borchmeyer took Goethe to task. The text of *Die natürliche Tochter* becomes "questionable" for Borchmeyer when, evading historical responsibility, the bourgeoisie in the figure of the Gerichtsrat shifts focus from political life to privacy and the family idyll. With this turn, Borchmeyer sees Goethe's drama embracing the reactionary values of *Hermann und Dorothea*. Instead of continuing on the progressive path of *Wilhelm Meister*, Goethe took a step backwards beyond even *Iphigenie*, the work that was at the center of Goethe denunciations in the classics war.

In an allusion to Rousseau's betrayal of political for private interests in *La Nouvelle Héloise*, Borchmeyer's "Nouvelle Iphigénie," Eugenie, lands "in the haven of marriage," and the world-embracing "Temple of Humanity" shrinks to the size of the bourgeois home. At the same time, with a nod to Hegel, Borchmeyer pronounces the European model of French classicist tragedy as instantiated in Goethe's *Iphigenie*, abandoned in favor of the privatized and particularized German specialty: the genre of *"bürgerliches Trauerspiel* [bourgeois tragedy]" that Goethe produced in *Die natürliche Tochter*.

Three years later the impact of Emrich made itself felt in the camp of the historicizers. Dieter Borchmeyer's account of *Die natürliche Tochter* in his *Weimarer Klassik* (1980) is an abbreviated version of his 1977 reading, with a notable change being a marked upward valuation of the drama. Following Emrich, instead of a decline in Goethe's dramatic writing to the level of *bürgerliches Trauerspiel* he now sees a progressive direction toward the modern, twentieth century form of epic drama developed by Brecht. On the other side stands Hans Rudolf Vaget's essay on *Die natürliche Tochter* in the Reclam volume *Goethes Dramen* of the same year (ed. Hinderer 1980). Vaget explicitly opposes Emrich on the central issues of theme, focus, and political import. Just as adamantly, if not explicitly, he contests Emrich's high aesthetic valuation. For the first time in the drama's postwar rise to classical standing in German criticism, Vaget stirs up the long history of critical objections, from Peacock all the way back to Kettner. In another first, he adds his own, severe criticism when he accuses Goethe of obscurantism, reductionism, and denunciation in matters political: "tendency toward obscurantism" with a "truly denunciatory accentuation in the presentation of any oppositional position, which [Goethe] reduces to the politically thin motive of envy" (214). On the drama's sociopolitical perspective Vaget differs emphatically from Bahr and Borchmeyer, both of whom saw the focus in the bourgeoisie's revolutionary role. For Vaget, the "political content" of the drama consists in a critical reflection on the historical role and fate of the aristocracy, which in his mind vastly reduces the significance for cultural critique claimed by Emrich. No visionary meditation of "historico-philosophical" depth, as Goethe himself and recent critics imagined, in Vaget's reading *Die natürliche Tochter* is merely a rather outdated comment on a limited aspect of social history: the crisis and demise of European feudalism.

The next round of the debate took place in the Goethe editions of the eighties. The commentators in the Munich and the new Hamburg editions mirrored the critical divide in perspective and evaluation. Stuart Atkins (*Hamburger Ausgabe* 1981) clearly marks his distance from both warring camps with his effort, first, to detach the drama from any sociohistorical or culture-critical messages by emphasizing its artful, even artificial aspect. Second, by reattaching the drama to Goethe's life-context he relativizes the supposedly objective historical perspective claimed in recent criticism. Atkins narrows the drama's view of history to the limited and sharply defined horizon of the known individual Goethe, for whom the history of the French Revolution was a personal experience. On the other hand, since Goethe was a creative individual, he would have recast his experience of historical reality into a literary form, according to the theoretical and programmatic principles of classicism. For evidence, Atkins points to the highly artificial language and the universalizing and essentializing effect of the drama's symbolism. He emphasizes Schiller's input in the classicist procedure of "dehistoricization" (601), which resulted in the production of ahistorical *Urphänomene* [archetypal phenomena] instead of the reproduction of historical events. Atkins's retrenchment is reinforced when he declares *Die natürliche Tochter* evidence of Goethe's "Rückzugsposition [position of withdrawal]" from public involvement into the privacy of *Bürgerlichkeit* [bourgeois lifestyle] and marriage. Atkins does not, however, mean to confirm the position of the sociohistorical critics, who had appropriated the drama for a progressive, even revolutionary history of the bourgeoisie. According to Atkins, the bourgeoisie in this drama is merely the lesser of two evils in an undialectical alternative between order and chaos.

The comment in the Munich edition (1986)[*] seems a direct rebuttal of Atkins's classicist retrenchment and confirms once again the amazing power of this drama to provoke diametrically opposed interpretations of identical textual features. Provocatively entitled "Das politische Trauer-

---

[*] The volume editor is Victor Lange. In contrast with other volumes, there is no attribution of the commentary to a particular author.

spiel," the commentary pronounces *Die natürliche Tochter* the founding work of this new genre, a work of multi-layered innovation and of supreme poetological importance. According to this view, Goethe's classicism is rooted in Sophoclean political tragedy as model of a negative poetics, which essentially, archetypally unmasks the "negativity of all temporal order" and therewith proclaims the archetypal necessity of the revolutionary principle. (The overuse of *archetypal* is striking in the Munich comment.) Precisely the opposite of a conservative-reactionary "Rückzugsposition," Goethe's dramatic experiment is an arch-progressive "Aufruf zur Begründung und Verwirklichung des immer wieder notwendigen Neuen [call to found and realize the new that is again and again necessary]" (863f.). For the Munich commentator, Schiller was no godfather to this sort of innovative classicism: Goethe's *Natürliche Tochter* is declared a sharp contrast to Schiller's nostalgic-reactionary *Braut von Messina* written at the same time. The abstraction of form and language is considered further evidence of the experimental poetological status of Goethe's text, anticipating the desubjectifying tendency of modern political drama. (We are in the neighborhood of Brechtian epic theater again.) Thus Goethe's "politisches Trauerspiel [political tragedy]" is to be seen properly as a drama of language, not of psychology or morals. By means of an objectifying linguistic form, Goethe here aimed to enable an aesthetic understanding of the historical process. At the time of the drama's composition, before Hegel and Marx, the historical process could not be understood by means of rational categories and therefore appeared to comtemporaries — including Goethe himself — as "demonic." It goes without saying that this reading ranks *Die natürliche Tochter* very highly indeed in the Goethe canon: "at the same time one of the most astonishing and most important productions of Goethe" (930).

The consistent interest in the drama since the mid eighties at the average rate of two special studies per year may be attributed to three factors. First and obviously, the comparatively new classic still offered a wide open horizon for critical approaches. Second, the contentious seventies in Germany had left a legacy: consensus was out, controversy in. The new critical paradigm of controversy commended *Die natürliche Tochter* to her major promoter during this period, Bernhard Böschenstein, who selected the drama as a significant instance of "controversies, old and new," one of the main topics of the seventh *Internationale Germanisten-Kongress* in 1985 (published 1986). And finally, next to *Faust II*, *Die natürliche Tochter* was the most "interdisciplinary" of Goethe's dramas. For the new historicist quest for contexts, this political-social-historical drama promised ample rewards, even though the new historicism in this case still looked a lot like the old positivism, complete with source studies now called intertextuality. However, since the old positivists had largely ignored our drama of then ill repute, source work still remained to be done. In another banner year for

Die natürliche Tochter, 1986 saw a total of three articles on the drama in addition to the comment of the Munich edition. In the *Jahrbuch des Freien Deutschen Hochstifts,* Stefan Bodo Würffel presented another one of Goethe's French sources, the historical work by Soulavie, while Werner Schultheis in *Euphorion* offered textual contexts for the meaning of *gothic* as Goethe used it in the stage directions.

Inevitably, propelled by the anniversary year of the French Revolution in 1989, Goethe's main source was reintroduced as well in an essay by Bernhard Böschenstein (1989) and then in his 1990 book publication of Stéphanie de Bourbon-Conti's memoirs (in German translation), together with the text of Goethe's drama and Böschenstein's essays on *Die natürliche Tochter.* (Böschenstein's third essay was first published in *Bausteine zu einem neuen Goethe* 1987.) Böschenstein explores the negativity of classicism from a Hölderlinian perspective, where political and historical questions recede before the central issue of the loss of spirit in a postreligious age. In this view *Die natürliche Tochter* figures art as compensatory compromise, as ersatz religion with Eugenie the dead goddess of an empty myth. The drama's language exhibits the inability to represent, and instead turns to self-reflexivity and deconstruction.

In tune with the sociohistorical tendency of mainstream *Germanistik,* the historicizing perspective found the largest group of followers in the eighties with four special studies in addition to a chapter in a monograph. The preferred focus of interest remained the role of the bourgeoisie: in question were, above all, the character of the Gerichtsrat and the significance of Eugenie's marriage. Concepts from the wider field of intellectual history entered to suggest new approaches: Adorno and Horkheimer's dialectic of instrumental reason, Hans Blumenberg's study of Goethean myth, Reinhard Koselleck's linkage between moral and political crises, and especially Jürgen Habermas's critique of the bourgeoisie. Opposing Vaget's focus on aristocracy, Herbert Uerlings in the *Goethe Jahrbuch* of 1987 reads in the drama a Habermasian critique of bourgeois economy and of the bourgeois state with its separation between morality and legality. (Karl Otto Conrady had borrowed Uerlings's critique of the bourgeoisie for the *Natürliche Tochter* chapter in his *Goethe* monograph 1982.) In a *Festschrift* for Viktor Zmegac (1989), Walter Weiss offers a new key to Goethe's drama about revolution, which he calls "metamorphology" but does not himself employ to unlock the mysteries of the text. A year later in *Sprachkunst,* a journal published by the Austrian Academy of Sciences, Robert von Dassanowski-Harris presents *Die natürliche Tochter* as a fullblown historical allegory, with "Eugenie/France's" dramatic fate intended to represent the "Eras of France" beginning with idealized chivalric feudalism, through the fall into a politicized aristocracy marked by hedonistic excesses (jewel scene) and despotic abuses (the royal decree) of the prerevolutionary times of Louis XVI, to end in the projection of the birth of a nation state under the auspices of the bourgeoisie (marriage). Klaus Gille's article in the *Zeitschrift für Germanistik* (formerly published by Rostock University in the German Democratic Republic) of 1991 demonstrates the state of agglomeration among historicizers as he tries out several keys to understanding the difficult work; among others, he offers reception aesthetics in rereading contemporary critics (Kotzebue, Schiller, Fichte), and in conclusion he considers, but does not engage, Koselleck's concept of eighteenth century moral criticism and political crisis.

It was a sign that *Die natürliche Tochter* had finally achieved a status of normalcy when criticism in the late eighties went beyond content-based competition between various lines of historiography, sociology, and ideology to involve the more canonical approaches from new developments in literary history and theory. In Rudolf Brandmeyer's study, *Heroik und Gegenwart: Goethes klassische Dramen* (1987), *Die natürliche Tochter* most distinctly makes the point of his thesis and therefore gets twice as much text as the established classics *Iphigenie* or *Tasso*. For Brandmeyer, the latecomer on the Goethe scene marks a watershed in Western thought. Focused on the generational split between father and daughter, the drama represents the end of one kind of history, that is, history as a heroic fiction of the past, and the painful beginning of another, that is, the modern concept of history as a factual account of reality.

Helmut Schanze in *Goethes Dramatik* (1989) rather slights our drama in a brief and very general treatment, but also finds of chief interest its concept of history. Karl Mickel's fascinating essay in the *Goethe Jahrbuch* of 1990, too, sees history at issue, but for Mickel the drama offers an innovative play with the traditional concept of history as nemesis. Supported by a host of Goethe documents new in this context, Mickel reads *Die natürliche Tochter* as a parody akin to *Reineke Fuchs*. Here Goethe presents the alienating look of the Noble Savage ("das blöde Lämmchen," as he names Eugenie), couched in deliberately alienating language in order to signal the fake character of the famed high civilization that is presently falling due to its self-destructive behavior. The function of language, finally, is at the center of an essay by Irmgard Wagner in the *Goethe Yearbook* of 1988. Within the concept of Foucauldian epochs of representation and based on Lacanian speech theory, Wagner examines the problematic status of characters, symbols, and rhetoric to argue that *Die natürliche Tochter* represents the failure of representation in language and as such marks a crisis point in the creative development of the poet, Goethe.

A fitting conclusion to the mottled postwar history of this drama, as it reflects the volatile nature of criticism itself in recent times, with its preference for divergence, controversy, and change in contrast to the earlier search for consensus, might be found in the Borchmeyer story. We have seen how the low valuation Borchmeyer accorded the drama in 1977 concerning political consciousness, language, and genre, underwent a remarkable change under the impact of Emrich and Bahr, until in 1980 he could consider the drama "one of the certainly most significant works of Goethe" — though still sounding a note of needing assurance in his "certainly." Both of Borchmeyer's judgments, however, were based on political-ideological criteria dominant in German criticism of the time. Thirteen years later, Borchmeyer's comment in the edition of the Deutscher Klassiker Verlag (1993) is far removed from such concerns. In matters of interpretation he defers, indeed he explicitly refers the reader to Böschenstein's "significant interpretation" of the absent divinity in an empty myth. Böschenstein's 1990 publication prompts, too, the big play Borchmeyer gives to Stéphanie's memoirs and his strong focus on the figure of Eugenie. For Borchmeyer now, she is a tragic heroine in the collective myth Goethe constructed from Stéphanie's individual life. Borchmeyer's other focus is the aesthetic of theater. He considers documents concerning the situation of theater director Goethe with his antirealist program, strung out between the radical theorist Schiller and a recalcitrant public.

Borchmeyer's inconclusive reading of 1993 signals another turn of the screw in the critical history of the new postwar classic: the return of the repressed. A decade and a half after the sociopolitical turn of *Germanistik,* artistic and aesthetic themes once more came to the fore. Furthermore, with the collapse of the East-West fault line, which had strongly influenced German criticism over the past two decades, political and ideological interests abated noticeably. In *Die natürliche Tochter,* only recently discovered as a major "political drama," the history of revolution now appears to Borchmeyer neutralized, aestheticized, and distanced as mythology ("reich mythologisch instrumentiert [with rich mythological instrumentation]"). It is the new historicist view of history as res gestae: fascinating, preferably odd events of the past with no import for the present, staged dramatically under a mythic-symbolic veil ("Schleier, verschleiert" 1149). History as myth is no longer relevant, merely signifying: "bedeutend" in a sort of "museale Vergötzung [museum-like idolization]" — as one of our critics once described his discipline's attitude to the classics.

Conclusion

IF AMONG THE three narratives of the afterlife of Goethe's classical dramas — *Iphigenie auf Tauris, Torquato Tasso, Die natürliche Tochter* — the one about *Tasso* appears the least satisfactory, the impression accords with the documentary record. Critical writing on *Tasso* leaves the historian, on the whole, unsatisfied. Having surveyed the century and a half leading up to the present, one is tempted to fall in with Atkins's and Magill's frustrated resignation in the early seventies. Tasso criticism does not seem to have gone anywhere. In a marked difference from the other two dramas studied here, with very few exceptions — Gundolf, Petsch, Wilkinson, Neumann — earlier Tasso criticism is no longer worth reading. Not even from strictly historical interest, since — again different from *Iphigenie* and *Natürliche Tochter* — the earlier writing on *Tasso* remained so completely uninvolved with history.

A closer look reveals some of the reasons for the barren Tasso landscape. One is the limited focus on two topics: the question about genre, and the figure of the poet. The second main reason is that critical approaches became trapped in an adversary pattern. Critics argued back and forth over whether *Tasso* was a tragedy or not, and they took sides for the poet or against him. This narrow perspective widened for a short time only, when the poet was read as the figure of the artist. The debate pro or contra tragedy, artist, or poet must needs turn repetitive and monotonous. And, since judgments of this sort are based on subjectivity, ideology, and sociohistorical positionality, the debate had to remain inconclusive. No arguments have yet convinced the opposition.

If we ask for the reasons underlying the limited scope of earlier Tasso criticism, the answer would point to the limited range of the topics and themes addressed in this drama. At the risk of offending professional self-interest, one could argue that the issues transacted in *Tasso* hold real interest only for artists, poets, and other intellectuals. Such an argument would point out that, by contrast, *Iphigenie* and *Die natürliche Tochter* involve a whole gamut of significant issues and questions concerning essential values of human existence in the cosmic world order. These two dramas lead to the very sources of human values and meaning: myth and momentous history.

The richest harvest in criticism, obviously, comes from *Iphigenie*. The issues involved in this work were always felt to be of central significance, touching the very foundations of human experience. Furthermore, *Iphigenie* as bearer of the Enlightenment message — secularization, humanism, emancipation from the myths of religion, state, and family — aroused lively reactions in an era of competing ideologies. *Iphigenie* remained a central text for Enlightenment critique, too; for catholics and conservatives from the turn of the twentieth century to Adorno and his disciples after the Second World War, all the way to Foucauldian revisionism and the postmodern revolt of the margins against dominant discourses.

Interest in *Die natürliche Tochter,* on the other hand, tended to be even more limited in scope than was the case for *Tasso.* With very few exceptions, it was the single issue of politics and revolution that drove *Natürliche Tochter* criticism. The German intellectual class of the nineteenth century, full of Francophobia and fear of revolution, had no use for this drama. No special interpretive study (excepting Düntzer's obligatory volume) exists before 1912. The amazing emergence of *Die natürliche Tochter* in the thirties was directly related, as we have seen, to the politicization of intellectual life. Incredible as it may seem after a near total silence since the First World War, this decade produced twice as many studies on the drama than on *Tasso.* The pattern was repeated in the revival after the Second World War. From the 1960s, as literary criticism in Germany became once again embroiled in politics, the political *Natürliche Tochter* could be played out against her apolitical sister, *Iphigenie.* This time, however, the political interest in *Die natürliche Tochter* took a pronounced turn toward historical perspectives. It should be noted, too, that interest in the drama has so far been limited to German scholars. It almost seems as though, in *Die natürliche Tochter,* a German history of revolution was to be claimed at least in literature and at least, too, for the greatest German author, Goethe.

Works Consulted

Editions of Goethe's Works Cited

1866–68. *Goethes Werke.* Ed. K[arl] G[oedeke]. Stuttgart: Cotta. Vol. 6.

1868–79. *Goethe's Werke.* Ed. Friedrich Strehlke. Berlin: Hempel. Vols. 7 (for *Iphigenie* and *Tasso*) and 10 (for *Die natürliche Tochter*).

1883. *Goethe's Werke.* Ed. Ludwig Geiger. Berlin: Grote. Vols. 4, 5.

1882–97. *Goethes Werke. Deutsche Nationallitteratur.* Ed. Karl J. Schröer. Berlin: Spemann. Vol. 9.

1900–08. *Goethes Werke.* Ed. Karl Heinemann. Leipzig: Bibliographisches Institut. Vol. 6.

1901. *Goethes sämtliche Werke.* Ed. Ludwig Geiger. Leipzig: Hesse. Vol. 1.

1902–07. *Goethes Werke. Jubiläums-Ausgabe.* Ed. Albert Köster. Stuttgart: Cotta. Vol. 12.

1910. *Goethes Werke in sechs Bänden.* [*Insel-Goethe.*] Ed. Erich Schmidt im Auftrage der Goethe-Gesellschaft. Leipzig: Insel. Vol. 2.

1923–24. *Goethes sämtliche Werke.* Berlin: Ullstein. Vol. 6 (for *Iphigenie*), ed. Paul Ernst. Vol. 7 (for *Tasso* and *Die natürliche Tochter*), ed. Ernst Hardt.

1926. *Goethes Werke. Festausgabe.* Ed. Robert Petsch. Leipzig: Bibliographisches Institut. Vol. 8.

1952. *Goethes Werke. Hamburger Ausgabe.* Hamburg: Wegner. Vol. 5, ed. Josef Kunz.

1954. *Goethe: Gedenkausgabe der Werke, Briefe und Gespräche.* Zurich: Artemis. Vol. 6, ed. Kurt May.

1981. *Goethes Werke. Hamburger Ausgabe.* New Edition. Hamburg: Wegner. Vol. 5, ed. Stuart Atkins.

1986 and 1990. *Goethe. Sämtliche Werke. Münchener Ausgabe.* Munich: Hanser. Vol. 6.1 (for *Die natürliche Tochter*), ed. Victor Lange. Vol. 3.1 (for *Iphigenie* and *Tasso*), ed. Hartmut Reinhardt.

1988 and 1993. *Goethe. Sämtliche Werke.* Ed. Dieter Borchmeyer. Frankfurt: Deutscher Klassiker Verlag. Vols. I.5 (for *Iphigenie* and *Tasso*) and I.6 (for *Die natürliche Tochter*). Ed. Dieter Borchmeyer.

Works Cited in Chronological Order

The following abbreviations are used throughout:

Gjb   *Jahrbuch der Goethe-Gesellschaft* (Weimar) (1880-). The title of the *GJb* varies, from the above quoted to *Goethe* and more recently *Goethe-Jahrbuch*.

GYb   *Goethe Yearbook.* Published by the Goethe Society of North America (1982–).

PEGS   *Publications of the English Goethe Society* (1886–)

Gervinus, Georg Gottfried. 1842. *Geschichte der deutschen Dichtung.* Quoted from the fourth edition 1853. Leipzig: Engelmann.

Rosencranz, Karl. 1847. *Göthe und seine Werke.* Königsberg: Bornträger.

Danzel, Theodor Wilhelm. 1848. "Goethe's *Iphigenie* und Diderot." Quoted from his *Zur Literatur und Philosophie der Goethezeit.* 1962. Stuttgart: Metzler, 164–72.

Bratranek, Franz Thomas. 1853. "Erläuterungen zu Göthe's *Iphigenie auf Tauris.*" In his *Ästhetische Studien.* Vienna: Gerold, 119–94.

Düntzer, Heinrich. 1854. *Goethes "Tasso." Zum erstenmal vollständig erläutert.* Leipzig: Wartig. Quoted from the fifth edition 1898.

Lewes, George Henry. 1855. *The Life and Works of Goethe.* London: Nutt. Quoted from the 1863 edition.

Düntzer, Heinrich. 1859a. *Goethes "Iphigenie auf Tauris." Erläutert.* Leipzig: Wartig. Quoted from the ninth edition 1899.

———. 1859b. *Goethes Trilogie "Die natürliche Tochter."* Leipzig: Wartig. Quoted from the second edition 1874.

Hettner, Hermann. 1870. *Geschichte der deutschen Literatur im achtzehnten Jahrhundert.* Quoted from his *Literaturgeschichte der Goethezeit.* Sonderausgabe. Munich: Beck, 1970.

Grimm, Herman. 1877. *Goethe Vorlesungen.* Berlin: Hertz. Quoted from the tenth edition 1915. Stuttgart: Cotta.

Schmidt, Julian. 1880. "Die Vollendung des *Tasso.* " *Preußische Jahrbücher* 46: 174–212.

Baumgartner, Alexander S. J. 1882. *Göthe: Sein Leben und seine Werke.* Freiburg: Herder. Vol. 1. Quoted from the second edition 1885.

Bulthaupt, Heinrich. 1882. *Dramaturgie der Classiker.* Oldenburg: Schulze. Vol. 1.

Schöll, Adolf. 1882. "Goethes *Tasso* und Schillers *Don Carlos.*" *Goethe in den Hauptzügen seines Lebens und Wirkens. Gesammelte Abhandlungen.* Berlin: Hertz, 304–40.

Scherer, Wilhelm. 1883. *Geschichte der deutschen Litteratur.* Berlin: Weidmann. Quoted from the eighth edition 1899.

Braun, Julius W. 1883–85. *Goethe im Urtheile seiner Zeitgenossen. Zeitungs-kritiken, Berichte, Notizen, Goethe und seine Werke betreffend, aus den Jahren 1773–1812.* 3 Vols. Berlin: Luckhardt. Reprinted edition 1969 Hildesheim: Olms.

Minor, Jacob. 1887. "Die Wielandschen Singspiele und Goethes *Iphigenie.*" *Zeitschrift für deutsche Philologie* 19: 232–39.

Fischer, Kuno. 1888. "Goethes *Iphigenie.*" Address to the third General Assembly of the Goethe-Gesellschaft. Quoted from his *Goethe-Schriften.* Heidelberg: Winter, 1900.

Huther, A. 1889. "Die heilung Orests: ein beitrag zur erklärung von Goethes *Iphigenie.*" *Neue Jahrbücher für Philologie und Pädagogik* 35: 32–43.

Reinhardt, K. 1889. "Über den künstlerischen Bau von Goethes *Tasso.*" *Berichte des Freien Deutschen Hochstifts* N.F. 5: 10–23.

Fischer, Kuno. 1890. *Goethes "Tasso."* Heidelberg: Winter.

von Loeper, Gustav. 1890. "Berlin und Weimar." *Deutsche Rundschau* 16: 30–39. Quoted from Mandelkow 1975–79, Volume 3: 197–207.

Grimm, Herman. 1892. "Leonore von Este." *Deutsche Rundschau* 18: 177–205.

Kern, Franz. 1892. *Goethes "Tasso" und Kuno Fischer.* Berlin: Nicolai'sche Verlagsbuchhandlung.

Büchner, Wilhelm. 1894. "Selbsterlebtes in Goethes *Tasso.*" *GJb* 15: 178–86.

Bielschowsky, Albert. 1895. *Goethe: Sein Leben und seine Werke.* Vol 1 (for *Iphigenie* and *Tasso*). Vol. 2 (for *Natürliche Tochter*) publ. posth. 1903. Munich: Beck. Quoted from the 23rd edition 1912.

Meyer, Richard M. 1895. *Goethe.* 3 vols. Berlin: Hofmann. Quoted from the one-vol. *Volksausgabe.* Berlin: Bondi, 1913.

Düntzer, Heinrich. 1896. "Der Ausgang von Goethes *Tasso.*" *Zeitschrift für deutsche Philologie* 28: 56–71.

Rößler, Constantin. 1896. "Das Tassoräthsel." *Preußische Jahrbücher* 84: 226–45.

Diekhoff, Tobias. 1897. "Note on Goethe's *Tasso,* ll. 1325–1337." *Modern Language Notes* 12: 345–47.

Grimm, Herman. 1897. "Weltcharaktere." *Deutsche Rundschau* 23: 86–125.

Scheidemantel, Eduard. 1897. "Neues zur Entstehungsgeschichte von Goethes *Torquato Tasso.*" *GJb* 18: 163–73.

Heinemann, Karl. 1899. "Die Heilung des Orest." *GJb* 20: 212–20.

Witkowski, Georg. 1899. *Goethe.* Leipzig: Seemann und Gesellschaft für graphische Industrie.

Wohlrab, Martin. 1899. "Die Entsühnung in Goethes *Iphigenie auf Tauris.*" *Neue Jahrbücher für klassisches Altertum* 4: 86–93.

Metz, Adolf. 1900. "Die Heilung des Orestes in Goethes *Iphigenie.*" *Preußische Jahrbücher* 102: 27–46.

Dalmeyda, Georges. 1902. "Goethes *Tasso* und Vignys *Chatterton.*" *GJb* 23: 177–85.

Witkowski, Georg. 1903. "Goethes *Torquato Tasso* als dramatisches Kunstwerk." *Jahrbuch des Freien Deutschen Hochstifts* 2: 265–81.

Dilthey, Wilhelm. 1905. *Das Erlebnis und die Dichtung.* Leipzig: Teubner. Quoted from the fourth edition 1913.

Metz, Adolf. 1905. "Die Tragödie in Goethes *Tasso.*" *Preußische Jahrbücher* 122: 292–308.

Meyer, Richard M. 1905. "Goethes italienische Dramen." *GJb* 26: 126–32.

Wessely, Rudolf. 1905. "Die erste Prosafassung von Goethes *Iphigenie* und die vollendete Dichtung." *Nord und Süd* 112: 419–40.

Hofmannsthal, Hugo von. 1906. "Unterhaltung über den *Tasso* von Goethe." Quoted from his *Gesammelte Werke in Einzelausgaben. Prosa II.* 1951. Frankfurt: Fischer, 212–28.

Castle, Eduard. 1907. "Tasso-Probleme: Ein Goethemosaik." *Zeitschrift für österreichische Gymnasien* 58: 97–123. [1905 lecture to Wiener Goethe-Verein.] Quoted from his *In Goethes Geist.* 1926, 161–92.

Schrempf, Christoph. 1907. *Goethes Lebensanschauung in ihrer geschichtlichen Entwicklung.* Stuttgart: Frommann. Vol. 2.

Pniower, Otto. 1908. "*Torquato Tasso.*" [Introduction to Pantheon edition of Goethe's works, vol. 28.] Quoted from his *Dichtungen und Dichter: Essais und Studien.* 1912. Berlin: Fischer, 58–78.

Engel, Eduard. 1909. *Goethe: Der Mann und das Werk.* Berlin: Concordia Deutsche Verlagsanstalt. Quoted from the third edition 1910.

Castle, Eduard. 1910. "*Die natürliche Tochter*: Ein Rekonstruktionsversuch des Trauerspiels von Goethe." *Chronik des Wiener Goethe-Vereins* 24: 37–50. Quoted from his *In Goethes Geist.* 1926, 237–65.

Rueff, Hans. 1910. *Zur Entstehungsgeschichte von Goethes "Torquato Tasso."* Marburg: Elwert. Quoted from the reprinted edition 1968. New York: Johnson.

Willenbücher, Hugo. 1910. "Antonio und Leonore Sanvitale in Goethes *Torquato Tasso.*" *Zeitschrift für den deutschen Unterricht* 24: 481–98.

Hoffmann, Paul. 1911. "*Die natürliche Tochter* und das Berliner Theater-Publikum." *Euphorion* 18: 482–84.

Kilian, Eugen. 1911. "*Die natürliche Tochter* auf der Bühne." *GJb* 32: 62–72.

Fries, Albert. 1912. *Goethes "Natürliche Tochter."* Berlin: Ebering.

Fries, Carl. 1912. "Parzenlied und Völuspa." *GJb* 33: 85–96.

Kettner, Gustav. 1912. *Goethes Drama "Die natürliche Tochter."* Berlin: Weidmann.

Lucerna, Camilla. 1912. "Der morphologische Grundriß und die religiöse Entwicklungsidee des Goetheschen Dramas *Iphigenie auf Tauris.*" *GJb* 33: 97–112.

Steinweg, Carl A. 1912. *Goethes Seelendramen und ihre französischen Vorlagen.* Halle: Niemeyer.

Brandes, Georg. 1915. *Wolfgang Goethe.* Copenhagen: Gyldental. Quoted from the English translation. New York: Frank-Maurice. 1925.

Gundolf, Friedrich. 1916. *Goethe.* Berlin: Bondi.

Mann, Thomas. 1917. *Betrachtungen eines Unpolitischen.* Berlin: S. Fischer.

Möller, Marx. 1917. *Unser großes vaterländisches Frauendrama. Studien zu Goethes "Natürlicher Tochter."* Berlin [publisher unavailable].

Baker, George M. 1918. "The Healing of Orestes." *Modern Philology* 15: 349–54.

Spieß, Otto. 1918. *Die dramatische Handlung in Goethes "Clavigo," "Egmont" und "Iphigenie."* Halle: Niemeyer.

Daffis, Hans. 1919. "Goethes *Tasso* und Kleists *Prinz von Homburg.*" *Das deutsche Drama* 2: 78–84.

Korff, Hermann August. 1921. "Zur *Iphigenie.*" *Zeitschrift für Deutschkunde* 35: 311–16.

Roethe, Gustav. 1922. "Der Ausgang des *Tasso.*" *GJb* 9: 119–32. [First publ. 1921 in *Funde und Forschungen. Festschrift Julius Wahle.* Leipzig: Insel, 92–109.]

Tiedge, Johannes. 1922. "Goethes Iphigenie als weibliche Gegengestalt zu Wagners Parsifal." *GJb* 9: 116–18.

Warncke, Pedro. 1922–24. "Die Entsühnung des Orest in Goethes *Iphigenie auf Tauris,* unter Berücksichtigung einer Entwicklung in des Dichters Auffassung von der 1. zur 4. Gestalt der Dichtung." *GJb* 9: 113–15, and 10: 131–38. The *GJb* suspended publication in the inflation year 1923.

Gerhard, Melitta. 1923. "Goethes Erleben der Französischen Revolution im Spiegel der *Natürlichen Tochter.*" *Deutsche Vierteljahresschrift für Literaturwissenschaft und Geistesgeschichte* 1: 281–301. Quoted from her *Leben im Gesetz: Fünf Goethe-Aufsätze.* 1966. Bern: Francke, 7–33.

Robertson, John George. 1924. "Goethe's *Iphigenie auf Tauris:* Some New Points of View." *PEGS* n.s. 1: 25–43.

Goldschmidt, Helene. 1925. *Das deutsche Künstlerdrama von Goethe bis R. Wagner.* Weimar: Duncker.

Schnapp, Friedrich. 1925. "Die Berliner Handschrift der *Natürlichen Tochter.*" *GJb* 11: 173–81.

Castle, Eduard. 1926. *In Goethes Geist.* Vienna: Österreichischer Bundesverlag für Unterricht, Wissenschaft und Kunst.

Schulze, Berthold. 1926. "Episches im Drama. Ein induktiver Versuch auf Grund von Goethes *Iphigenie.*" *Zeitschrift für Ästhetik und Allgemeine Kunstwissenschaft* 20: 238–41.

Linden, Walther. 1927. "Die Lebensprobleme in Goethes *Tasso.*" *Zeitschrift für Deutschkunde* 41: 337–55.

Robertson, John George. 1927. *Goethe.* London: Routledge. Quoted from 1973 reprint of the 1932 edition *The Life and Work of Goethe.* New York: Haskell House.

Schreiber, Carl F. 1927. "Nochmals 'Die drei losen Nymphen'." *GJb* 13: 96–105.

Robertson, John George. 1928. "The Tragedy of Goethe's *Tasso.*" *PEGS* n.s. 5: 46–59.

Levy, Erna. 1929. *Die Gestalt des Künstlers im deutschen Drama von Goethe bis Hebbel.* Berlin: Ebering.

Ernst, Fritz. 1930. "Iphigeneia." *Mélanges d'histoire littéraire générale et comparée offerts à Fernand Baldensperger.* Republished 1946 as "Der Weg Iphigeniens" in his *Essais.* Zurich: Wasmuth. Vol. 2: 116–41.

Korff, Hermann August. 1930. *Geist der Goethezeit.* Vol 2. Leipzig: Weber.

Viëtor, Karl. 1930. *Der junge Goethe.* Leipzig: Quelle & Meyer. Second revised edition 1951.

Burkhard, Arthur. 1931. "German Dramas, Classic and Romantic." *German Quarterly* 4: 141–63.

Fairley, Barker. 1932. *Goethe as Revealed in His Poetry.* London and Toronto: Dent. Quoted from the second edition 1963. New York: Ungar.

Furtmüller, Carl. 1932. "*Iphigenie auf Tauris.*" *Internationale Zeitschrift für Individualpsychologie* 10: 328–39.

Hérenger, Alexandre. 1932. "La Religion de la Vérité dans *Iphigenie.*" *Revue de Littérature Comparée* 12: 43–48.

Sprengel, Johann Georg. 1932. "*Iphigenie auf Tauris* als Erlebnis und Sinnbild." *Zeitschrift für deutsche Bildung* 8: 126–31.

Engel, Pepi. 1933. *Der dramatische Vortrieb in Goethes "Torquato Tasso."* Halle: Niemeyer.

Grabowsky, Adolf. 1933. "Goethes *Natürliche Tochter* als politisches Bekenntnis." *Zeitschrift für Politik* 22: 92–109. Republished 1951 with substantial changes as "Goethes *Natürliche Tochter* als Bekenntnis." *GJb* 13: 1–27.

Lüdtke, Ernst. 1933. *Vom Wesen deutscher und französischer Klassik: Versuch einer Stildeutung an Goethes "Iphigenie" und Racines "Mithridate."* Stettin: Ostsee-Verlag.

Michéa, René. 1934a. "L'élément pictural de *Torquato Tasso.*" *Revue de l'Enseignement des Langues Vivantes* 51: 109–17.

————. 1934b. "L'Italianisme de *Torquato Tasso*." *Revue Germanique* 25: 209–17.

Willige, Wilhelm. 1934. "Wachstum und Verantwortung: Betrachtungen über Goethes Mannesjahre, besonders über *Die natürliche Tochter*." *Zeitschrift für Geschichte der Erziehung und des Unterrichts* 24: 249–59. Republished with minor revisions 1935 as "Verantwortung und Gemeinschaftsgesinnung in Goethes Mannesjahren" in *Zeitschrift für Deutschkunde* 49: 111–19.

Butler, E. M. 1935. *The Tyranny of Greece over Germany*. Cambridge University Press. Quoted from the reedition 1958. Boston: Beacon Press.

Kommerell, Max. 1936. "Goethes Ballade vom vertriebenen Grafen." *Die Neue Rundschau* 47: 1209–19.

Petsch, Robert. 1937. "*Iphigenie auf Tauris*." *GJb* N.F. 2: 163–83.

Boyd, James. 1938. "Four Prayers in Goethe's *Iphigenie*." *German Studies. Festschrift H. G. Fiedler*. Oxford University Press, 33–61.

Schröder, Rudolf Alexander. 1938. "Ein Wort über die *Natürliche Tochter*." *Goethe-Kalender* 31: 63–100. Reprinted in his *Die Aufsätze und Reden*. Vol. 1 (*Gesammelte Werke* Vol. 2). Frankfurt: Suhrkamp. 1952, 472–95.

Beck, Adolf. 1939. "Goethes *Iphigenie* und Maler Müllers *Niobe*." *Dichtung und Volkstum*. N.F. *des Euphorion* 40: 157–74.

Bradish, Joseph A. von. 1939. "Die Entstehung der *Iphigenie auf Tauris* 1779. Nach Goethes Tagebüchern und Briefen." *German Quarterly* 12: 140–52.

May, Kurt. 1939. "Goethes *Natürliche Tochter*." *GJb* 4: 147–63.

Staiger, Emil. 1939. *Die Zeit als Einbildungskraft des Dichters: Untersuchungen zu Gedichten von Brentano, Goethe und Keller*. Zurich: Atlantis. Quoted from the 1953 reprinted edition.

Müller, Joachim. 1940. "Goethes *Iphigenie*." *Zeitschrift für Deutschkunde* 54: 273–84.

Boyd, James. 1942. *Goethe's "Iphigenie auf Tauris."* Oxford: Blackwell.

Jockers, Ernst. 1942. *Soziale Polarität in Goethes Klassik*. Philadelphia: [Jockers with grant from the Committee on the Publication of Research of the University of Pennsylvania].

Emrich, Wilhelm. 1943. *Die Symbolik von "Faust II": Sinn und Vorformen*. Berlin: Junker und Dünnhaupt. Quoted from the second edition 1957. Bonn: Bouvier.

Staiger, Emil. 1943. "Goethes *Torquato Tasso*." *Jahrbuch der literarischen Vereinigung Winterthur* 20: 5–18.

Peacock, Ronald. 1946. "Goethe's Version of Poetic Drama." *PEGS* n.s. 16: 29–53.

Staiger, Emil. 1946. "Goethe: *Die natürliche Tochter*." *Trivium* 4: 227–28.

Wilkinson, Elizabeth M. 1946. "Goethe's *Tasso*: The Tragedy of a Creative Artist." *PEGS* n.s. 15: 96–127. Quoted from Wilkinson and L. A. Willoughby *Goethe: Poet and Thinker.* 1962. London: Arnold, 75–94.

Adorno, Theodor W. and Max Horkheimer. 1947. *Dialektik der Aufklärung: Philosophische Fragmente.* Amsterdam: Querido.

Fairley, Barker. 1947. *A Study of Goethe.* Oxford: Clarendon.

Kahn, Ludwig W. 1947. "Goethes *Iphigenie*, Kleists *Amphitryon* und Kierkegaard." *Monatshefte* 39: 234–36.

Stegmeyer, Franz. 1947. "Iphigeneia oder: Die Geburt der Humanität des Abendlandes." In his *Europäische Profile.* Wiesbaden: Limes, 56–64.

Appelbaum, Ilse. 1948. "Goethe's *Iphigenie* und Schiller's *Braut von Messina.*" *PEGS* n.s. 17: 43–73.

Wiese, Benno von. 1948. *Die deutsche Tragödie von Lessing bis Hebbel.* Hamburg: Hoffmann und Campe. Quoted from the sixth edition 1964.

Atkins, Stuart. 1949. "On the Opening Lines of Goethe's *Iphigenie.*" *The Germanic Review* 24: 116–23.

Heller, Erich. 1949. "Goethe and the Avoidance of Tragedy." *The Listener* 42: 1045–46. Quoted from his *The Disinherited Mind.* 1952. Cambridge: Bowes and Bowes, 35–63.

Leibrich, Louis. 1949. "*Iphigénie en Tauride* à la lumière de la philosophie d'aujourd'hui." *Etudes Germaniques* 4: 129–38.

Seidlin, Oskar. 1949. "Goethe's *Iphigenie* and the humane ideal." *Modern Language Quarterly* 10: 307–20.

Viëtor, Karl. 1949. *Goethe the Poet.* New York: Russell and Russell. Quoted from the 1970 edition.

Voser, Hans-Ulrich. 1949. *Individualität und Tragik in Goethes Dramen.* Zurich: Artemis.

Wilkinson, Elizabeth M. 1949. "'Tasso — ein gesteigerter Werther' in the light of Goethe's principle of 'Steigerung'." *Modern Language Review* 44: 305–28. [German translation 1951 *GJb* 13: 28–58.] Quoted from Wilkinson and Willoughby *Goethe: Poet and Thinker.* 1962, 185–213.

Blumenthal, Lieselotte. 1950. "Die Tasso-Handschriften." *GJb* 12: 89–125.

Brendel, Otto J. 1950. "*Iphigenie auf Tauris.*" *Goethe Bicentennial Studies.* Ed. Hubert J. Meessen. Bloomington: Indiana University Press, 1–47.

Blumenthal, Lieselotte. 1951. "Goethes Bühnenbearbeitung des *Tasso.*" *GJb* 13: 59–85.

Wolff, Hans M. 1951. *Goethes Weg zur Humanität.* Munich: Lehnen.

Adorno, Theodor W. 1952. *Versuch über Wagner.* Berlin: Suhrkamp.

Ernst, Fritz. 1952. "Fragment über Goethes *Torquato Tasso.*" *Merkur* 6 (1): 65–70. [Lecture 1949 on Goethe's birthday in Olten, Switzerland.]

Jenkins, Sylvia P. 1952. "The Image of the Goddess in *Iphigenie auf Tauris.*" *PEGS* n.s. 21: 56–80.

Manasse, Ernst Moritz. 1952. "Iphigenie und die Götter." *Modern Language Quarterly* 13: 377–91.

Stahl, Ernest L. 1952. "Tasso's Tragedy and Salvation." *German Studies. Festschrift L. A. Willoughby.* Oxford: Blackwell, 191–203.

Staiger, Emil. 1952. *Goethe.* Zurich: Atlantis. Vol. 1 for *Iphigenie* and *Tasso.* Vol. 2 (1956) for *Natürliche Tochter.*

Wolff, Hans M. 1952. *Goethe in der Periode der "Wahlverwandtschaften" (1802–1809).* Bern: Francke.

Fambach, Oscar. 1953. *Goethe und seine Kritiker. Die wesentlichen Rezensionen, aus der periodischen Literatur seiner Zeit, begleitet von Goethes eigenen und seiner Freunde Äußerungen zu deren Gehalt. In Einzeldarstellungen mit einem Anhang: Bibliographie der Goethe-Kritik bis zu Goethes Tod.* Düsseldorf: Ehlermann.

Müller, Günther. 1953. "Das Parzenlied in Goethes *Iphigenie.*" *PEGS* n.s. 22: 84–106.

Mulot, Arno. 1953. "Goethes *Tasso*: Eine Interpretation von vier Szenen." *Wirkendes Wort* 3: 23–34.

Storz, Gerhard. 1953. "*Iphigenie auf Tauris.*" In his *Goethe-Vigilien oder Versuche in der Kunst, Dichtung zu verstehen.* Stuttgart: Klett, 5–18.

Ernst, Fritz. 1954. "Goethes *Natürliche Tochter.*" *Neue Zürcher Zeitung*, June 6. Quoted from his *Späte Essais.* 1963. Zurich: Atlantis, 138–45.

Hock, Erich. 1954. "Grillparzers Lustspiel [and *Iphigenie*]." *Wirkendes Wort* 4: 12–13.

Rasch, Wolfdietrich. 1954. *Goethes "Torquato Tasso": Die Tragödie des Dichters.* Stuttgart: Metzler.

Seidlin, Oskar. 1955. "Goethes *Iphigenie* — 'verteufelt human'?" *Wirkendes Wort* 5: 272–80.

Boeschenstein, Hermann. 1956. "Goethe's *Natürliche Tochter.*" *PEGS* n.s. 25: 21–40.

Burckhardt, Sigurd. 1956. "Die Stimme der Wahrheit und der Menschlichkeit: Goethes *Iphigenie.*" *Monatshefte* 48: 49–71. Quoted from Burckhardt 1970, 33–56.

Lindenau, Herbert. 1956. "Die geistesgeschichtlichen Voraussetzungen von Goethes *Iphigenie*: Zur Geschichte der Säkularisierung christlicher Denkformen in der deutschen Dichtung des 18. Jahrhunderts." *Zeitschrift für deutsche Philologie* 75: 113–53.

Moenkemeyer, Heinz. 1956. "Das Politische als Bereich der Sorge in Goethes Drama *Die natürliche Tochter.*" *Monatshefte* 48: 137–48.

Silz, Walter. 1956. "Ambivalences in Goethe's *Tasso*." *The Germanic Review* 31: 243–68.

Bänninger, Verena. 1957. *Goethes "Natürliche Tochter": Bühnenstil und Gehalt.* Zurich: Atlantis.

Browning, Robert M. 1957. "The Humanity of Goethe's *Iphigenie*." *German Quarterly* 30: 98–113.

Burckhardt, Sigurd. 1957. "Methodische Voraussetzungen zu geistesgeschichtlichen Untersuchungen: Randbemerkung zu Herbert Lindenaus Iphigenie-Aufsatz." *Zeitschrift für deutsche Philologie* 76: 228–30.

———. 1958. "The Consistency of Goethe's *Tasso*." *Journal of English and Germanic Philology* 57: 394–402. Quoted from Burckhardt 1970, 57–65.

Klein, Johannes. 1958. "*Nathan, Iphigenie, Don Carlos:* Bemerkungen zum vor- und frühklassischen Drama." *Wirkendes Wort* 8: 77–84.

Wiese, Benno von, ed. 1958. *Das deutsche Drama vom Barock bis zur Gegenwart.* Düsseldorf: Bagel. Vol. 1.

Includes:

Hass, Hans-Egon. "Goethe: *Die natürliche Tochter*." 215–47.

Henkel, Arthur. "Goethe: *Iphigenie auf Tauris*." 169–92.

Wilkinson, Elizabeth M. "Goethe: *Torquato Tasso*." 195–214.

Allison, D. E. 1959. "The Spiritual Element in Schiller's *Jungfrau* and Goethe's *Iphigenie*." *German Quarterly* 32: 316–29.

Blumenthal, Lieselotte. 1959. "Arkadien in Goethes *Tasso*." *GJb* 21: 1–24.

Burger, Heinz Otto. 1959. "Zur Interpretation von Goethes *Iphigenie*." *Germanisch-Romanische Monatsschrift* N.F. 6: 266–77.

Jenkins, Sylvia P. 1959. "Goethe's *Die natürliche Tochter*." *PEGS* n.s. 28: 40–63.

Mantey, Johannes. 1959. *Der Sprachstil in Goethes "Tasso."* Berlin: Akademie-Verlag.

1959. *The Era of Goethe: Essays Presented to James Boyd.* Oxford: Blackwell. Quoted from the reprinted edition 1968. Freeport, N.Y.: Books for Libraries Press.

Includes:

Pascal, Roy. "Some Words of Pylades." 106–17.

Peacock, Ronald. "Incompleteness and Discrepancy in *Die natürliche Tochter*." 118–36.

Peacock, Ronald. 1959. *Goethe's Major Plays.* Manchester University Press.

Apelt, Hermann. 1960. "Zwischen Euripides und Goethe." *GJb* N.F. 22: 54–63.

Burckhardt, Sigurd. 1960. "*Die natürliche Tochter,* Goethes *Iphigenie in Aulis?*" *Germanisch-Romanische Monatsschrift* N.F. 10: 12–34. Quoted from Burckhardt 1970, 66–93.

Emrich, Wilhelm. 1960. *Protest und Verheißung: Studien zur klassischen und modernen Dichtung.* Frankfurt: Athenäum.

Friederici, Hans. 1960. "Die Konflikte in Goethes *Iphigenie* als Abbildungen gesellschaftlicher Widersprüche." *Weimarer Beiträge* 6: 1055–65.

Hodler, Werner. 1960. "Zur Erklärung von Goethes *Iphigenie.*" *Germanisch-Romanische Monatsschrift* N.F. 10: 158–64.

Schumann, Detlev W. 1960. "Die Bekenntnisszenen in Goethes *Iphigenie*: Symmetrie und Steigerung." *Jahrbuch der Deutschen Schiller-Gesellschaft* 4: 229–46.

Böckmann, Paul. 1961. "Die Symbolik in der *Natürlichen Tochter* Goethes." *Worte und Werte. Festschrift Bruno Marckwardt.* Ed. Gustav Erdmann and Adolf Eichstaedt. Berlin: de Gruyter, 11–23.

Leppmann, Wolfgang. 1961. *The German Image of Goethe.* Oxford: Clarendon Press.

Stahl, E[rnest] L. 1961a. *Goethe: "Iphigenie auf Tauris."* London: Arnold.

———. 1961b. "Fluch und Entsühnung in Goethes *Iphigenie auf Tauris.*" *Germanisch-Romanische Monatsschrift* N.F. 11: 179–84.

Bräuning-Oktavio, Hermann. 1962. "Der Einfluß von Johann Heinrich Mercks Schicksal auf Goethes *Faust* (1774) und *Tasso* (1780/88)." *Jahrbuch des Freien Deutschen Hochstifts,* 9–57.

Hamburger, Käte. 1962. "Iphigenie." In her *Von Sophokles zu Sartre: Griechische Dramenfiguren antik und modern.* Stuttgart: Kohlhammer, 95–120. Quoted from the third edition 1965.

Peacock, Ronald. 1962. "Goethes *Die natürliche Tochter* als Erlebnisdichtung." *Deutsche Vierteljahresschrift für Literaturwissenschaft und Geistesgeschichte* 36: 1–25.

Politzer, Heinz. 1962. "No man is an island: A Note on Image and Thought in Goethe's *Iphigenie.*" *The Germanic Review* 37: 42–54. Quoted from his *Das Schweigen der Sirenen.* 1968. Stuttgart: Metzler, 285–311.

Eissler, Kurt Robert. 1963. *Goethe: A Psychoanalytic Study.* 2 Vols. Detroit: Wayne State University Press.

Hatfield, Henry. 1963. *Goethe. A Critical Introduction.* New York: New Directions. Quoted from the Harvard University Press edition 1964.

Staroste, Wolfgang. 1963. "Symbolische Raumgestaltung in Goethes *Natürlicher Tochter.*" *Jahrbuch der Deutschen Schiller-Gesellschaft* 7: 235–52.

Hatfield, Henry. 1964. *Aesthetic Paganism in German Literature from Winckelmann to the Death of Goethe.* Harvard University Press.

Papst, Edmund. 1964. "Doubt, Certainty, and Truth: Tasso's Vision of Reality." *PEGS* n.s. 34: 122–52.

Colby, Ursula J. 1965. "The Sorrows of Iphigenie." *PEGS* n.s. 35: 38–67.

Emrich, Wilhelm. 1965. *Geist und Widergeist: Wahrheit und Lüge der Literatur. Studien.* Frankfurt: Athenäum.

Neumann, Gerhard. 1965. *Konfiguration: Studien zu Goethes "Torquato Tasso."* Munich: Fink.

Ryan, Lawrence. 1965. "Die Tragödie des Dichters in Goethes *Torquato Tasso.*" *Jahrbuch der Deutschen Schiller-Gesellschaft* 9: 283–322.

Walser, Martin. 1965. "Imitation oder Realismus." [Paper read at the *Germanistentag* in Essen 1964.] *Erfahrungen und Leseerfahrungen.* 1965. Frankfurt: Suhrkamp, 66–93.

Stammen, Theo. 1966. *Goethe und die Französische Revolution: Eine Interpretation der "Natürlichen Tochter."* Munich: Beck.

Adorno, Theodor W. 1967. "Zum Klassizismus von Goethes *Iphigenie.*" *Die Neue Rundschau* 78: 586–99.

Gray, Ronald. 1967. *Goethe. A Critical Introduction.* Cambridge University Press.

Melchinger, Siegfried. 1967. "Das Theater Goethes: Am Beispiel der *Iphigenie.*" *Jahrbuch der Deutschen Schiller-Gesellschaft* 11: 297–319.

Mitscherlich, Alexander and Margarete. 1967. *Die Unfähigkeit zu trauern: Grundlagen kollektiven Verhaltens.* Munich: Piper.

Emrich, Wilhelm. 1968. *Polemik: Streitschriften, Pressefehden und kritische Essais um Prinzipien, Methoden und Maßstäbe der Literaturkritik.* Frankfurt: Athenäum.

Includes:

———. 1964. "Marquis de Sade und die natürliche Tochter." 52–56.

Nahler, Horst. 1968. "Dichtertum und Moralität in Goethes *Torquato Tasso.*" *Studien zur Goethezeit. Festschrift Lieselotte Blumenthal.* Ed. Helmut Holtzhauer and Bernhard Zeller. Weimar: Böhlau, 285–301.

Werner, Hans-Georg. 1968. "Antinomien der Humanitätskonzeption in Goethes *Iphigenie.*" *Weimarer Beiträge* 14: 361–84.

Angst, Joachim and Hackert, Fritz. 1969. *Erläuterungen und Dokumente. Johann Wolfgang Goethe: Iphigenie auf Tauris.* Stuttgart: Reclam.

Forster, Leonard. 1969. "Thoughts on Tasso's Last Monologue." *Essays on German Language, Culture, and Society. Festschrift for Roy Pascal.* Ed. Siegbert Prawer. London: Institute of Germanic Studies, 18–23.

Magill, C. P. 1969. "Torquato Tasso oder Die Feindlichen Brüder." *German Life and Letters* n.s. 23: 39–47.

Müller, Joachim. 1969. "Das Wagnis der Humanität: Goethes *Iphigenie.*" In his *Neue Goethe-Studien.* Halle: Niemeyer, 7–25. [Substantially revised version of his 1940 article.]

Burckhardt, Sigurd. 1970. *The Drama of Language.* Baltimore: Johns Hopkins University Press.

Canaris, Volker. 1970. *Goethe u. a. "Torquato Tasso": Regiebuch der Bremer Inszenierung.* Frankfurt: Suhrkamp.

Holmes, T. M. 1970. "Homage and Revolt in Goethe's *Torquato Tasso.*" *Modern Language Review* 65: 813–19.

Waldeck, Marie-Luise. 1970. "The Princess in *Torquato Tasso*: Further Reflections on an Enigma." *Oxford German Studies* 5: 14–27.

Abbé, Derek van. 1971. "Truth and Illusion about *Die natürliche Tochter.*" *PEGS* n.s. 41: 1–20.

Boulby, Mark. 1972. "Judgment by Epithet in Goethe's *Torquato Tasso.*" *PMLA* 87: 167–81.

Schlaffer, Hannelore. 1972. *Dramenform und Klassenstruktur: Eine Analyse der dramatis persona "Volk."* Stuttgart: Metzler.

Weiss, Hermann F. 1972. "Image Structures in Goethe's *Iphigenie auf Tauris.*" *Modern Language Notes* 87: 433–49.

Atkins, Stuart. 1973. "Observations on Goethe's *Torquato Tasso.*" *Carleton Germanic Papers* 1: 41–59.

Fowler, Frank M. 1973. "Storm and Thunder in Gluck's and Goethe's *Iphigenie auf Tauris* and in Schiller's *Die Jungfrau von Orleans.*" *PEGS* n.s. 43: 28–56.

Graham, Ilse. 1973. *Goethe and Lessing: The Wellsprings of Creation.* New York: Barnes and Noble.

Ivo, Hubert. 1973. "Die politische Dimension des Deutschunterrichts. Zum Beispiel: Goethes *Iphigenie.*" *Diskussion Deutsch* 4: 5–36.

Jauß, Hans Robert. 1973. "Racines und Goethes *Iphigenie*: Mit einem Nachwort über die Partialität der rezeptionsästhetischen Methode." *Neue Hefte für Philosophie* 4: 1–46.

Menhennet, Alan. 1973. *Order and Freedom: Literature and Society in Germany from 1720 to 1805.* New York: Basic Books.

Prudhoe, John Edgar. 1973. *The Theatre of Goethe and Schiller.* Totowa N.J.: Bowman and Littlefield.

Lamport, F. J. 1974. "'Entfernten Weltgetöses Widerhall': Politics in Goethe's Plays." *PEGS* n.s. 44: 41–62.

Lorenz, Rolf. 1974. "Utopie contra Entfremdung? Eine Entgegnung auf H. Ivos Versuch, Goethes *Iphigenie* politisch zu verstehen." *Diskussion Deutsch* 5: 181–92.

Pascal, Roy. 1974. "Der Versdialog. Ein Gespräch über Goethes *Iphigenie auf Tauris.*" *Festschrift Friedrich Beißner.* Ed. Ulrich Gaier and Werner Volke. Bebenhausen: Rotsch, 333–40.

Redslob, Edwin. 1974. "*Torquato Tasso.*" *Neue deutsche Hefte* 21: 521–31.

Ziolkowski, Theodore. 1974. "The Imperiled Sanctuary: Toward a Paradigm of Goethe's Classical Dramas." *Studies in the German Drama. Festschrift Walter Silz.* Ed. Donald H. Crosby and George C. Schoolfield. Chapel Hill: University of North Carolina Press, 71–87.

Fischer-Lichte, Erika. 1975. "Goethes *Iphigenie* — Reflexion auf die Grundwidersprüche der bürgerlichen Gesellschaft: Zur Kontroverse Ivo/ Lorenz." *Diskussion Deutsch* 6: 1–25.

Mandelkow, Karl Robert. 1975–79. *Goethe im Urteil seiner Kritiker: Dokumente zur Wirkungsgeschichte Goethes in Deutschland.* 4 volumes. Munich: Beck.

Farrelly, Daniel J. 1976. "Iphigenie as 'schöne Seele'." *New German Studies* 4: 55–76.

Heukenkamp, Rudolf. 1976. "*Torquato Tasso* im Deutschen Theater." *Weimarer Beiträge* 22 (6): 137–45.

Marahrens, Gerwin. 1976. "Die organisch-vegetative Metaphorik in Goethes klassischen Dramen *Iphigenie auf Tauris, Torquato Tasso* und *Die natürliche Tochter.*" *Kommunikative Metaphorik: Die Funktion des literarischen Bildes in der deutschen Literatur von ihren Anfängen bis zur Gegenwart.* Ed. Holger A. Pausch. Bonn: Bouvier, 96–116.

Rohmer, Rolf. 1976. "Klassizität und Realität in Goethes Frühweimarer Dramen (besonders *Iphigenie auf Tauris*)." *GJb* 93: 38–50.

Schaum, Konrad. 1976. "Der historische Aspekt in Goethes *Iphigenie.*" *Versuche zu Goethe. Festschrift Erich Heller.* Ed. Volker Dürr and Geza von Molnar. Heidelberg: Stiehm, 248–68.

Borchmeyer, Dieter. 1977. *Höfische Gesellschaft und Französische Revolution bei Goethe: Adliges und bürgerliches Wertsystem im Urteil der Weimarer Klassik.* Kronberg: Athenäum.

Bürger, Christa. 1977. *Der Ursprung der bürgerlichen Institution Kunst im höfischen Weimar: Literatursoziologische Untersuchungen zum klassischen Goethe.* Frankfurt: Suhrkamp.

Conrady, Karl Otto, ed. 1977. *Deutsche Literatur zur Zeit der Klassik.* Stuttgart: Reclam.

Includes:

Bahr, Ehrhard. "Goethes *Natürliche Tochter:* Weimarer Hofklassik und Französische Revolution." 226–42.

Bürger, Christa. "Der bürgerliche Schriftsteller im höfischen Mäzenat: Literatursoziologische Bemerkungen zu Goethes *Tasso.*" 141–53.

Fischer-Lichte, Erika. "Probleme der Rezeption klassischer Werke — am Beispiel von Goethes *Iphigenie.*" 114–40.

Emrich, Wilhelm. 1977. "Goethes Trauerspiel *Die natürliche Tochter:* Zur Ursprungsgeschichte der modernen Welt." *Aspekte der Goethezeit. Festschrift Victor Lange.* Ed. Stanley Corngold et al. Göttingen: Vandenhoeck & Ruprecht, 163–82.

Graham, Ilse. 1977. *Goethe, Portrait of the Artist*. Berlin: de Gruyter.

Grimm, Reinhold. 1977. "Dichterhelden: Tasso, Empedokles und die Folgen." *Basis. Jahrbuch für deutsche Gegenwartsliteratur* 7: 7–25.

Kaiser, Gerhard. 1977. "Der Dichter und die Gesellschaft in Goethes *Torquato Tasso*." In his *Wandrer und Idylle: Goethe und die Phänomenologie der Natur in der deutschen Dichtung von Geßner bie Gottfried Keller*. Göttingen: Vandenhoeck & Ruprecht, 175–208.

Williams, J. R. 1977. "Reflections in Tasso's Final Speech." *PEGS* n.s. 47: 47–67.

Yuill, William F. 1977. "Lofty Precepts and Well-Tempered Madness: Generalisation and Verbal Pattern in Goethe's *Torquato Tasso*." *German Life and Letters* n.s. 31: 114–29.

Dye, Robert Ellis. 1978. "Zu Gleichem Gleiches: The Idea of Correspondence in *Iphigenie auf Tauris*." *The Germanic Review* 53: 147–55.

Pfaff, Peter. 1978. "Die Stimme des Gewissens: Über Goethes Versuch zu einer Genealogie der Moral, vor allem in der *Iphigenie*." *Euphorion* 72: 20–42.

Bennett, Benjamin. 1979. *Modern Drama and German Classicism: Renaissance from Lessing to Brecht*. Ithaca: Cornell University Press.

Muenzer, Clark S. 1979. "Virginity and Tragic Structure: Patterns of Continuity and Change in *Emilia Galotti*, *Iphigenie auf Tauris*, and *Die Jungfrau von Orleans*." *Monatshefte* 71: 117–30.

Rasch, Wolfdietrich. 1979. *Goethes "Iphigenie auf Tauris" als Drama der Autonomie*. Munich: Beck.

Sims-Gunzenhauser, William D. 1979. "Conflict of the Inner Life in Goethe's *Iphigenie* and Shelley's *Cenci*." *Neophilologus* 63: 95–107.

Borchmeyer, Dieter. 1980. *Die Weimarer Klassik. Eine Einführung*. Königstein: Athenäum.

Cottrell, Alan P. 1980. "On Speaking the Good: Goethe's *Iphigenie* as 'moralisches Urphänomen'." *Modern Language Quarterly* 41: 162–80.

Dyer, Denys. 1980. "*Iphigenie*: The Role of the Curse." *PEGS* 50: 29–54.

Hinderer, Walter, ed. 1980. *Goethes Dramen. Neue Interpretationen*. Stuttgart: Reclam.

Includes:

Hackert, Fritz. "*Iphigenie auf Tauris*." 144–68.

Hermann, Helmut G. "Auswahlbibliographie zu Goethe und seinem dramatischen Werk." 313–52.

Hinderer, Walter. "*Torquato Tasso*." 169–96.

Vaget, Hans Rudolf. "*Die natürliche Tochter*." 210–25.

Hobson, Irmgard. 1980. "Updating the Classics: *Faust* and *Iphigenie* in Stuttgart, 1977." *German Studies Review* 3: 435–55.

Kreutzer, Leo. 1980. "Schnee ohne Maß und Ordnung: Über Torquato Tasso, Werther und die Phantom-Gesellschaft." In his *Mein Gott Goethe: Essays*. Reinbek bei Hamburg: Rowohlt, 12–28.

Reed, T[erence] J[ames]. 1980. *The Classical Centre: Goethe and Weimar 1775–1832*. Totowa N.J.: Barnes and Noble.

Vaget, Hans Rudolf. 1980. "Um einen Tasso von außen bittend: Kunst und Dilettantismus am Musenhof von Ferrara." *Deutsche Vierteljahresschrift für Literaturwissenschaft und Geistesgeschichte* 54: 232–58.

Borchmeyer, Dieter. 1981. "Johann Wolfgang von Goethe: *Iphigenie auf Tauris*." In Harro Müller-Michaels, ed. *Deutsche Dramen: Interpretationen zu Werken von der Aufklärung bis zur Gegenwart*. Königstein: Athenäum, 52–86.

Fowler, Frank M. 1981."The Problem of Goethe's Orest: New Light on *Iphigenie auf Tauris*." *PEGS* 51: 1–26.

Girschner, Gabriele. 1981. *Goethes "Tasso": Klassizismus als ästhetische Regression*. Königstein: Hain.

Grawe, Christian, ed. 1981. *Johann Wolfgang Goethe. "Torquato Tasso": Erläuterungen und Dokumente*. Stuttgart: Reclam.

Malek, James S. and Carson, Franklin D. 1981. "Tragic Effects in Euripides' *Iphigenia in Tauris* and Goethe's *Iphigenie auf Tauris*." *Classical and Modern Literature* 1: 109–19.

Pestalozzi, Karl. 1981. "Goethes *Iphigenie* als Antwort an Lavater betrachtet." *GJb* 98: 113–30.

Salm, Peter. 1981. "Truthtelling and Lying in Goethe's *Iphigenie*." *German Life and Letters* 34: 351–58.

Conrady, Karl Otto. 1982. *Goethe: Leben und Werk*. Königstein: Athenäum. Vol. 1 for *Iphigenie* and *Tasso*. Vol. 2 (1985) for *Die natürliche Tochter*.

Emrich, Wilhelm. 1982. "Goethes Tragödie des Genius: Von *Götz* bis zur *Natürlichen Tochter*." *Jahrbuch der Deutschen Schiller-Gesellschaft* 26: 144–62.

Fowler, Frank M. 1982. "'Doch mir verzeih Diane . . .': Thoas and the Disputed Ending of Goethe's *Iphigenie*." *New German Studies* 10: 135–50.

Grappin, Pierre. 1982. "Die Idee der Entwicklung im Spiegel des Goetheschen Schauspiels *Iphigenie auf Tauris*." *GJb* 99: 32–40.

Horsley, Ritta Jo. 1982. "'Dies Frauenschicksal': A Critical Appraisal of Goethe's *Iphigenie*." *Beyond the Eternal Feminine: Critical Essays on Women and German Literature*. Ed. Susan Cocalis and Kay Goodman. Stuttgart: Akademischer Verlag Hans-Peter Heinz, 47–74.

Kraft, Herbert. 1982. "Das magre Licht von der Humanität über Goethes Schauspiel *Iphigenie auf Tauris*." *AUMLA* 58: 113–25.

Sternberger, Dolf. 1982. "Parabel von der Verfolgung: Gedanken zu Goethes *Natürlicher Tochter*." *Frankfurter Allgemeine Zeitung*. December 4.

Brückner, Christine. 1983. *Wenn du geredet hättest, Desdemona. Ungehaltene Reden ungehaltener Frauen.* Hamburg: Hoffmann und Campe.

Dahnke, Hans-Dietrich. 1983. "Im Schnittpunkt von Menschheitsutopie und Realitätserfahrung: *Iphigenie auf Tauris.*" *Impulse* 6: 9–36.

Kimpel, Dieter. 1983. "Ethos und Nomos als poetologische Kategorien bei Platon-Aristoteles und das Problem der substantiellen Sittlichkeit in Goethes *Iphigenie auf Tauris.*" *Germanisch-Romanische Monatsschrift* N.F. 33: 367–93.

Wierlacher, Alois. 1983. "Ent-fremdete Fremde: Goethes *Iphigenie auf Tauris* als Drama des Völkerrechts." *Zeitschrift für deutsche Philologie* 102: 161–80.

Barner, Wilfried, Eberhard Lämmert, and Norbert Oellers, eds. 1984. *Unser Commercium: Goethes und Schillers Literaturpolitik.* Veröffentlichungen der deutschen Schillergesellschaft. Stuttgart: Cotta. [Symposium held at Marbach, 6–9 September 1982.]
Includes:

Pütz, Peter. "Nähe und Ferne zur Antike: *Iphigenie* und *Maria Stuart.*" 289–302.

Weimar, Klaus. "Ihr Götter!" 303–27.

Furst, Lilian R. 1984. "Mythology into Psychology: *Deus ex Machina* into God Within." *Comparative Literature Studies* 21: 1–15.

Girschner, Gabriele. 1984. "Vom Verhältnis zwischen Dichter und Gesellschaft in Goethes *Torquato Tasso.*" *GJb* 101: 162–86.

Hobson, Irmgard W. 1984a. "Goethe's *Iphigenie*: A Lacanian Reading." *GYb* 2: 51–67.

———[Wagner, Irmgard]. 1984b. "Hans Robert Jauss and Classicity." *Modern Language Notes* 99: 1173–84.

Martin, Günther. 1984. "Tasso oder der Augenblick — Goethe und die Zeit." *GJb* 101: 187–204.

Wittkowski, Wolfgang. 1984a. "'Bei Ehren bleiben die Orakel und gerettet sind die Götter'? Goethes *Iphigenie*: Autonome Humanität und Autorität der Religion im aufgeklärten Absolutismus." *GJb* 101: 250–68.

———. 1984b, ed. *Goethe im Kontext: Kunst und Humanität, Naturwissenschaft und Politik von der Aufklärung bis zur Restauration. Ein Symposium.* Tübingen: Niemeyer. [Symposium held in October, 1982, at SUNY Albany].
Includes:

Borchmeyer, Dieter. "Der unfruchtbare Lorbeer: Über ein Existenzsymbol des modernen Dichters. Goethe — Grillparzer — Wagner." 148–57. "Diskussion." 158–62.

Crosby, Donald H. "Goethes *Tasso* in der Inszenierung von Peter Stein." 136–43. "Diskussion." 144–47.

Wittkowski, Wolfgang. "Goethe und Kleist: Autonome Humanität und religiöse Autorität zwischen Unbewußtsein und Bewußtsein in *Iphigenie, Amphitryon, Penthesilea.*" 205–29.

Borchmeyer, Dieter. 1985. "Tasso oder das Unglück Dichter zu sein." *Allerhand Goethe. Seine wissenschaftliche Sendung.* [Goethe anniversary symposium and lectures given at Frankfurt University 1982.] Ed. Dieter Kimpel and Jörg Pompetzki. Frankfurt: Lang, 67–88.

Geyer-Ryan, Helga. 1985. "Prefigurative Racism in Goethe's *Iphigenie auf Tauris.*" *Europe and Its Others.* Proceedings of the Essex Conference on the Sociology of Literature, July 1984. Ed. Francis Barker et al. Colchester: University of Essex. Vol. 2, 112–19.

Ockenden, R. C. 1985. "On Bringing Statues to Life: Reading Goethe's *Iphigenie auf Tauris* and *Torquato Tasso.*" *PEGS* 55: 69–106.

Prandi, Julie D. 1985. "Goethe's Iphigenie as Woman." *The Germanic Review* 60: 24–31.

Reed, Terence James. 1985. "Iphigenies Unmündigkeit: Zur weiblichen Aufklärung." *Germanistik: Forschungsstand und Perspektiven. Vorträge des deutschen Germanistentages 1984.* Ed. Georg Stötzel. Berlin: de Gruyter, 505–24.

Ronell, Avital. 1985. "Taking it Philosophically: *Torquato Tasso*'s Women as Theorists." *Modern Language Notes* 100: 599–631.

Böschenstein, Bernhard. 1986. "Antike und moderne Tragödie um 1800 in dreifacher Kontroverse: Goethes *Natürliche Tochter* — Kleists *Penthesilea* — Hölderlins *Antigone.*" *Kontroversen, alte und neue. Akten des VII. Internationalen Germanisten-Kongresses Göttingen 1985.* Vol. 8. Ed. Albrecht Schöne. Tübingen: Niemeyer, 204–15.

Gille, Klaus F. 1986. "Erlaubt ist, was sich ziemt . . . — Hermeneutische Überlegungen zum Umgang mit Klassischem." *Neophilologus* 70: 256–69.

Hart, Gail K. 1986. "Goethe's *Tasso*: Reading the Directions." *GYb* 3: 125–38.

Meier, Albert. 1986. "Amarilli auf Tauris: Der Einfluß von Guarinis *Pastor fido* auf Goethes *Iphigenie.*" *Germanisch-Romanische Monatsschrift* N.F. 36: 455–57.

Schultheis, Werner. 1986. "Goethe: *Die natürliche Tochter.* Gotisch und modern." *Euphorion* 80: 326–39.

Schulz, Karlheinz. 1986. *Goethes und Goldonis "Torquato Tasso."* Frankfurt: Lang.

Würffel, Stefan Bodo. 1986. "' . . . Ein Werk das einen nicht los lässt . . .': Goethes Soulavie-Lektüre und *Die Natürliche Tochter.*" *Jahrbuch des Freien Deutschen Hochstifts*, 91–117.

Brandmeyer, Rudolf. 1987. *Heroik und Gegenwart: Goethes klassische Dramen.* Frankfurt: Lang.

Chiarini, Paolo, ed. 1987. *Bausteine zu einem neuen Goethe*. Frankfurt: Athenäum.

Includes:

Böschenstein, Bernhard. "Goethes *Natürliche Tochter* als Antwort auf die Französische Revolution." 93–106.

Emrich, Wilhelm. "Goethes Tragödie des Genius. Vom *Götz* bis zur *Natürlichen Tochter*." 22–42.

Hewitt, Regina. 1987. "Torquato Tasso — A Byronic Hero?" *Neophilologus* 71: 431–46.

Kraft, Herbert. 1987. "Goethes *Tasso*: Nachfrage zu einem Bündnis zwischen Kunst und Politik." *GJb* 104: 84–95.

Uerlings, Herbert. 1987. "*Die natürliche Tochter*: Zur Rolle des Bürgertums in Goethes Trauerspiel." *GJb* 104: 96–112.

Ugrinsky, Alexej, ed. 1987. *Goethe in the Twentieth Century*. New York: Greenwood. [Conference held at Hofstra University April 1982.]

Includes:

Dietrich, Donna and Marshall, Harry. "Thoas and Iphigenie: A Reappraisal." 61–66.

Wittkowski, Wolfgang. "Goethe's *Iphigenie:* Autonomous Humanity and the Authority of the Gods in the Era of Benevolent Despotism." 77–83.

Villwock, Jörg. 1987. "Zu einigen Entsprechungen zwischen Goethes *Iphigenie* und der Gebetsrhetorik des Origenes." *Euphorion* 81: 189–216.

Brown, Kathryn and Anthony Stephens. 1988. "'... Hinübergehn und unser Haus entsühnen': Die Ökonomie des Mythischen in Goethes *Iphigenie*." *Jahrbuch der Deutschen Schiller-Gesellschaft* 32: 94–115.

Merkl, Helmut. 1988. "Spiel zum Abschied: Betrachtung zur Kunst des Leidens in Goethes *Torquato Tasso*." *Euphorion* 82:1–24.

Reynolds, Susan Helen. 1988. "'Erstaunlich modern und ungriechisch?' Goethe's *Iphigenie auf Tauris* and its Classical Background." *PEGS* 57: 55–74.

Wagner, Irmgard. 1988. "*Die natürliche Tochter* and the Problem of Representation." *GYb* 4: 185–207.

Weisinger, Kenneth D. 1988. *The Classical Facade: A Nonclassical Reading of Goethe's Classicism*. University Park: Pennsylvania State University Press.

Reed. T. J. 1989. "Tasso und die Besserwisser." *Texte, Motive und Gestalten der Goethezeit*. Festschrift Hans Reiss. Ed. John L. Hibberd et al. Tübingen: Niemeyer, 95–112.

Schanze, Helmut. 1989. *Goethes Dramatik: Theater der Erinnerung*. Tübingen: Niemeyer.

Weiss, Walter. 1989. "Goethe: *Die natürliche Tochter*: Metamorphose durch Revolution?" *Politik und Geschichte. Festschrift Viktor Zmegac*. Ed. Dieter Borchmeyer. Tübingen: Niemeyer, 55–62.

Ammerlahn, Hellmut. 1990. *Aufbau und Krise der Sinn-Gestalt: Tasso und die Prinzessin im Kontext der Goetheschen Werke.* Bern: Lang.

Böschenstein, Bernhard. 1990. *Goethe: "Die natürliche Tochter. Trauerspiel": Mit den Memoiren der Stéphanie-Louise de Bourbon-Conti und drei Studien von Bernhard Böschenstein.* Frankfurt: Insel.

Dassanowski-Harris, Robert von. 1990. "Classicism Subverted and the Eras of France: Goethe's *Die natürliche Tochter.*" *Sprachkunst* 21: 219–30.

James, Dorothy and Silvia Ranawake, eds. 1990. *Patterns of Change: German Drama and the European Tradition. Festschrift Ronald Peacock.* New York: Lang.

Includes:

Reiss, Hans. "The Consequences of 'Theological' Politics in Goethe's *Iphigenie auf Tauris.*" 59–71.

Sengle, Friedrich. "*Egmont, Iphigenie, Tasso*: Goethes klassizistische Dramen in Ronald Peacocks Sicht." 73–85.

Krockow, Christian Graf von. 1990. *Die Deutschen in ihrem Jahrhundert 1890–1990.* Reinbek bei Hamburg: Rowohlt.

Kruse, Jens. 1990. "Die Innenwelt der Außenwelt der Innenwelt: Tassos Ende und kein Ende." *GYb* 5: 103–20.

Larkin, Edward. 1990. "Aggression and Dialogue in Goethe's *Iphigenie auf Tauris*: Competing Principles of Societal and Personal Intercourse." *Crossings — Kreuzungen. Festschrift Helmut Kreuzer.* Ed. Edward R. Haymes. Columbia, S.C.: Camden House, 92–103.

Mickel, Karl. 1990. "*Die natürliche Tochter* oder: Goethes soziologischer Blick." *GJb* 107: 6–70.

Wagner, Irmgard. 1990. "Vom Mythos zum Fetisch: Die Frau als Erlöserin in Goethes klassischen Dramen." *GYb* 5: 121–43.

Ameri, Sussan Milantchi. 1991. *Die deutschnationale Sprachbewegung im Wilhelminischen Reich.* New York: Lang.

Boyle, Nicholas. 1991. *Goethe. The Poet and the Age.* Vol. 1: *The Poetry of Desire (1749–1790).* Oxford University Press.

Gille, Klaus. 1991. "*Die natürliche Tochter* — Zu Goethes Versuch einer Kritik der Krise." *Zeitschrift für Germanistik* N.F. 1: 352–63.

Wilson, Jean. 1991. *The Challenge of Belatedness: Goethe, Kleist, Hofmannsthal.* Lanham: University Press of America.

Index

Gramley Library
Salem College
Winston-Salem, NC 27108